# Trumpism

# Trumpism

## Race, Class, Populism, and Public Policy

Carter A. Wilson

LEXINGTON BOOKS
*Lanham • Boulder • New York • London*

Published by Lexington Books
An imprint of The Rowman & Littlefield Publishing Group, Inc.
4501 Forbes Boulevard, Suite 200, Lanham, Maryland 20706
www.rowman.com

6 Tinworth Street, London SE11 5AL, United Kingdom

British Library Cataloguing in Publication Information Available

**Library of Congress Cataloging-in-Publication Data**

Names: Wilson, Carter A., author.
Title: Trumpism : race, class, populism, and public policy / Carter A. Wilson.
Description: Lanham : Lexington Books, [2021] | Includes bibliographical references
    and index. | Summary: "Although Trump supporters depict him as a champion of the
    working class and a friend of minorities, this text demonstrates that the preponderance
    of evidence indicates that Trump promoted a right-wing public policy agenda that
    exacerbated inequality, benefited the economic elite, and hurt low-income white
    workers and minorities"— Provided by publisher.
Identifiers: LCCN 2021038041 (print) | LCCN 2021038042 (ebook) |
    ISBN 9781793617514 (cloth) | ISBN 9781793617538 (paperback) |
    ISBN 9781793617521 (ebook)
Subjects: LCSH: Trump, Donald, 1946—Influence. | Populism. | United States—Social
    policy—History—21st century. | United States—Economic policy—History—21st
    century. | United States—Politics and government—2017-
Classification: LCC E912 .W547 2021 (print) | LCC E912 (ebook) |
    DDC 973.933092—dc23
LC record available at https://lccn.loc.gov/2021038041
LC ebook record available at https://lccn.loc.gov/2021038042

*To my beautiful and supportive wife,*
*Khadijah Rasheed Wilson*

# Contents

# Acknowledgments

I greatly appreciate editing and critical comments from a number of sources, especially from Bruce Larson, Katherine Larson, and Steve Nelson who read, edited, and critiqued the first draft of the first few chapters and the reviewer who read and critiqued the initial draft. The editing and critical comments contributed to a much improved text.

# Introduction

*Trumpism: Race, Class, Populism, and Public Policy* examines racial and working-class issues related to Trump's brand of populism and his public policy agenda. The text reviews both the factors that enabled the Trump phenomenon and Trump's domestic policy agenda. It is divided into two parts. Part I, chapters 1–5, covers the political, ideological, and economic context of Trumpism. Part II, chapters 6–10, covers select domestic public policies of the Trump administration.

Chapter 1, "Populism," reviews different forms of populism. The goal of this chapter is to identify Trump's particular brand of populism and the public policy agenda associated with it. It contrasts left-wing populism with right-wing populism and demonstrates that Trump is a right-wing populist. Despite the promises from Trump, this form of populism does not bode well for low-income workers or minorities.

Chapter 2, "Trumpism," examines Trump's world view or ideology. It rejects the notion that he is chaotic or erratic. It draws from his own writings and investigates various sources to create a portrait of Trump's ideas and political perspectives. It reviews his several books (*The Art of the Deal, Great Again,* and *Think Big*), many speeches, and countless Tweets. Although many critics claim that Trump is not a conservative, he has been enthralled with Ayn Rand, especially the John Galt, super-masculine entrepreneur character. Trump's writings and speeches reflect many aspects of both neoliberal and neoconservative thought. Trump's opposition to free trade is a misplaced indicator of a progressive ideology. Indeed, Herbert Hoover and other past conservatives would support Trump's trade war. This chapter identifies and elaborates on four dimensions of his political world view and character: neoliberalism, authoritarianism, nationalism, and racism. The evidence presented in this chapter supports the contention that Trump is a right-wing reactionary populist who appeals to the white working class by exploiting fears, stoking prejudices, and promising economic revitalization, while promoting a policy agenda that favors the rich and corporate sector at the expense of low-income workers and minorities.

Chapter 3, "Trump Voters," summarizes the demographics of Trump supporters in terms of age, gender, income, race, and attitudes. It reviews the literature on Trump's base of support: Trump voters and the political movements that enabled his election. It investigates whether Trump's election was a product of economic populism or cultural populism. It examines whether white workers voted for Trump, because they felt left behind or because of social status threats, immigration fears, and racial resentment. It looks at the true believers, the disenchanted and disaffected, and the gullible voters who put him in the White House. Republicans and white males with less than a college degree overwhelmingly supported Trump. Economic distress and racial resentment were also factors in explaining Trump's success.

Chapter 4, "Perfect Storm," identifies the four political movements that provided the foundation for the current right-wing populist movement that enabled the ascension of Donald Trump. These movements included the economic elite or corporate insurgency movement, the Tea Party movement, the Christian right movement, and the white nationalist movement. There was no conspiracy among these movements. There was no intention to build a populist movement. These movements emerged like a perfect storm. Disconnected jet streams and unrelated temperature shifts interacted in the right space and at the right time to produce a powerful and destructive storm.

The revolt of multi-billionaires/corporate leaders, the economic elite, is a key factor in precipitating the current political storm, yet it is too often neglected in most the studies of the current U.S. populist movement. However, political scientists examining contemporary public policy changes have concluded that understanding this movement is essential in understanding the current populist movement. It is also important in understanding the disconnection between public opinion and public policy changes favoring the rich and the corporate sector (Page and Gilens 2017; Hacker and Pierson 2011, 2016; MacLean 2017). This factor is often overlooked in the populist literature primarily because multi-billionaire business leaders had absolutely no intention of producing a populist movement. Most of these leaders are libertarians. Most were appalled by Trump's racism, misogyny, mendacity, and baseless conspiracy theories. Nevertheless, key multi-billionaire leaders contributed to anti-government movements. They supported the Christian right, which included conservative evangelicals, fundamentalist, and other Christian groups. Some multi-billionaires like Charles Koch, and his now deceased brother David Koch, contributed heavily to the Tea Party movement. These economic elites emerged as a dominant political force in the twenty-first-century politics and public policy making. These leaders inadvertently set in motion political forces that elected Trump in 2016.

The Tea Party movement was a Republican insurgency movement, as it emerged in opposition to moderate Republicans. This movement was energized to oppose the Obama administration. Insofar as it was driven by anger and resentment, it was a populist movement. It constituted a major bloc of the Republican Party coalition. At the same time, it formed the core foundation of Trump's political power base. Trump did not take over the Republican Party. He emerged as a central leader in the Tea Party movement, especially when he led the birther movement, the movement to discredit Obama's presidency on the false grounds that Obama was not born in the United States.

The conservative Christian right movement was incompatible with Trump's moral values exhibited by his liaison with porn star Stormy Daniels, the Access Hollywood tape, and the complaints of sexual harassment and assaults from over twenty women (Eliza 2020). However, Trump made a Faustian bargain with leaders of this movement. In exchange for their support, Trump solemnly pledged to grant all of their political wishes: a Supreme Court that would reverse *Roe V Wade* and allow states to outlaw abortions, the end of LGBT rights, and support for religious rights and religious schools, and many others. Trump also bargained with the white nationalist and alt-right movement. He enabled this bloc to move from the dark fringes of American politics into the mainstream as part of his coalition.

Chapter 4 also examines the formation of a right-wing media ecosystem and the realignment of the Republican Party. The right-wing media pushed U.S. politics into a post-truth era where power and emotions matter more than facts, evidence, and truth. Indeed, this ecosystem enables the promotion of the level of disinformation that accelerated the current right-wing populist movement.

Finally, this chapter demonstrates that the contemporary Republican Party is no longer the same as the Republican Party of the twentieth century. It is a party in turmoil, divided between traditional libertarians who represent economic elites and the Christian right, Tea Party, white nationalists who constituted the masses. Indeed, although the white nationalists constituted a minority faction, it played a key role in organizing and leading the January 6, 2021 assault on the Capitol.

Chapter 5, "Inequality," surveys the literature on the growth and consequences of extreme inequality. This chapter begins by demonstrating the shift of the U.S. economy from a plus sum economy to a zero sum economy. Indeed, from 1945 to 1980, all income groups benefited from an expanding economy and lower income groups enjoyed modest upward social mobility. These circumstances defined the plus sum society. These circumstances changed after 1980. As the economy expanded, the top quintile gained income, while the bottom quintile lost income and upward social mobility declined. These circumstances defined the zero sum society. Whereas most pundits and economists attributed these changes to abstract economic forces, such as globalization and technological change, this chapter presents considerable evidence that an assault on the equal opportunity, inclusive state played a central role in the production of extreme inequality. This inequality is partially related to the ascension of today's right-wing populist movement.

Chapter 6, "Labor Policy," covers labor policy changes under the Trump administration. It examines the issues of wages and working hours, collective bargaining, and health and safety in the workplace. Whereas candidate Trump promised to favor American workers, his actual policies hurt workers. In almost every labor issue area, President Trump's policy changes favored management over labor. These changes weakened labor unions and substantially weakened the bargaining power of workers. His refusal to raise the minimum wage further contributed to stagnant wages. His commitment to deregulation eroded health and safety protections in the work place. Despite the pre-Covid-19 expanding economy and declining unemployment rate, wages have stagnated, workplace safety has eroded, and the overall wellbeing of American workers has diminished. The overall impact of Trump's labor policies has been the immiseration of American workers.

Chapter 7, "Healthcare Policy," covers healthcare policy. It demonstrates the extent to which Trump used the neoliberal policy playbook. His approach to making healthcare policy better was to follow the free market solution advocated not by neoliberal scholars but by neoliberal extremists. Trump engaged in a relentless assault on the Affordable Care Act (ACA). He hacked away at the parts of this policy designed to expand healthcare access and improved the life chances of low-income American workers, without healthcare benefits.

Chapter 8, "Social Welfare, Education, and Tax Policies," examines changes in social welfare, education, and tax policies. It illustrates Trump's continual assault on the equal opportunity, inclusive state. His proposed budget cuts to social welfare programs have been much more draconian that those of the Reagan administration. This chapter reviews the proposed budget cuts and the Jobs and Tax Cut Act of 2017. The tax cuts had a ;modest economic stimulus effect. However, although these cuts were expected to increase the average salaries of working-class families by about $4,000, the combination of the tax cuts and the budget cuts redistributed income upward, made the rich richer and increased inequality.

Chapter 9, "Voter Suppression," identifies the voter suppression movements, a political movement designed to make it more difficult for voting aged citizens to vote. It notes the role of the Republican Party in initiating this movement, but focuses on Trump's direct efforts to suppress the right to vote: his establishment of a voter fraud commission and his deliberate efforts to reduce the resources for mail-sorting machines in the post office to undermine the ability of the U.S. Post Office to deliver mail-in ballots. It draws a parallel between the Redeemer movement lead by the Southern Democratic Party over a hundred years ago to suppress the right to vote among African Americans and minorities and the role of Trump and the contemporary Republican Party to suppress the votes of African Americans and poor whites. Both movements used big lies and conspiracy theories to expand popular support and to legitimize a profoundly anti-democratic movement.

Chapter 10, "Trumpism: Race, Class, and Police Policy," reiterates the theme of the text and focuses on violence and police administration under the Trump administration. The theme is that Trump was a right-wing reactionary populist whose public policies have had their most devastating impacts of low-income white workers and minorities. This chapter focuses on factors associated with violent crime, the process of racializing violent crime, the problem of police violence, and the role of Trump in encouraging police violence, increasing unaccountable police power, and moving the United States in the direction of a repressive police state.

*Part I*

# THE POLITICAL, IDEOLOGICAL, AND ECONOMIC CONTEXT OF TRUMPISM

# *Chapter 1*

# Populism

Trump is a polarizing, divisive enigma—a paradox best understood after the exposure of his brand of populism, his worldview, his base of support, and the context of excessive inequality out of which he emerged. This chapter notes the contradictory characterizations of Trump and exposes his brand of populism.

## THE TRUMP PARADOX

In 2016, President Trump was elected on a promise to make America great again. He promised to bring back manufacturing and mining jobs, expand the economy, reduce unemployment, renegotiate trade deals, reduce the flow of undocumented immigrants crossing the southern border from Mexico, and build a wall to prevent future immigration crises.

In 2020, in spite of the damage to the economy produced by the coronavirus-19 pandemic, Trump boasted about fulfilling his promises. He bragged about expanding the economy, revitalizing the manufacturing sector, providing job opportunities for American workers, promoting religious freedom, and maintaining law and order. On multiple occasions, Trump claimed to have done more for African Americans than any other president since Lincoln. Among his public policy accomplishments, he listed the Tax Cut and Jobs Act of 2017 and the First Step Act of 2018. He insisted that his policies reformed the prison system, reduced poverty to its lowest level, and created more jobs among African Americans ever. He pointed to the creation of Opportunity Zones, a program designed to stimulate inner city economic development and expand inner city jobs. He allocated federal money to historic black colleges and universities.

Scholars have disagreed over Trump's public policy accomplishments. Conservative scholars offered positive evaluations of the Trump administration. They claimed that Trump's public policy agenda responded to the concerns and needs of those victimized by globalization and technological change and those left behind by the economic recovery from the 2008–2010 recession. They argued that Trump expanded healthcare services for veterans, established transparency in hospital prices, and increased the number of conservative judges on federal courts. His most striking accomplishments included the expansion of the economy and the reduction of unemployment and poverty rates before the Covid-19 pandemic. They attributed this success primarily to tax cuts and deregulation.

Liberal scholars offered negative evaluations. They saw Trump driven by racism, xenophobia, and misogyny. They claimed he was devoid of a coherent ideology and lacked a constructive policy agenda. They argued that he targeted and attacked the progressive public policies of the Obama administration. They exposed his sadistic policy of taking young children from the families of asylum seekers at the southern border and herding them into cages to discourage other Central American asylum seekers from wanting to come to the United States. They highlighted his attack on the Clean Energy Plan and other environmental regulations. They accused Trump of encouraging a nationwide movement to make voting more difficult for minorities and of inciting an assault on the Capitol.

Despite the disagreement among scholars, the preponderance of the evidence suggests that Trump promoted a policy agenda that had its most devastating impact on low-income white workers and minorities. He opposed raising the minimum wage. He pushed to establish work requirements for food benefits. He engaged in a relentless assault on the Affordable Care Act. He hacked away at provisions of this bill that had expanded healthcare access for low-income workers. His labor policy agenda was designed to eviscerate labor power, weaken collective bargaining rights, and rollback workplace health and safety regulations. Although unemployment rates dropped to record low levels, stagnant wages and underemployment persisted especially for workers with a high school degree or less (Blanchflower 2021; Autor 2019).

After several decades of increases in life expectancy and declines in morbidity rates, over the past decade-and-a-half, life expectancy declined and morbidity rates increased for middle-aged whites between the ages of 45 and 54. Economists have referred to these rising death rates among middle-aged whites as despair-related deaths (Burke 2017; Blanchflower 2021; Case and Deaton 2017, 2020; Metzl 2019). They associated it with the rise of extreme inequality (Case and Deaton 2020; Blanchflower 2021). Rather than adopting a policy agenda to mitigate both the extreme inequality and the increase in rates of despair-related deaths, Trump's public policies agenda focused on expanding the economy. This policy focus combined with the failure to raise the minimum wage—the relentless assault on the Affordable Care Act, the rollback of labor regulations, and the deliberate effort to reduce the social safety net—had a devastating impact on low-income workers and minorities. This impact was predictable given Trump's brand of populism, the political movements that formed his base of political support, and his rhetoric and worldview (Green 2018; Hacker and Pierson 2020).

## TRUMP AND POPULISM

Almost all scholars and pundits characterized Trump as a populist, although the literature on Trump and populism has been inconsistent. Characterizations of Trump's brand of populism have been contradictory. Definitions of populism have been ambiguous.

Trump supporters have portrayed him as a positive populist. Some presented him as an economic populist who helped common working-class Americans. In her book, *The New American Revolution: The Making of a Populist Movement*, Kayleigh McEnany, journalist and Trump's press secretary, claimed that he was a revolutionary populist in the tradition of the American Revolution, promoting freedom everywhere and responding to those Americans who had been forsaken by a corrupt and unresponsive government. She presented Trump as responsive to workers who were stressed over the decline of the manufacturing sector and threatened by crime, immigration, and terrorism (McEnany 2018). In his book on Trump, the former Republican Speaker of the U.S. House of Representatives, Newt Gingrich, insisted that Trump's strategy of cutting taxes and rolling back regulations revitalized the economy and made economic conditions better for both black and white Americans. Gingrich maintained that liberals lied when they claimed that Trump's tax cuts provided far more benefits to rich people and major corporations than to middle-class Americans (Gingrich 2018). Of course, Gingrich neglected to mention that Trump's Jobs and Tax Cuts Act of 2017 reduced corporate taxes from 35 percent down to 21 percent. In their book, *The Great Revolt: Inside the Populist Coalition Reshaping American Politics*, Slaena Zito and Brad Todd documented a revolt among working-class Americans who played a pivotal role in the 2016 election of Trump. These authors demonstrated that thousands of working-class Democrats, who voted for Barack Obama in 2008 and 2012, switched parties and voted for Trump in 2016, enabling Trump to win the election. They interviewed many union leaders who voted for Trump, because they felt betrayed by the Democrats. The common complaint was that Bill Clinton and Barack Obama

supported free trade deals that hurt workers and Trump promised to renegotiate the deals to favor American workers (Zito and Todd 2018).

Other supporters saw Trump as a Christian populist enabled by divine
intervention. Victor Hanson claimed that America is suffering from a cultural
divide between the godless coastal big-city liberal elites, on the one side, and
ordinary God-fearing traditional Americans living in rural areas and small
towns in Middle America, on the other side. For Hanson, Trump's populism
appealed to traditional rural and small-town Christian Americans, whose culture and way of life was threatened by godless liberalism. Hanson characterized Trump as chemotherapy, strong medicine for flushing out the diseases of
liberalism and socialism (Hanson 2019). Many conservative evangelicals saw
Trump as a gift from God, comparable to Cyrus, the Biblical era Persian King
who liberated the Hebrews from the Babylonians (Wallnau 2016; Strang
2020). Lance Wallnau referred to President Trump as God's wrecking ball,
chosen by God to protect and save his people (Wallnau 2016). Televangelist
Mike Evans called Trump God's imperfect vessel chosen to fulfill God's plan
(Mitchell 2017).

Critical scholars painted a negative view of Trump and his form of populism. They characterized him as ascending into the White House on the crest
of a cultural backlash, a powerful political movement driven by fear, anger,
and prejudice (Norris and Inglehart 2019; Jardina 2019; Sides et al. 2018)).
This backlash was provoked by the perception, real or imagined, that white
Christian Americans faced multiple existential threats: Hispanic immigrants
flooding across the southern border, taking American jobs and threatening the
dominant and privileged status of white Americans; and Muslim immigrants
from the Middle East bringing terrorists among them; and leftist Democrats
violating the values, beliefs, and sensitivities of white Christians by legalizing
same-sex marriage and tolerating homosexuality.

Scholars Are Divided over the Definition and Characteristics of Populist
Movements

A number of scholars have defined populist movements as anti-pluralist
(Muller 2016; Galston 2018). Pluralism is a political process in which the
government creates public policy in response to multiple competing interest
groups. This process involves bargaining and compromise. Populists respond
to the people as a whole, not competing special interest groups. Scholars
who see populist movements as anti-pluralist define populist movements as
both mass movements and democratic movements, but inherently illiberal
(Galston 2018; Mounk 2018; Mudde 2007; Norris 2019). These scholars
maintained that populists see the people as virtuous and sovereign and elites
as corrupt and in opposition to the people. The view of the people as virtuous and the notion of popular sovereignty are consistent with the concept of
democracy. However, illiberalism arises when populists define the people as

homogeneous. For example, when a populist movement defines the people as primarily white Christians, it tends to exclude non-whites and non-Christians. Illiberalism is exacerbated when populists expand the definition of despised elites to include the educated, urban, and liberal elites. Democracy is undermined when populists define themselves as the people and opponents as enemies of the people (Muller 2016; Galston 2018).

Disagreements over the definition of populism persist. Some scholars have characterized populist movements as emotional, conspiratorial, paranoid, and anti-intellectual (Hofstadter 1948; 1964). Other scholars have complained about the tendency of researchers to confuse the characteristics of contemporary right-wing illiberal, authoritarian populist movements with the characteristics of all other forms of populist movements. These scholars recognize liberal-democratic populist movements (Frank 2020; Goodwyn 1978).

Despite disagreements among scholars over the definition and characteristics of populist movements, there are some characteristics exhibited by almost all populist movements. These characteristics offer a more consistent definition of populism. Although ideas undergird populist movements, there is no one specific ideology that defines a populist movement. Although populist leaders express ideological themes, populist movements are rarely ideological movements. They are generally emotional movements, driven by anger and resentment. They are precipitated by grievances, real or imagined. They are anti-establishment and anti-elitist. Populist leaders tend to be charismatic. They identify with and speak the language of the people. Sometimes supporters have an emotional attachment to these charismatic populist leaders. There are different types of populist movements, distinguished by two sets of factors.

First, populist movements can be distinguished by the target of their anger and resentment, their base of political support, and their demands on government. These factors provide a clearer distinction between left-wing liberal populist and right-wing illiberal populist movements. Left-wing populists target the economic elite and tend to be supported by organizations representing farmers, workers, and minorities. They demand an expanded role for government. While right-wing populists blame the economic elite, they target scapegoats. Their base tends to cut across class lines and include the rich, poor, and middle class.

Right-wing movements vary in their demands on government. Nationalist right-wing movements tend to call for an expanded role for government, which may include investment in infrastructure, support for social security, and possibly spending for social welfare programs for deserving white families but not undeserving minority families and emphatically not for immigrant families. Plutocratic or conservative right-wing movements call for a diminished role of government: tax cuts, spending cuts, deregulation, and privatization of public services. Both nationalist and conservative movements call for increased police powers to maintain law and order, suppress dissent, and target scapegoats. Nationalist movements tend to support racially repressive police states.

Second, populist movements can be either authoritarian-illiberal or liberal-democratic. Authoritarians favor order and hierarchy. They distinguish between the deserving and the underserving. They tend to see the world in black-and-white terms: divided between good and evil, between us and them. They oversimplify conflicts and are more likely to resort to the use of force or violence. Authoritarian populist movements favor strong leaders committed to promoting law and order and willing to engage in state violence. Leaders strive for power and dominance. Followers are generally obsequious and submissive to the leader, but hostile toward outsiders. Authoritarian movements cut across ideological lines. Both right-wing and left-wing populist movements can be authoritarian and illiberal.

Authoritarian movements are inherently illiberal. Authoritarian leaders use democratic institutions and principles to get into power. Once in office, authoritarian leaders strive to maintain and enhance their power. When members of the press become critics, authoritarian leaders tend to classify them as enemies of the people. Authoritarian leaders use power not just to promote their political agendas but to discredit opponents, suppress political opposition, and silence critics. This use of power threatens democratic principles, promotes incivility, and disregards truth and justice. Illiberal authoritarian leaders are likely to violate basic freedoms of speech, press, and assembly and disregard basic human rights.

Liberal-democratic movements are by definition anti-authoritarian. They advocate expanding democracy: amplifying the voices and political influence of all people, especially minorities who tend to be politically marginalized. They support making the vote a guaranteed constitutional right for all voting-aged citizens and limiting the political influence of major corporations. They favor civil rights: extending the same rights and privileges enjoyed by dominant groups to subordinate groups, identifiable on the basis of race, ethnicity, nationality, religion, gender, sexual orientation, and disabling conditions. They promote civil liberties: the protection of the freedom of speech, religion, press and assembly, and the limiting of police powers to protect those suspected of crimes from unreasonable search and seizure and excessive force. The civil rights movement in the United States exhibited these liberal-democratic populist features. Liberal-democratic movements favor a robust role of government in improving the quality of the lives of its citizens: sustaining a livable wage, promoting health and safety in the workplace, protecting collective bargaining rights, recognizing health care as a human right, investing heavily in education from pre-school through higher education, and improving environmental quality.

## Left-Wing Populists

Left-wing populist movements tend to direct anger and resentment toward economic elites: leaders of major banks, corporations, and businesses. The base of support for these types of movements tends to come predominately from workers, farmers, minorities, and the poor. Organizations of farmers, labor unions, civil rights, and anti-poverty groups dominate the base of these movements. These movements tend to demand government intervention to restrain the power of banks and corporations and to improve the quality of the lives of all citizens, especially low-income workers, farmers, and disadvantaged populations. Left-wing movements tend to favor progressive taxes, an extensive social safety net, and educational programs calculated to increase upward social mobility.

A left-wing populist movement arose in the United States in the 1880s. The leaders of this movement criticized what they saw as corporate and financial elites cheating and exploiting farmers and workers. These leaders believed that both farmers and workers were victims of an unfair economic system. They supported an expanded government role to protect workers from excessive exploitation and dangerous working conditions (Hofstadter 1955; Frank 2020; Goodwyn 1978).

This populist movement was initiated by multiple farmers' alliances responding to rising costs and declining profits among farmers. The movement was anchored by the National Farmers' Alliance (Goodwyn 1978; Hoftstadter 1955; Schwartz 1988; Woodward 1938). This organization of farmers formed alliances with labor unions and black workers. It engaged in sympathetic strikes and boycotts to support the rights of workers to unionize and engage in collective bargaining. It promoted a progressive policy agenda that called for the federal government to regulate railroads rates, protect the collective bargaining rights of workers, mandate a shorter workweek, and impose a progressive income tax (Goodwyn 1978; Schwartz 1988).

Tom Watson of the Georgia People's Party was a leader who began his career as a left-wing populist. He advocated public ownership of railroad, steamship, telephone, and telegraph companies; opposed the convict lease system that exploited prison labor; condemned lynching; demanded direct elections of senators; and supported a progressive income tax. The young Tom Watson spoke of how the welfare of white workers and farmers depended on government programs that also benefited black workers and farmers. While recruiting for the People's Party, he warned of the tendency of unscrupulous economic elites to deliberately incite racial hatred and divisions among black and white farmers and workers in order to super-exploit both:

The white tenant lives adjoining the colored tenant. Their houses are almost equally destitute of comfort. Their living is confined to bare necessities . . . Now the People's Party says to these two men, "You are kept apart that you may be separately fleeced of your earnings. You are made to hate each other because upon that hatred is rested the keystone of the arch of financial despotism which enslaves you both. You are deceived and blinded that you may not see how this race antagonism perpetuates a monetary system which beggars both." (Watson 1892)

By the end of the nineteenth century, the left-wing populist movement was crushed in the South. Rich landowners engaged in a crusade against the movement. They used both legal and extra-legal means to destroy labor unions, especially those that attempted to organize agricultural workers. They were exceptionally violent toward those who attempted to organize black workers and sharecroppers (Foner 1982). They stoked racial fears and prejudices in order to capture the support of white workers and poor whites. Racial stereotypes and fears were pervasive in southern newspapers, schools, and churches. Racism saturated southern culture. Skillful political leaders exploited anger, provoked fear, and promoted stereotypes. Southern populist leaders, including the older Tom Watson, succumbed to racism.

Thomas Frank offered a different perspective on left-wing populism. He traced the origins of American populist movements back to Thomas Paine and Thomas Jefferson (Frank 2020). Paine and Jefferson argued for limited governmental police powers to prevent unreasonable search and seizure, self-incrimination, excessive use of force, and cruel and unusual punishment. They favored restricting governmental powers to protect basic freedoms, such as the freedom of speech, press, assembly, and religion. Paine and Jefferson both opposed monopolies. However, Paine advocated for an expansive role of government to improve the quality of the lives of its citizens (Hitchens 2008).

Frank maintained that genuine populists opposed unrestrained capitalism. They promoted democracy and individual and civil rights. They demanded the expansion of the right to vote. They supported government regulations to ensure a fair economy and to protect the health and safety of consumers and workers. They called for empowering workers through labor unions and insisted upon a robust social safety net. Frank insisted that the New Deal and Great Society programs were products of genuine populist movements.

He argued that what scholars define as contemporary populism is not populism. It is anti-populism, the antithesis of original populism. He claimed that for centuries, skillful, unscrupulous, and wealthy political leaders undermined genuine populism by stoking fears, exploiting anger, and promoting racial stereotypes. He insisted that the anti-populist movements of the early twentieth century were racist and anti-immigration. Frank pointed out that anti-populists promoted protectionist trade policies. His main point was that Donald Trump was not a populist. He was an anti-populist. Although Trump's support for tariffs have people confused over whether he is a conservative or not, Frank insisted that Trump's ideas were not much different from those of conservatives like William McKinley and Herbert Hoover. McKinley and Hoover were supported by the superrich, favored limited government, and promoted protective tariffs. Frank's point is well taken. However, it oversimplifies a wide variety of different forms of populism. It is useful to distinguish between left-wing and right-wing populist movements.

## Right-Wing Populists

Right-wing populist movements have characteristics similar to most other populist movements. Like all other populist movements, right-wing movements are driven by anger. They target elites and the establishment. They acknowledge grievances. However, there are many characteristics of the right-wing populist movement that distinguishes it from other populist movements. The political base of right-wing populist movements often constitute what some scholars refer to as an alliance between capital and labor or the dominant economic class and the masses (Arendt 1951; Frank 2020). Right-wing movements attract supporters from all economic classes. Typically, right-wing populist leaders criticize economic elites and acknowledge the grievances of the workers in public. However, they redirect grievances toward scapegoats. When they are in power, their actual public policy agenda responds primarily to the interests of the economic elites they criticize. Often they include intellectuals and opposition political leaders among the elite.

There is a dispute in the literature over how much right-wing movements helped white workers, especially in the former Confederate states. There is no dispute that during the New Deal era, Southern Democrats and populist leaders supported programs that helped poor whites even though they opposed benefits going to poor blacks. Southern right-wing populists tended to be white nationalist. White nationalist movements have favored anti-poverty programs that helped poor whites, the deserving poor, but opposed helping non-whites, the undeserving poor. These movements support increasing the power of their leaders and their parties, but oppose the empowerment of labor unions and minorities. Right-wing movements engage in a form of us versus them politics. That is, right-wing leaders tend to define themselves and their base as the people and their opponents, including news critics, as enemies of the people. They tend to criminalize their opponents and refer to liberals as socialists. They campaign for law and order and against corruption in government. They favor increasing police powers, and they encourage police violence.

A classic, but extreme, example of right-wing populism is the German Nazi movement of the 1920s and 1930s. This movement was precipitated by the extreme resentment and anger over the defeat of Germany in World War I, the severe economic stress imposed on Germany by the war reparation payments, the inflation of the 1920s, the depression of the 1930s, and the paralyzing and polarizing political conflicts of this time period. The Nazi Party blamed Germany's defeat on Jews, liberals, and socialists. The Nazi Party claimed that these groups stabbed Germany in the back. It redirected anger and resentment at scapegoats—Jews, liberals, socialists, and non-Germans. The political base of this German populist movement was what Hannah Arendt referred to as an alliance between German corporate leaders and the mob, all other classes (Arendt 1951). While the Nazi Party claimed to favor workers, once in power, it engaged in an all-out assault on labor unions. The party and its leaders presented themselves as the people and their critics as enemies of the people. These leaders claimed that pure German or Aryan people were not just virtuous. They were superior. The party, the people and the leader were all one and the same. The Nazi Party promoted and dramatically increased state violence and terror. The Nazi movement engaged in an aggressive campaign of spreading disinformation—deliberate lies calculated to validate stereotypes, stoke anger, provoke strong emotions, and generate support for extreme and violent actions that would ordinarily appear appalling.

A particular form of a right-wing populist movement bears mention because this form is related to Trump's populism: reactionary populism. Reactionary populist movements are the same as right-wing populist movements, except they are generally preceded and precipitated by an era of expansionary progressive policies. Right-wing reactionary populist movements have emerged periodically throughout U.S. history typically in response to the passage of a flood of progressive public policies or a progressive era. Generally, these movements have been initiated by economic elites threatened by progressive taxes and public policies that contribute to the rapid upward social mobility of the lower classes. Leaders of these movements not only exploit racial prejudices. They tend to racialize progressive policies to provoke anger and opposition to these policies. A classic example of a right-wing reactionary populist movement is the Redeemer movement.

## The Redeemer Movement

The Redeemer movement was a southern reactionary movement. It was partially a reaction to the defeat of the Confederacy during the Civil War and largely a reaction to the Reconstruction regime. This movement was committed to restoring the glory of the Antebellum South. Although this movement involved many different political and social interests and classes, it was led by wealthy landowners and business leaders, the Southern aristocracy. It defined the people as virtuous and superior, but it limited this characterization of the people to white Christians. African Americans were characterized as inferior, ignorant, immoral, and dangerous if there were not submissive and controlled. Redeemer leaders characterized the south as the victim of northern exploitation and northern aggression.

An avalanche of progress Reconstruction policies enacted just after the Civil War incited this movement. These policies included the 13th, 14th, and 15th amendments and more. The 14th amendment defined anyone born in the United States as a citizen entitled to due process and equal protection under the law. The 15th prohibited states from denying citizens the right to vote on account of race. Reconstruction laws included the Civil Rights Acts of 1866, 1870, 1871, and 1875. Indeed, the 1866 act prohibited denying former slaves the right to purchase real estate, to serve on juries, and to be free from forced labor. The 1875 act prohibited racial segregation in public accommodation. Other progressive policies included taxes on rich landowners in order to finance infrastructure projects to build roads and bridges and to finance a public school system. There was not much of a public school system in the Antebellum South. Slave states had the highest illiteracy rate in the nation among white males (Merritt 2017). The Reconstruction education system was designed to educate both former slaves and poor whites. These policies encouraged equal opportunity, inclusiveness, and democracy. They were a precursor of what can be called the equal opportunity state, which emerged out of the New Deal and the Great Society programs. These policies were the product of the Republican Party. The Southern Republican Party was a racially integrated party committed to protecting the rights of black and white sharecroppers and workers. This party enabled the election of former slaves to federal and state legislative offices that had previously been once held exclusively by white males, primarily from the southern aristocracy. These policies and the Southern Republican Party provoke a powerful backlash which became the Redeemer movement.

The Redeemer movement was not just a reaction to Reconstruction policies. It was an all-out assault on these policies and the Southern Republican Party. The movement characterized the Southern Republican Party as incompetent and corrupt and as a threat to the southern way of life and to the system of white supremacy. This movement declared war on the Southern Republican Party. It engaged in a campaign to overthrow the Reconstruction regime by any means necessary. The movement targeted progressive taxes. It created a profoundly inequitable system that favored rich white school children and disadvantaged poor white and black school children. It was hostile to labor rights and lethal to civil rights. It disenfranchised almost all voting-aged black male voters and most voting-aged poor white voters. It established the Jim Crow system of racial segregation. It created an excessively punitive criminal justice system. It enabled an upward redistribution of wealth. For example, between 1896 and 1900 in Louisiana, the number of registered voters fell from about 127,000 to about 3,300 (Gossett 1971, 266). In Texas, voter participation among white males declined from a rate of 80 percent in 1900 to 27 percent by 1904 (Bloom 1987, 49). Whereas spending for K-12 public school education increased in the south in the early 1900s, it increased dramatically for the rich, marginally poor whites, and very little for blacks. For example, in Mississippi in 1907, public school spending averaged about $3.50 per pupil for blacks, $5.65 per pupil for poor whites, and about $80 per pupil for well-to-do whites (Bloom 1987, 55–56). As a result of the Redeemer movement, poor whites lost the right to vote, suffered inadequately funded schools, and experienced harsh working conditions (Bloom 1987).

Even though this movement hurt them, working-class and lower class whites supported the Redeemer movement for two reasons. First, they supported the movement because of a phenomenon that historian W.E.B. DuBois referred to as "the wages of whiteness." Poor whites benefit from the enhanced esteem and status afforded to white identity. When white people were defined as a virtuous and superior people, poor whites could count themselves among the virtuous and superior. Second, southern political leaders and the southern media engaged in a disinformation campaign. Poor whites joint the chorus of other whites in condemning the Reconstruction regime as corrupt and repeating stories of ignorant, bribed, and manipulated black voters. Many believed the images of uncontrolled, immoral, and dangerous black males threatening young, virtuous southern women. These narratives, stories, and images influenced whites of all social classes to oppose Reconstruction and to fear unrestrained black males.

Leaders of the Redeemer movement deliberately engaged in a campaign of disinformation, false narratives, and lies to discredit and destroy the opposition party, the Republican Party. They characterized the entire Republican regime as corrupt and irrational. They promoted racial stereotypes and stoked fear. They depicted young black males as dangerous subhuman creatures that roam the south searching for innocent white women to rape and murder (Foner 2014; Alexander 2004). They used both illegal violent and legal means to silence opposition, suppress the right to vote, established racial caste system, and super exploit both black and white workers.

Although there is little consensus over the factors that enabled the rise of right-wing populist movements, these movements do not spring up out of nowhere. They seem be associated with economic stress, extreme inequality, and concentrated wealth among the economic elites. The form that a populist movement takes appears to be related to the political leaders. Globalization, corporate greed, and public policy changes—that weaken labor bargaining power, reduce labor costs, increase corporate power, weaken the social safety net, and enabled upward social mobility—provided the fertile ground for the growth of these movements. Jon Kofas offered this observation, "To some extent, populism is a reaction to globalization and neoliberal policies that have accounted for massive capital concentration in the top ten percent of the population at the expense of the middle class and workers" (Kofas 2017). David Blanchflower demonstrated that economic stress, particularly in rural areas, was strongly associated with the rise of these movements (2021).

Trump appealed to disgruntled white workers who had experienced stagnant wages. He promised economic nationalism and stoked animus toward minorities and China. However, once in office, he hacked away at social programs designed to help struggling Americans, while he offered massive tax cuts for corporations and the rich. He made vague grandiose promises and exploited fears and prejudices to capture support from white workers and some minorities, but then promoted a public policy agenda that harmed both.

## TRUMP'S RIGHT-WING POPULIST MOVEMENT AND PUBLIC POLICY

Despite the tremendous effort by many talented, creative, and articulate Trump supporters to depict him as a champion of working-class Americans and a friend of minorities, the preponderance of the evidence suggests that Trump is a right-wing, reactionary populist engaged in an assault on the equal opportunity, inclusive state. The equal opportunity inclusive state is an artificial construct that defines the accumulation of progressive public policies that emerged over the past 120 years. These policies never equalized opportunities. Neither the government nor the free market can equalize opportunities. However, the government can establish rules to enhance fairness in the market, create policies to reallocate resources to alleviate the harsh effects of poverty, and to invest in all levels of education, from pre-school to higher education. Public policies and public resources can assist in upward social mobility. These types of progressive public policies are the product of multiple left-wing populist movements. These movements produced progressive federal income taxes, the New Deal, the Great Society, civil rights, and anti-poverty programs. The New Deal empowered workers and increased their political influence through labor unions, raised the standard of living of American workers, and expanded the middle class. Whereas the anti-poverty programs of the 1960s failed to eliminate poverty, many of these programs eliminated diseases associated with poverty and improved the living conditions of low-income families. Great Society programs enhanced upward social mobility by increasing investments in public education: pre-school, K-12, and higher education. Civil rights policies expanded the right to vote and equalized opportunities for well-qualified minorities in the job market. In short, the equal opportunity, inclusive state abstractly refers to a political and governmental commitment to invest in programs that enhance upward social mobility, improve the quality of the lives of all citizens, protect the rights of minorities, as well as non-minorities, support social welfare programs, and guarantee the right to vote for all voting-aged citizens.

Donald Trump's actions and politics mirrored the defining characteristics of a right-wing populist movement. Trump engaged in an "us versus them" style of politics. He defined himself and his supporters as the people and characterized his critics, including the media, as enemies of the people. In the 2016 election, he effectively criminalized his opponent, Hillary Clinton. In the 2020 election, he attempted to criminalize his opponent, Joe Biden. Like other right-wing populists, Trump referred to himself as the law and order president. In his speeches, he encouraged increased police violence. He specifically encouraged police officers to "rough up suspects." During the 2020 summer riots, advocated the shooting of looters. He called the Black Lives Matter movement violent and dangerous. He stoked prejudices in ways that redirected anger from corporate leaders to various scapegoats—immigrants, China, and the Black Lives Matter movement. He acknowledged the impact that the slow recovery of the manufacturing mining sectors of the economy had on working-class America. While he criticized corporate leaders for moving manufacturing facilities and jobs out of the country, he shifted the blame to China. In a number of public speeches, he stated that China was taking our jobs and eating our lunch. His solution was not a set of policies to penalize corporations for closing down facilities in the United States. His solution was to engage in a trade war with China. This trade war hurt American farmers and did little for American workers.

Trump's renegotiated NAFTA agreement promised to solve the problem of the loss of automobile jobs. However, this trade agreement only applied to Mexico and Canada, not other countries. It did not establish a monitoring system nor provide any specific penalties to ensure compliance with the agreement. Moreover, Trump scapegoated Latino as well as Chinese Americans. He blamed the Covid-19 pandemic on China. He blamed Mexico and China for the loss of American jobs. He characterized Central American immigrants as invaders, crossing the U.S. border. Whether done deliberately or not, he provoked rage toward Chinese and Latino Americans and redirected anger away from corporate leaders.

Trump was not just a right-wing populist. He exhibited all of the traits of a reactionary populist. Although he supported Social Security and Medicare, which benefited a substantial bloc of his base, he accelerated the assault on progressive policies. He tried to cut funding for Medicaid and turn it into a block grant, something that wealthy opponents of the welfare state had been trying to accomplish since the election of Ronald Reagan. He pushed for work requirements for food assistance. He engaged in a relentless attack on the Affordable Care Act. He repealed policies that protected the rights of transgender persons in the military. He attempted to roll back workplace health and safety regulations. His Justice Department revoked consent decrees with local police departments. These decrees, negotiated by Obama's Justice Department, addressed issues of the excessive and unconstitutional use of police violence that targeted young black males. The Trump administration cut higher education grants for low-income college students and obstructed efforts initiated by the Obama administration to provide some relief for student loans. Unlike left-wing populists, Trump never advocated a redistribution of wealth and income downward. Contrary to Newt Gingrich, Trump's tax cuts favored the rich and corporations.

Whereas the voter suppression movement predates the Trump administration, Trump intensified this movement. Just like the leaders of the Redeemer movement of the late nineteenth century, Trump not only lied about voter fraud. He incessantly promoted incredible, bold faced lies about millions of fraudulent votes and left-wing conspiracies to steal elections. These lies and conspiracy theories were used to justify the passage of voter suppression laws, laws that made it more difficult for American citizens to vote, especially the more vulnerable citizens. After he lost the 2020 election by over 7 million votes, he lied and claimed the election was stolen from him. He endorsed conspiracy theories that largely blamed cities with substantial black populations for stealing the election: Atlanta, Detroit, Milwaukee, and Philadelphia.

Trump's assault on the equal opportunity, inclusive state is no trivial, coincidental, or isolated matter. This assault is a major defining feature of the Trump administration. Trump did not initiate this assault. It had been occurring for decades. The very same political movements that ushered Trump into the White House in 2016 were engaged in this assault. Trump simply accelerated and intensified the assault. He expanded it into a full-fledged reactionary movement and an all-out war on the opposition party. Trump was far more successful in leading this assault and fighting this partisan war than any other Republican candidate. Trump's personal attributes and ideological disposition endowed him with the power to promote this war beyond all expectations. His blend of nationalism with neoliberalism, his authoritarian/narcissistic character type, his common, vulgar, and unrestrained communication style and his ability to read crowds enabled him to emerge as a powerful and charismatic right-wing reactionary populist leader.

Understanding the Trump phenomenon requires a careful review of three factors: Trump himself, Trump supporters, and the historical circumstances that contributed to the rise of Trump. These circumstances include the right-wing political movements that put him in the White House, the Realignment of the Republican Party, and the formation of a right-wing media-ecosystem. These circumstances also include the rise of extreme inequality and the decline of the real wages of workers with just a high school degree or less. Once these three factors are understood, Trump's domestic policy agenda becomes clear and predictable. This agenda accelerated the assault on the equal opportunity, inclusive state.

During the 2020 presidential campaign, Trump drew a stark contrast between the Republican Party and the Democratic Party. He persistently referred to Democratic candidates as radical Marxists and socialists (Epstein and Qui 2019). In the summer of 2019, he stated, "A vote for any Democrat in 2020 is a vote for the rise of radical socialism and the destruction of the American dream" (quoted by Reid and Qui 2019). By the fall of 2020, he was intimating that some Democrats were communists. He added, "If Joe Biden doesn't have the strength to stand up to wild-eyed Marxists like Bernie Sanders and his fellow radicals—and there are many, many, we see them all the time, it's incredible, actually—then how is he ever going to stand up for you?" (quoted by Martin 2020).

There is indeed a contrast between Trump and the Democratic Party, but the contrast is not between capitalists and socialists. Socialism is defined as government ownership and control over the means of production. A socialist healthcare system is one in which physicians work for the government and hospitals are owned and run by the government. Although Bernie Sanders calls himself a democratic socialist, his public policy agenda is inconsistent with a socialist agenda. His public policy agenda falls under the tradition of an expanded New Deal program. His political perspectives are more consistent with Franklin Delano Roosevelt. When questioned about his agenda, Sanders admits that his brand of socialism is not a form of Marxist socialism, but more in the tradition of the New Deal and Sweden's social welfare state. Sanders does not advocate a government-owned and -controlled healthcare system. He calls for "Medicare for all," which is based on the current capitalistic system in which hospitals are privately owned and controlled; doctors are allowed to operate their own private practice; and publicly financed health insurance is supplemented with private health insurance (Frizell 2019; Golshan 2019; Tupy 2016). For Bernie Sanders, health care is a human right. For Donald Trump, it is a private choice. The difference between Sanders and Trump is not a difference between socialism and capitalism. It is the difference between Franklin Delano Roosevelt's brand of capitalism and Herbert Hoover's brand of capitalism. As this text will demonstrate, it is the difference between democratic capitalism and plutocratic, nationalistic capitalism. It is the difference between a political system that strives to work for all of the people, including minorities, poor people, and low-income workers, and a political system that advocates nationalistic pride and America first, promotes laissez-faire capitalism along with protective tariffs, and redistributes wealth and income upward. The difference between Sanders and Trump is the difference between left-wing populism and right-wing reactionary populism.

## Chapter 2

# Trumpism

When explaining the formation of public policies, political scientists have generally focused on interest group pressure (Dahl 1989, 2005; Lindblom 1980; Lowi 1969; Truman 1950), strategic political elites (Carmine and Stimson 1990), or public attention cycles (Downs 1972). The more recent literature has examined the role of discourse, problem definition, and ideology (Bamgartner and Jones 2009; Cobbs and Elder 1983; Jost and Napier 2009; Robin 2012). Problem definition and ideology provide the rational, intellectual, cognitive, and emotive basis for public policy change. This chapter examines the cognitive and emotive foundation of Trumpism.

Scholars and journalist disagree about Trump's ideology. Some portray him as erratic, impulsive, inconsistent, and devoid of any coherent ideology (Woodward 2020). Others point to Steve Bannon and Steve Miller as major influences (Green). The Republican Party's public policy agenda is shaped by ideology (Grossman and Hopkins 2016). As head of the Republican Party, Trump has exercised considerable influence in reshaping the party's ideology.

This chapter investigates Trump's ideas and worldview that set his policy agenda, reshaped the party's ideology, and resonated with his political base. This chapter demonstrates that despite the common perspective of Trump as unpredictable and chaotic, he has a core set of ideas and views. This set is a blend of neoliberalism, nationalism, authoritarianism/narcissism, and racialism.

## IDEOLOGY AND MODUS OPERANDI

Based on extensive interviews with Trump and members of his administration, Bob Woodward presents a clear picture of Trump's administrative style.

Woodward shared a summary perspective from Trump's senior adviser and son-in-law, Jared Kushner. Kushner referenced four pieces of literature to summarize Trump's administrative style: Lewis Carole, *Alice in Wonderland*; Chris Whipple, *The Gatekeepers: How the White House Chiefs of Staff Define Every President*; Scott Adams, *Win Bigly: Persuasion in a World Where Facts don't Matter*, and Peggy Noonan's opinion piece in *The Wall Street Journal*. Kushner likened Trump to the Cheshire Cat in *Alice in Wonderland*, always running, but never having a destination. *The Gatekeepers* underscored the importance of the chief of staff in advising the president and managing of the presidency. Trump rarely followed their advice. In *Win Bigly*, Adams, the creator of the Dilbert comic strip, emphasized Trump's ability to invent any reality for most voters on most issues and "all you will remember is that Trump provided reasons, he didn't apologize, and his opponents called him a liar, like they always do (Woodward 2020, 258)." Noonan characterized the Trump administration as crazy, not unpredictable, or crafty like a fox, but unstable and unhinged (Woodward 2020, 257–258). Woodward pointed out that Trump did occasionally listen to advisers, especially during the early weeks of the covid-19 pandemic, but he seemed more concerned with the economy and winning re-election. According to Woodward, Trump argued that he wanted to avoid hysteria. Woodward concluded, "Trump has, instead, enshrined personal impulse as a governing principle of his presidency" (Woodward 2020, 392).

Several books emphasized Trump's insecurity, inability to empathized with others, cruelty, and dishonesty. John Bolton, former National Security Adviser to Trump, suggested that Trump lacked basic knowledge, had a short attention span, was easily distracted, and had difficulties sticking to a single subject. Trump was often more concerned with his own self-aggrandizement and popularity than the best interest of the country (Bolton 2020). Michael Cohen insisted that Trump did not care about facts or truth. He cared about his success, popularity, and power (Cohen 2020).

Despite the characterization of Trump as unpredictable and chaotic, there are two major dimensions of Trump's political perspectives: transactional and ideological. The transactional dimension arises from Trump's career as a business leader, contract negotiator, and reality television personality. A business transaction is a simple exchange, something of value in exchange for something of value. Trump understands that he needs a broad base of support from millions of voters to win the presidential election. To secure this support, he has engaged in a transactional or a quid pro quo relationship with two groups. That is, he makes promises in exchange for something in return.

As Trump's devotion to Christianity was somewhat ambiguous, he established a transactional relationship with the Christian right movement. He was never part of this movement, although he was clearly a Christian. In his book

*Great Again,* Trump claimed to be a religious person (Trump 2016). Indeed, he is a confirmed Presbyterian. He posted his June 1959 confirmation photograph on Twitter during the 2016 campaign (Burke 2016). In the 1960s, he was a follower of Norman Vincent Peale, the author of *The Power of Positive Thinking* and a promoter of prosperity Christianity, the view that salvation in Christ is demonstrated by the accumulation of wealth. During this period, Trump held many political positions that were antithetical to the Christian right perspective. Throughout most of his life, he was pro-choice. Moreover, Trump harbored values and engaged in forms of behavior incompatible with conservative Christian norms and expectations. These non-Christian values and forms of behavior were evident in the Access Hollywood video and in his liaisons with porn star Stormy Daniels and playboy bunny Karen McDougal. He seemed incapable of repenting, another trait incompatible with Christianity. He was known to hold grudges and to seek revenge on critics and opponents. In a February 2020 annual National Prayer Breakfast meeting, he disagreed with the keynote speaker who urged listeners to commit to civility and heed Jesus' command to love your enemies (Crary 2020). Trump was never a part of the Christian right movement.

His relationship to the Christian right was largely transactional. It was somewhat of a Faustian bargain. Trump offered to realize all of their political aspirations, hopes, and dream, in exchange for their loyalty and support. These political aspirations included the appointment of pro-life judges to the Supreme Court and other federal courts, the promotion of Christian values, the privileging of religious rights, and the exclusion of non-Christian immigrants. Trump delivered on his transactional promises to the Christian right. To this day, conservative evangelical followers are devout supporters of Trump. Although this relationship is clearly transaction, a number of scholars insist that it was not really a bargain, but an ideological commitment. Although Trump offered a bargain, he provided an ideological perspective that resonated with many on the Christian right, especially the implied idea of making the United States a white Christian nation, barring Muslims and people of color from coming into the country.

## Neoliberalism

Although there is little evidence that Trump is versed on the neoliberal literature, there is considerable evidence that Trump ascribes to a neoliberal perspective, modified with a mixture of nationalism and authoritarianism. Neoliberalism emerged in opposition to the New Deal regime and Keynesian economic theory, which favored the expansion of the administrative state and the formation of a welfare and equal opportunity state. Neoliberalism calls for market solution to public problems, the shrinking of government, and the shifting of public services to the private for profit or non-profit sector. Its primary method for stimulating the economy is to cut taxes, roll back regulations, and shrink government. Neoliberalism has no concept of social justice. It is hostile to labor unions. It has a negative concept of freedom, that is, freedom is the absence of government restrictions (Harvey 2005; Saad-Filho and Johnston 2005). For neoliberals, expanding government is antithetical to freedom.

Trump's domestic policy agenda is well grounded in neoliberalism. In his book, *Crippled America*, after claiming that the Affordable Care Act was an absolute disaster, Trump offered this neoliberal solution:

> I have a big company. I have thousands of employees. If I'm negotiating for health insurance for my people in New York or California or Texas, I usually have one bidder in each state. Competition brings down prices, and the way the law is now, it discourages real competition between insurance companies for customers. They have virtual monopolies within the states . . .
>
> Nobody understands business better than I do. You want better plans at a better price? Increase competition for customers.
>
> The government doesn't belong in health care except as the very last resort. The main way the government should be involved is to make sure the insurance companies are financially strong so that if there is a catastrophic event or they make some kind of miscalculation, they have the resources they'll need to handle it. (Trump 2015, 75–76)

According to the neoliberal perspective, competition constrains businesses to produce a better product for a cheaper price. Thus, most problems are solved with more competition and less government. Trump applied this neoliberal perspective to the problems of public schools as well:

> The problem with public schools is that in many places there is no way to take an honest measurement of how they're doing. If a charter school isn't doing the job, it closes. That's the type of accountability we need throughout our educational system.
>
> One huge obstacle is the strength of the teacher unions. Teacher unions don't want school choice because it means a potential reduction in union-protected jobs. (Trump 2015, 55)

Neoliberals are hostile to labor unions and so was Trump. Despite efforts to appeal to union workers, claiming that he built the Trump Tower in New

York City with union labor, the overall thrust of his approach was anti-union, as he explained a February 2016 radio interview praising right-to-work laws:

> We've had great support from [union] workers, the people that work, the real workers, but I love the right to work . . . I like it better because it is lower. It is better for the people. You are not paying the big fees to the unions. The unions get big fees. A lot of people don't realize they have to pay a lot of fees. I am talking about the workers. They have to pay big fees to the union. I like it because it gives great flexibility to the people. It gives great flexibility to the companies. (Trump, quoted by Higgins 2016)

Indeed, the New York Trump Tower was built in a state where the law required the use of union workers. By contrast, at the time of the interview, Trump was embroiled in a bitter dispute with service workers in Las Vegas, where no such law existed: The service workers at the Trump International Las Vegas Hotel had voted to unionize. Trump's organization fought to dispute the election.

This neoliberal perspective was evident in Trump's economic policies as well. He advocated cutting corporate and individual taxes; repealing or rolling back government regulations; shrinking government; and substantially reducing spending for social programs. He insisted that these policies would produce a robust economy, expand productivity, reduce unemployment, and increase jobs. Like most neoliberals, Trump had no qualms about slashing taxes to produce a deep budget deficit and then using the deficit to reduce government spending and shrink government programs.

Trump is a longtime admirer of Ayn Rand, a political theorist who maintains that greed is good, government is bad, and involuntary taxation is theft. This admiration for Rand appears inconsistent with his apparent willingness to use government to persuade major corporations to keep production facilities inside the United States. However, Rand's philosophy of unrestrained selfishness and her deification of the alpha male capitalist entrepreneur resonates with Donald Trump. Whereas Trump has few favorite books, Rand's *The Fountainhead* is one of them. Moreover, in his own books, Trump glorified the tough, risk-taking, unorthodox, overly aggressive, and domineering entrepreneur. Indeed, he defined himself as a smart, rich, multi-billionaire real estate investor. In an article published in the *Guardian*, Jonathan Freedland explains Trump's idolization of Rand:

> Rand scholars find this affinity of Trump's puzzling. Not least because Trump's offer to the electorate in 2016 was not a promise of an unfettered free market. It was a pledge to make the US government an active meddler in the market, negotiating trade deals, bringing back jobs. His public bullying of big

companies—pressing Ford or the air-conditioner manufacturer Carrier to keep
their factories in the US—was precisely the kind of big government intrusion
upon the natural rhythms of capitalism that appalled Rand.

So why does Trump claim to be inspired by her? The answer, surely, is that
Rand lionises the alpha male capitalist entrepreneur, the man of action who tow-
ers over the little people and the pettifogging bureaucrats—and gets things done.
As Jennifer Burns puts it: "For a long time, she has been beloved by disruptors,
entrepreneurs, venture capitalists, people who see themselves as shaping the
future, taking risky bets, moving out in front of everyone else, relying only
on their own instincts, intuition and knowledge, and going against the grain."
(Freedland 2017)

## Nationalism

Trump's nationalism operated to reconcile the inconsistencies between his
neoliberalism and his right-wing populism. His neoliberalism appealed to the
rich. His nationalism shifted blame for the economic problems of workers
from the rich and projected it on out-groups: foreign countries, immigrants,
and minorities. His inaugural address illustrates this point:
One by one, the factories shuttered and left our shores, with not even a
thought about the

millions upon millions of American workers left behind. The wealth of our
middle class has been ripped from their homes and then redistributed across the
entire world. But that is the past.

From this day forward, a new vision will govern our land. From this moment on,
it's going to be America First. Every decision on trade, on taxes, on immigration, on foreign affairs, will be made to benefit American workers and American
families. We must protect our borders from the ravages of other countries making our products, stealing our companies, and destroying our jobs. Protection
will lead to great prosperity and strength. (Trump 2017)

The problem is not the greed and callousness of American corporate leaders. The problem is not the redistribution of wealth and income upward from
the working and middle classes to the upper class. Indeed, Trump skillfully
shifts the blame for these problems from corporate leaders to invading immigrants and foreign countries. Trump claimed that wealth and income left the
country. He blamed the problem on other countries, most notably China, for
stealing American jobs and wealth (Trump 2015). He blamed the problem on
invaders from Mexico. He insisted that "we must protect our borders from

the ravages of other countries . . . stealing our companies and destroying our jobs" (Trump 2017). He added, "We need to bring manufacturing jobs back home—the jobs China is stealing" (Trump 2011).

Trump's rhetoric is neo-nationalistic and neoliberal. His assertion that "[t] he wealth of our middle class has been ripped from their homes and then redistributed across the entire world" was demonstrably false. Wealth had not left the county. Wealth and income had been redistributed from America's workers to America's corporate and Wall Street leaders (Bartels 2008; Hacker and Pierson 2011; Hacker and Pierson 2016; Lafer 2017; Page and Gilens 2017; Piketty 2014; Reich 2016; Smith 2012; Stiglitz 2012).

## Authoritarianism/Narcissism

Trump is authoritarian and narcissistic.

The concept of authoritarianism was popularized by the Frankfurth School, Institute for Social Research in Frankfurth, Germany. Authoritarianism is not an ideology. It is a particular orientation to the world that generally arises out of anxiety and insecurity alleviated by discipline, order, and strict obedience to authority. Erich Fromm associated authoritarianism with sado-masochistic dynamics: The masochism takes the form of reverence for powerful leaders and submission and loss of self to the in-group. Fromm defines sadism as the impulse to control, humiliate, and destroy. This impulse is directed at critics, enemies, or members of the out-group—minorities, Jews, immigrants, gays, lesbians, etc. (Fromm 1994). Theodore Adorno and others developed the concept of the authoritarian personality type. This personality type had nine identifying characteristics, which included authoritarian submission, aggression, destructiveness, superstition, homophobia, and several others. Adorno and others developed the so-called "F" test for measuring the authoritarian personality (Adorno et al. 1950). This test was rejected as too complex, involving too many factors, and lacking validity and reliability (Altemeyer 1988). In the 1980s a Canadian scholar, Bob Altemeyer, revised the "F" test, limiting it to three factors: authoritarian submission, convention, and aggression. By the end of the twentieth century, scholars had revised authoritarian surveys down to four forced-choice questions focused on preferred childhood behavior: independence versus respect for elders; curiosity versus good manners; self-reliance versus obedience; and being considerate versus being well behaved (Hetherington and Weiler 2009; MacWilliams 2016). Authoritarians favored respect over independence, good manners over curiosity, obedience over self-reliance, and good behavior over consideration for others.

Scholars also distinguished between right-wing authoritarianism and social dominance. Right-wing authoritarians were more likely to be religious and revered tradition. Social dominant personalities were less likely to be religious, but more aggressive, domineering, and cruel. Trump's form of authoritarianism was more like social dominance than right-wing authoritarianism.

By 2016, a large number of authoritarian voters had migrated to the Republican Party (Hetherington and Weiler 2009). Hetherington and Weiler documented the migration of authoritarians into the Republican Party over the past several decades (Hetherington and Weiler 2009). At least since Richard Nixon proclaimed Republicans to be the party of "law and order," authoritarians have been self-selecting into this party. During the 2016 primarily, Trump emerged as the most authoritarian candidate (MacWilliams 2016). Trump won the primary because he was the most aggressive and socially dominant, alpha male, authoritarian candidate. He had set out to destroy and humiliate his opponents. He expected absolute loyalty.

Trump saw the world divided between winners and losers, predators and prey. He made this point clear in the book *Think Big*:

> Lions kill for food. People kill for sport . . . . The same burning greed that makes people loot, kill, and steal in emergencies like fires and floods, operates daily in normal everyday people. It lurks right beneath the surface, and when you least expect it, it rears its nasty head and bites you. Accept it. The world is a brutal place. People will annihilate you just for the fun of it or to show off to their friends. (Trump and Zanker 2009)

For Trump, this is a dog-eat-dog world in which only the strong survives.

Trump exhibited another trait common among socially dominant or authoritarian populist leaders: narcissism (Lee 2017; Frances 2017). Three characteristics of narcissist populist leaders are problematic. First, they are self-centered and have a need for admiration. They see themselves and the people as one. They view the people as a homogenous whole (Muller 2016). This orientation is problematic because these types of leaders are likely to interpret criticism of themselves as an attack on the people or the nation. They tend to define critics as enemies of the people or, worse, as traitors to the nation. This type of orientation is a threat to liberal democracy, which requires free speech and open criticism of political leaders to function properly.

Second, narcissists have difficulty to empathize with others (APA 2013). They are capable of inflicting pain on others without remorse. In Trump's case, this characteristic was evident in his policy of separating young children, including mere babies younger than 2 years old, from their mothers to punish refugee families for attempting to seek asylum in the United States. In the Trump administration, this was a deliberate policy to discourage asylum seekers.

Third, they are driven to maintain power at all costs. Neither truth nor facts matter to them (Kakutani 2018). What matters is loyalty, adoration, and dominance. Their goal is not to be consistent, truthful, or reasonable but to prevail, to win, to dominate, and to control. Their assault on truth undermines the ability of the public to engage in honest discourse and enhances their power (Kakutani 2018).

The narcissistic authoritarian leader often believes he is creating a better world, making the country great again. This belief gives him the moral high ground. At the same time, he is relentless in destroying and humiliating critics and opponents. In his drive to dominate others, power is all that matters. Truth and fairness are irrelevant. The world is divided in black-and-white terms, good and evil. Authoritarianism correlates strongly with prejudice, anti-Semitism, racism, and other forms of bigotry.

## Racialism

There is no question more polarizing and divisive than this one: Is Trump a racist? According to public opinion polls, about 51 percent of white Americans do not see him as a racist (Eltagouri 2018; Shropshire 2018; Quinnipiac University 2018). While 86 percent of Democrats see him as a racist, only 11 percent of Republicans do (Quinnipiac University 2018). Even after his attack on four congresswomen of color in July 2019, telling them to go back to where they came from, opinion polls did not change much. The Quinnipiac polls indicated that by the end of July 31, 2019, 50 percent of white Americans still claimed that Trump was not a racist. The nation was polarized on this question along gender lines as well; 55 percent of men claimed Trump was not a racist; 59 percent of women claimed he was (Quinnipiac 2019).

Those Americans who say Trump is not racist generally understand racists to be hate-filled, uneducated, ignorant white supremacists. For some, racist are expected to have ties with neo-Nazis or the KKK. They burn crosses and use the "N" word. In contrast, Trump supporters see Trump's offer to help save African Americans from urban violence and unemployment as clear evidence that he is not a racist. This evidence is confirmed by the presence of a few black supporters. Thus, Trump supporters are offended by critics who accuse Trump of being a racist.

They see the accusation of racism as an outrageous, cowardly act by hysterical liberals and Trump haters.

The absence of a basic definition of racism makes it difficult for Trump defenders to see racism. A basic dictionary definition of racism is, "Prejudice, discrimination or antagonism directed against a person or people on the basis of their membership in a particular racial or ethnic group . . . The belief that different races possess distinct characteristics, abilities, or qualities, especially so as to distinguish them as inferior or superior" (Bling 2019). Encyclopedia Britannica offers a broader definition:

> Racism, also called racialism, the belief that humans may be divided into separate and exclusive biological entities called races; that there is a causal link between inherited physical traits and traits of personality, intellect, morality, and other cultural and behavioral features; and that some races are innately superior to others. (Britannica 2020)

Given these definitions, racism is not limited to the ignorant, uneducated, hate-filled white supremacists.

Race is an artificial social construct associated with oppression—violence, conquest, exclusion, segregation, exploitation, slavery, or dehumanization. The word "race" entered the English language during the period in which the English were conquering Ireland (Smedley and Smedley 2018). The English racialized the Irish; that is, defined them as belonging to a different race and ascribing demeaning behavioral characteristic on them. The English characterized the Irish as wild, promiscuous, drunken, and savage, asserted that they belonged to a different race. This characterization of the Irish justified the conquest (Rolston 1993; Smedley and Smedley 2018). Racism was about a collection of definitions, narratives, stories, images, and characterizations that enable and normalized oppression—conquest, slavery, domination, exploitation, violence, exclusion, and dehumanization and other manifestations of oppression.

Racism emerged in the United States to normalize and legitimize slavery. The prominent antebellum senator and intellectual leader from South Carolina, John Calhoun, offers a good example of how racism works. Calhoun insisted that the institution of slavery was good for the nation because it expanded the economy and produced wealth that benefited all Americans, including African Americans. He insisted that slavery lifted Africans from savagery, saved their bodies from cannibalism by taking them out of Africa, and saved their souls from damnation by making them Christians. He was passionately opposed to the abolitionist movement, because he believed that freeing the slaves would return them to barbarism and savagery. He, like most southerners, considered abolitionist to be dangerous radicals. Calhoun was a racist, not because he hated black people. He was racist because he categorized people with darker skin color as belonging to a separate race, with distinct behavioral characteristics and because he promoted narratives and lies that legitimized and normalized slavery and forms of oppressive treatment of people of color.

Trump is a racist, not because he says that he hates people of color. He is a racist because he categorizes people of color as belonging to a separate race with distinct behavioral characteristics. He claims that people of color as threatening and dangerous. He insists that Mexicans coming across the border are murderers and rapists. He trafficked in the use of racial stereotypes. He states that Jews are good at counting money and blacks are lazy. He is quoted saying, "laziness is a trait in blacks" (O'Donnell 1991; Cohen 2020; Lopez 2019). Throughout most of his life and especially during his presidency, Trump exhibited different forms and levels of racism: aversive, dominative, and symbolic.

Aversive racism involves the belief that a racialized group is undesirable or repulsive (Kovel 1982; Wilson 1996, 2015). This belief is often followed by efforts to exclude members of the racial group in question from neighbor-hoods, housing, employment, public accommodations, or other spaces or institutions. Trump exhibited this form of racism in the early 1970s. A num-ber of individuals and organizations filed complaints with the Urban League, the Justice Department, and other organizations claiming that the Trump Management Company, Fred Trump and Donald Trump, had engaged in deliberate racial exclusion. A community organization, Operation Open City, had sent out testers, white couples and black couples, to apply for apartments at the Trump Village located in Brooklyn. White couples had little or no prob-lem getting an apartment. For black couples, there were no apartments avail-able (Graham et al. 2019). After subpoenaing documents from the company, the Justice Department discovered that black applications for apartments were labeled with a large letter C. In reference to Donald Trump's attitude, a Justice Department lawyer said, "He was exactly the way he is today. He said to me at one point during a coffee break, You know, you don't want to live with them either" (quoted in Graham et al. 2019).

According to a rental agent at the time, Stanley Leibowitz, who worked for the Trump rental business, the Trump's (Donald Trump and his father, Fred Trump) had a clear and explicit policy of not renting to blacks (Punish 2020).

Aversive racism is about exclusion and separation. It often involves the use code words for racialized and undesirable groups, such as inner city, welfare, urban underclass, or welfare queen. Trump displayed this form of racism when he claimed a decade after the Justice Department suit, "What we didn't do was rent to welfare cases, white or black" (Trump 1987). The belief that most black women are on welfare and are undesirable as neighbors is an example of aversive racism.

Dominative racism entails characterizing racial groups as erratic, violent, dangerous, and murderous (Kovel 1983). These types of characterizations, in turn, incite efforts to dominate, control, or punish members of these groups. They also encourage the use of state violence to protect society from the sup-posedly menacing members of these groups. Trump did this, in an incident reminiscent of the 1930s "Scottsboro boys," a 1931 case in which Scottsboro,

Alabama, arrested and falsely accused nine African American teenagers of raping two white women. Trump campaigned to bring back the death penalty to punish the Central Park Five, four African American teenagers and one Puerto Rican teenager, who in 1989 were charged and convicted of raping and brutally assaulting a white woman. The only evidence used against them were their coerced confessions. When DNA evidence exonerated Central Park Five, Trump continued to insist on their guilt and death penalty punishment. He simply could not accept their innocence.

Symbolic racism pertains to indirect attacks on minorities, undergirded by an unspoken racial bias. Two examples of Trump's engagement in symbolic racism stand out. In one example, Trump's symbolic racism was expressed in his attack on Obama's academic record. Although Obama graduated magna cum laude from Harvard Law School and served as president of the Harvard Law Review, without a shred of evidence, Trump rejected Obama's academic credentials. Instead, Trump made up lies to defame Obama's record and character. In a 2011 interview, Trump asserted, "I heard he was a terrible student, terrible. How does a bad student go to Columbia and then to Harvard?" (quoted in Fouhy 2011). The only real evidence that Trump had was the color of Obama's skin. The belief that black men are inherently not as competent as white men and incapable of earning the academic record to get into Columbia and Harvard is the very definition of racism. This form of racism was not much different that the racism that faced the Tuskegee Airmen, African American fighter pilots who were believed to be incompetent, simply because of the color of their skin.

In another example of symbolic racism, Trump promoted the birther movement. Undergirding this movement was the inability to accept an African American as president of the United States. The movement resonated with people who could not accept a black president, but could not reject him solely on the basis of his race because such a rejection was socially unacceptable. Although Obama could trace his lineage to relatives who fought in the American Revolution with George Washington and although his grandfather fought to defend American in World War II, these facts were irrelevant. In the context of the American racialized culture, being of African descent is the only fact that mattered.

The birther movement originated from the racist right. Trump brought this movement into mainstream. Just after Obama announced his candidacy for president in 2007, the racist right WorldNetDaily website began promoting the false idea that Obama was not born in the United States and was a Muslim. Even though in 2008 Obama released the short form of his birth certificate showing that he was born in the State of Hawaii, WorldNetDaily continued to promote the claim that he was in Kenya or elsewhere. The birther movement gained traction with the publication of books by a senior staff writer for

WorldNetDaily, Jerome Corsi. *Obama Nation* (2008) and *Show Me the Birth Certificate* (2011) were used by birthers promoted by right-wing radio shows and websites, such as Alex Jones, InfoWars, which Corsi joined in 2017. Trump played a major role in bringing the birther movement into mainstream media, giving the movement more visibility and legitimacy than it would have had otherwise. He made numerous appearances on major television programs: The View, ABC News, Fox News, NBC's Today Show, MSNBC's Morning Joe, and CNN. In a May 2012 interview with Wolf Blitzer, Trump said, "An 'extremely credible source' has called my office and told me that Barack Obama's birth certificate is a fraud" (Quoted in Krieg 2016). Trump did not relent in his campaign against Obama until after Trump was nominated as the Republican Party's candidate for president in 2016.

Obama released and shared birth certificates with the public, the short form in 2008 and the long form in 2011. Hawaii's attorney general, governor, and director of health all verified that Obama was born in Hawaii, that he was a U.S. citizen, and that his birth certificate was authentic. Hawaii governor Neil Abercrombie stated, "No rational person can question the president's citizenship" (quoted in Sakahara 2011). Nevertheless, Donald Trump did.

Trump's personal attorney, Michael Cohen, claimed that Trump was disturbed by Obama's popularity and election to the presidency. Trump promoted the birther movement, not because he believed in the movement, but because he both envied Obama and had utter contempt and racist hatred for Obama:

> Watching Obama's Inauguration in 2008 with Trump, with the massive, adoring, joyful crowd on the Mall, incensed the Boss in a way I'd never seen before—he was literally losing his mind watching a handsome and self-evidently brilliant young black man take over, not only as Commander in Chief, but also as a moral world leader and guiding light. It was just too much for Trump. I thought I'd seen the worst of Trump, but when Obama won the Nobel Prize, Trump went ballistic . . . it was almost like he was hearing voices the way he rated and raved. (Cohen 2008, 107)

Trump is not the only modern president with a reputation for racism. Richard Nixon and Ronald Reagan have been accused of racism. Both used the so-called southern strategy, which had the goal of attracting southern to the Republican Party by enticing voters who were angry with the Democratic Party's support for civil rights, voting rights, busing, welfare, and other programs that were seen as benefiting blacks. Nixon's campaign consultant, Lee Atwater, summed up this strategy by suggesting that in the 1950s politicians could use the "N" word to attract support from among racist voters. By the 1970s, that strategy had become unacceptable. The new strategy employed seemingly race-neutral phrases such as state's rights, welfare, neighborhood schools, and law and order. These "dog-whistles" constituted symbolic racism. Instead of overtly saying that blacks are lazy and live on welfare, both Nixon and Reagan referred to welfare cheats taking advantage of the system (Lopez 2014).

Donald Trump's racism was different from Nixon's racism in a number of fundamental ways. Compared to Nixon, Trump's racism was more blatant, dehumanizing, provocative, and dangerous. Trump provoked fear and outrage. He not only characterized Mexicans as rapists and murderers, he called undocumented immigrants criminals. He referred to a caravan of asylum seekers as invaders. He conflated young Mexican immigrants with a violent gang in the New York area known as MS-13. He called gang members animals. These racist characterizations enabled state violence against Latino immigrants at the border. It made it easier for state agents to forcibly take children younger than 2 years old, babies, from their mothers with the goal of punishing the mothers and discourage other immigrants. Trump's acting director of Immigration and Customs Enforcement claimed that when he looked into the eyes of young detainees, no more than 17 years old, he could tell which ones would become MS-13 members.

Trump's public statements mattered not only in terms of promoting his public policy agenda but also in enabling violent racist behavior. Journalist Philip Rucker made this point. For example, in an August 4, 2019 article in the *Washington Post*, he drew a connection between a mass shooting in El Paso, Texas, and Trump's anti-immigration rhetoric. Rucker described a Trump rally in the Florida Panhandle where Trump characterized asylum seekers as invaders and asked, "how do you stop these people?" A voice in the audience shouted, "shoot them." Trump responded, "Only in the Panhandle can you get away with that statement" (quoted in Rucker 2019). Rucker adds:

> Patrick Crusius has been named as the [shooting] suspect. Portions of [his] the 2,300-word essay, titled "The Inconvenient Truth," closely mirror Trump's rhetoric, as well as the language of the white nationalist movement, including a warning about the "Hispanic invasion" of Texas.

> The author's ideology is so aligned with the president's that he decided to conclude the manifesto by clarifying that his views predate Trump's 2016 campaign and arguing that blaming him would amount to "fake news," another Trump phrase. (Rucker 2019)

Trump's dangerously racist statements served to bring the views of white supremacist extremists into the mainstream, giving them far greater currency. For example, he re-tweeted a profoundly inaccurate and provocative statement from a white supremacist claiming that black people were responsible for 81 percent of white homicides. That same lie was cited by Dylan Roof to justify his murder of nine worshippers in a black church in Charleston, South Carolina. Unlike any other modern president, Trump embraced and energized white supremacist groups as part of his political base (Green 2018). Prominent white supremacist leaders supported of his presidency, including Ku Klux Klan leader David Duke, who said in 2015:

> Voting for these people [Republican primary opponents Marco Rubio and Ted Cruz], voting against Donald Trump at this point is really treason to your heritage. I'm not saying I endorse everything about Trump, in fact I haven't formally endorsed him. But I do support his candidacy and I support voting for him as a strategic act. I hope he does everything we hope he will do. (quoted in Kessler 2016)

Trump's response to the murder of Heather Heyer provided a vivid example of his association with white supremacists. Heyer was murdered by James Field. Field drove his car into a crowd of non-violent, anti-racist, counter protesters. The counter protesters were opposed to a white supremacist, "Unite the Right" rally, organized by several white supremacist organizations including the Ku Klux Klan and a number of neo-Confederate, neo-fascist, and neo-Nazi groups. Organizers of this rally claimed that its goal was to unify the American white nationalist movements and to oppose the removal of a statute of Confederate General Robert E. Lee from Charlottesville's Lee Park.

In his initial response to the murder of Heather Heyer, Trump drew a moral equivalency between proponents of racism and opponents of racism. Trump claimed that there was blame on both sides and that there were fine people on both sides. Adding that there was "hatred, bigotry and violence on many sides," he asserted that the Klan, neo-Nazis, and other white supremacists were no better and no worse than the anti-racists. The next day, in the face of widespread outrage, Trump read aloud a different, carefully prepared statement: "Racism is evil. And those who cause violence in its name are criminals and thugs, including the KKK, neo-Nazi, white supremacists and other hate groups that are repugnant to everything we hold dear as Americans" (quoted by Nakamura 2017).

The third day at a news conference and without his prepared statement in hand, Trump reverted back to his original position:

> "I think there is blame on both sides," the president said in a combative exchange with reporters at Trump Tower in Manhattan. "You had a group on one side that was bad. You had a group on the other side that was also very violent. Nobody wants to say that. I'll say it right now."

Mr. Trump defended those gathered in a Charlottesville park to protest the removal of a statue of Robert E. Lee. "I've condemned neo-Nazis. I've condemned many different groups," he said. "Not all of those people were neo-Nazis, believe me. Not all of those people were white supremacists by any stretch." (Shear and Haberman 2017)

Trump's perspective of viewing anti-fascists and anti-racists as not much different from neo-Nazi and white supremacists, normalized racist and white supremacists in ways never imagined by Nixon.

Trump and Nixon represented different public policy regimes. Despite his southern strategy and opposition to busing, Nixon operated under a Keynesian policy perspective, which supported a robust role for government and government programs. Nixon offered substantial public policy benefits to workers of all colors, such as the Comprehensive Employment and Training Act, which provided jobs for teenagers over the summer and public service jobs, support for both small businesses and minority businesses, and other forms of support for high poverty urban areas. Nixon maintained a decent minimum wage and promoted workplace health and safety regulations. During recessions, he offered counter-cyclical revenue sharing, which benefited white and black public sector workers at the state and local levels. He introduced the so-called Philadelphia plan, which was designed to stimulate black business development and which evolved into minority set-aside programs. Whereas Nixon saw urban problems as an opportunity to offer help and expand his political base, Trump used urban problems to condemn Democrats and frighten suburbanites. Nixon's secretary of housing and urban development, George Romney, promoted scatter site housing, the spreading of low-income housing throughout metropolitan areas instead of concentrating it in segregated inner city areas. Of course as a result of pressure from local white opposition, Nixon overruled Romney (Hannah-Jones 2015). Trump used the possibility of scatter site housing to frighten suburban residents. During his 2020 campaign, Trump said, "I am happy to inform all of the people living their suburban lifestyle dream that you will no longer be bother or financially hurt by having low-income housing built in your neighborhood . . . Your housing prices will go up based on the market, and crime will go down. I have rescinded the Obama-Biden AFFH rule. Enjoy!" (Trump 2020).

The message couldn't have been clearer: white suburban voters should vote for Trump for protection from low-income, crime-committing, inner-city blacks

## TRUMPISM

Trump's worldview is eclectic. He is not a doctrinaire libertarian nor a traditional neoliberal. His worldview is a blend of neoliberalism, nationalism, and racialism, couched in authoritarianism. He has adopted the perspectives of the Christian right as his own perspective. More than any other Republican, his ideology, if his worldview qualifies as an ideology, resonates with the base of the Republican Party. Like neoliberals, he was committed to expanding the economy by following a simple formula: cut taxes, roll back regulations, shrink government, and privatize programs were feasible. His formula for making health care better is to rely more on the market, increase competition, and make prices more transparent. He acknowledged the problems of American workers and job losses in the Rustbelt and rural areas. He offers a nationalistic solution: campaign for America First, American protectionary tariffs, a NAFTA agreement that protects American workers. Trump opposes raising the minimum wage and protecting collective bargaining rights. His commitment to rolling back regulations favors corporate interests. Insofar as the rollbacks include workplace health and safety regulations, they hurt American workers. Trump's authoritarianism commits him to increasing police powers and opposing the Black Lives Matter movement. As will be demonstrated in the succeeding chapters, Trump's public policy agenda is consistent with his worldviews.

# Chapter 3

# Trump Voters

The previous chapter examined Trump's ideas. This chapter focuses on Trump voters in the 2016 election. It examines demographic factors strongly associated with votes for Trump and it analyzes three theories explaining this election. It demonstrates that basic demographic factors explain the vote for Trump: party identification, race, religion, education, age, and region. White, evangelical, less-than-college-educated, rural, Republican voters 55 years old plus elected Trump. Whereas this chapter acknowledges that many different people voted for Trump for many different reasons—dislike of Clinton, belief in Trump's promises, disenchantment with Obama, and the Democratic Party—this chapter investigates three prominent theories or hypotheses that explain Trump's success in the 2016 election:

1. White working-class economic distress and political neglect
2. Racism, sexism, and xenophobia
3. The interactive effect of 1 and 2.

## DEMOGRAPHIC FACTORS

Table 3.1 provides a summary of a range of demography variables explaining the outcome of the 2016 presidential election. Party identification has long been a strong determinant of how a voter would vote. According to the *New York Times* exit poll survey summarized in this table, about 90 percent of self-identified Republicans voted for Trump. The survey indicated that race, gender, age, education, and geography were strongly associated with a respondent's choice of candidate for president. As Table 3.1 indicates, whites were overwhelming more likely to vote for Trump than people of color. About 58 percent of white voters voted for

Trump. In contrast, only 8 percent of black voters voted for him. Only about 29 percent of Hispanic or Asian Americans voted for Trump. Gender also mattered. Men were more likely to vote for Trump than women. About 53 percent of male voters cast their votes for Trump, compared to only 42 percent for women. Age also made a difference. Young people were far less likely to vote for Trump than older people. Only about 37 percent of voters between the ages of 18 and 29 voted for Trump, compared to 53 percent of voters over the age of 45 (See Table 3.1).

Level of education was also associated with the vote for Trump. Table 3.1 indicates that voters with a college degree or more were decidedly less likely

**Table 3.1   2016 Presidential Election Exit Poll**

| | Percentage Vote for | |
|---|---|---|
| Demographics | Clinton | Trump |
| Party Identification | | |
| Democrats | 89 | 9 |
| Republican | 7 | 0 |
| Race | | |
| White | 37 | 58 |
| Black | 88 | 8 |
| Hispanic/Latino | 65 | 29 |
| Asian | 65 | 29 |
| Other | 56 | 37 |
| Gender | | |
| Male | 41 | 53 |
| Female | 54 | 42 |
| Age | | |
| 18–29 | 55 | 37 |
| 30–44 | 50 | 42 |
| 45–64 | 44 | 53 |
| 65+ | 45 | 53 |
| Religion | | |
| Protestant | 39 | 58 |
| Catholic | 45 | 52 |
| Jewish | 71 | 24 |
| Something else | 62 | 29 |
| None | 68 | 26 |
| Education | | |
| High School or less | 45 | 51 |
| Some College-Assoc. degree | 43 | 52 |
| College Graduate | 49 | 45 |
| Postgraduate | 58 | 37 |
| Resident | | |
| City with population of 50,000+ | 59 | 35 |
| Suburb | 45 | 50 |
| Small city or rural area | 34 | 62 |

*Source*: Huang, Jon, Samuel Jacoby, Michael Strickland, and K.K. Rebecca Lai. Election 2016: Exit Polls. *New York Times*, November 8, 2016.
https://www.nytimes.com/interactive/2016/11/08/us/politics/election-exit-polls.html.com.

to vote for Trump than less educated voters. Slightly over half of those with some college or less voted for Trump. Only 45 percent of those with a college degree voted for Trump. Among those with a post-graduate education, only 37 percent voted for Trump.

Place of residence mattered. About 62 percent of voters who resided in small towns or rural areas voted for Trump. Only 35 percent of residents in cities with populations over 50,000 voted for Trump.

Table 3.2 summarizes the results of 2016 exit polls that accounted for the intersection of race, religion, gender, and education. In regards to race and gender, white men were strong Trump supporters, about 63 percent of white men voted for him. About 53 percent of white women voted for him. Black women were the strongest Trump opponents, as 94 percent of black women voted for Clinton. Although only 13 percent of black males voted for Trump, this figure

Table 3.2   Race, Religion, Age, Gender, and Education

| | Percentage Vote of White Evangelical or White Born Again *for | |
|---|---|---|
| | Clinton | Trump |
| Yes, White Evangelical | 16 | 81 |
| No, White Evangelical | 59 | 35 |
| White Voters by Age | | |
| 18–29 | 43 | 48 |
| 30–44 | 37 | 55 |
| 45–64 | 34 | 63 |
| 65+ | 39 | 58 |
| Race and Gender** | | |
| White men | 31 | 63 |
| White women | 43 | 53 |
| Black men | 80 | 13 |
| Black women | 94 | 4 |
| Race, Gender, and Education** | | |
| White college grad men | 39 | 54 |
| White college grad women | 51 | 45 |
| White men w/o college degree*** | 23 | 72 |
| White women without*** | | |
| College degree | 34 | 62 |

*Sources:*
*Huang, Jon, Samuel Jacoby, Michael Strickland, and K.K. Rebecca Lai. Election 2016: Exit Polls. *New York Times*, November 8, 2016.
https://www.nytimes.com/interactive/2016/11/08/us/politics/election-exit-polls.html
**Tyson, Alec, and Shiva Maniam. "Behind Trump's Victory: Divisions by Race, Gender, Education". Factank, Pew Research Center, November 9, 2016.
https://www.pewresearch.org/fact-tank/2016/11/09/behind-trumps-victory-divisions-by-race-gender-education/
***Colem Nicki Lisa. "How Did Race, Gender, Class, and Education Influence the Election?" *Thoughtco*, July 9, 2019.
https://www.thoughtco.com/race-gender-class-and-education-4111369

Table 3.3   Economic Factors

|  | Percentage Vote for | |
|---|---|---|
|  | Clinton | Trump |
| Income* | | |
| Under $30,000 | 53 | 41 |
| $30,000–$49,000 | 51 | 42 |
| $50,000–$99,999 | 46 | 50 |
| $100,000–$199,999 | 47 | 48 |
| $200,000–$249,999 | 46 | 48 |
| $250,000+ | 46 | 48 |
| Union household** | 51 | 43 |
| Union member** | 56 | 37 |
| Non-union household** | 46 | 48 |

Source: Roper Center for Public Opinion Research. 2016. "How Groups Voted in 2016."Cornell University. https://ropercenter.cornell.edu/how-groups-voted-2016

is higher than the percentage of black men who voted for Mitt Romney in 2012. About 81 percent of self-identified white evangelical or born-again Christians claim to have voted for Trump. Among white men without a college degree, 72 percent voted for Trump. This figure dropped down to 62 percent for white women without a college degree. This gender difference persisted with college-educated white men and college-educated white women. Whereas about 54 percent of college-educated white men voted for Trump, only 45 percent of college-educated white women voted for Trump.

According to table 3.3, most low-income voters supported Clinton over Trump. The lowest income group was the least likely to vote for Trump. Less than 42 percent of voters making less than $50,000 a year voted for Trump. Voters with higher incomes were more likely to vote for Trump. The income group with the highest vote for Trump, 50 percent, had incomes between $50,000 and $99,999. As income increased above $100,000, the Trump vote hovered around 48 percent, compared to less than 47 percent for Clinton. Higher income voters leaned slightly in favor of Trump.

The majority of voters from unionized households voted against Trump. Unionized voters were even more likely to vote against Trump. Indeed, only 37 percent of unionized voters voted for Trump, compared to 56 percent who voted for Clinton.

## WHITE WORKING-CLASS ECONOMIC DISTRESS AND POLITICAL NEGLECT

The most common hypothesis used to explain Trump's election in 2016 is the economic distress and political neglect narrative. This narrative is based on the premise that white workers, particularly those in manufacturing and mining sectors, suffered job losses, wage stagnation, and economic insecurity as a result of the decline of these sectors. It maintains that white workers were alienated from both political parties, as both had supported NAFTA and free trade. As mentioned in chapter one, Zito and Todd quoted union leaders who had voted for Obama in 2008 and 2012, but voted for Trump in 2016. In his book, *The New Minority: White Working Class Politics in an Age of Immigration and Inequality*, Justin Gest insisted that in the minds of white workers, the slogan "Make America Great Again" did not mean make America white or racist. It meant restore the manufacturing sector and bring jobs back:

> . . . Trump promised to spread his winnings around and to punish companies that take their manufacturing overseas—a direct appeal to the Rust Belt. The "Again" in his campaign slogan, "Make America Great Again," plugs into this sense of nostalgia and suggests a return to better times. "I guess I want things back to the way they were," Campanella says in Youngstown. "And in his odd, crude way, he makes sense. I know he's not a woman-hater and he's not going to reverse what liberalism has done for us the last 40 years. He just wants to get our country stabilized and back on track [. . .] I know it's never going to be like the way it was. But we need to concentrate on this country. We're lowering our standards more than we're raising standards in third world countries. We can't worry about other people's problems." (Gest 2016, 194)

Proponents of this narrative find strong support from county-level election data. They maintain that Trump won because hundreds of counties that had supported Obama flipped in 2016 to support Trump. Uhrmacher, Schaul, and Keating state: "Of the nearly 700 counties that twice sent Obama to the White House, a stunning one-third flipped to support Trump. Trump also won 194 of the 207 counties that voted for Obama either in 2008 or 2012" (Uhrmacher et al. 2016).

Uhrmacher *et al* point out that the counties that flipped were primarily in swing states, older manufacturing areas, and majority white working-class counties.

This narrative minimizes the role of racism. It assumes that white workers supported Trump for rational, self-interest, pocketbook reasons. White workers voted for Trump, because he was going to get the economy on track in ways that would benefit them.

Expanding on this perspective on Trump supporters, Musa al-Gharbi wrote a blistering critique of what he describes as a prejudice against Trump among scholars. He claimed that this prejudice was a function of motivated reasoning and confirmation bias "due to the relative homogeneity and intensity of scholars' views" toward Trump and his supporters (al-Gharbi 2018). Al-Gharbi reacted against what he sees as the entire community of scholars portraying Trump supporters as racists. He critiqued the works of Ta-Nehisi Coates, Thomas Wood, and Arlie Hochschild.

Al-Gharbi insisted that Coates was driven by flawed logic. Because Trump made racist statements, and because whites voted for Trump, Coates fallaciously concluded that therefore the whites who voted for Trump must be racists. Contradicting Coates, al-Gharbi argued that the whites who decided the 2016 election were neither racists nor anti-Obama:

> First, many of the white voters who proved most decisive for Trump's victory actually voted for Obama in both 2008 and 2012 (Uhrmacher et al. 2016). If the white voters who ostensibly decided the 2016 election were horrified at the very prospect of a black president, it is unclear why they would have supported Barack Obama's initial campaign. (al-Gharbi 2018, 500)

Al-Gharbi claimed that Trump's racist rhetoric actually turned whites off and dissuaded many of them from voting in 2016. Al-Gharbi added that it is likely that gains among people of color put Trump in the White House:

> Second, Trump did not mobilize or energize whites toward the ballot box (Mellnik et al. 2017). Given Trump's lower share among whites, it was likely these gains (and Democrats' attrition) among people of color put Trump in the White House. Coates et al therefore seem committed to arguing that millions of these blacks, Latinos and Asians who voted for Trump were also primarily or exclusively motivated by "white rage" or their commitment to white supremacy—or else conceding that it is possible to vote for Trump for other reasons (and of course, if this is true of minorities, it stands to reason what whites could be similarly motivated by other factors [al-Gharbi 2018, 501]).

Al-Gharbi argued that although Woods and Hochschild depicted Trump supporters as racist, a careful review of their actual data proves otherwise. Al-Gharbi pointed out that Wood, author "Racism Motivated Trump Voters More Than Authoritariam," neglected to point out that his data actually indicate that whites who voted for Trump were "less racist than those who voted for Romney" (al-Gharbi 2018, 10).

Al-Gharbi considered Hochschild's study of Louisiana irrelevant in understanding the 2016 election because close to 90 percent of the voters were Republicans: And so, empirically speaking, it is not clear how Hochschild's project—which basically attempts to understand why whites in a solidly red state vote Republican—would explain much about why so many former Obama supporters, more of them minorities, voted for Donald Trump over Hillary Clinton in 2016 (al-Gharbi 2018, 509).

Al-Gharbi claimed that he identified serious flaws in the academic research on the 2016 presidential election. He concluded that because of these flaws and the obsession with demonstrating that Trump supporters are racist, it is understandable that conservatives see academics as biased and their research as liberal propaganda.

There is no doubt that a small percentage of Obama supporters—white workers and black males—shifted and voted for Trump in 2016 and that this shift was a factor in deciding the outcome of the 2016 election. However, the problem with al-Gharbi's argument is not with this shift from Obama to Trump factor. The problem is that al-Gharbi relies exclusively on this single factor and ignores other factors that also explain Trump's election, particularly the shift in voter turnout among white and black voters.

Table 3.4 provides 2012 and 2016 data on changes in black and white voter turnout rates for the nation and for five Midwestern swing states: Illinois, Michigan, Ohio, Pennsylvania, and Wisconsin. Nation-wide, white voter turnout increased by 1.2 percentage points, while black voter turnout declined by 7.1 percentage points. In 2012, the white voter turnout was 64.1 percent and the black voter turnout was 66.2 percent. In 2016, the white voter turnout increased to 65.3 percent, while the black voter turnout

**Table 3.4   Black and White Citizen Voter Turnout Rates for Select Midwest Swing States**

| States | 2012 | 2016 | Percentage Change |
| --- | --- | --- | --- |
| Illinois | | | |
| White | 62.2 | 67.8 | + 5.6 |
| Black | 71.8 | 58.7 | -13.1 |
| Michigan | | | |
| White | 67.9 | 66.5 | -1.4 |
| Black | 63.3 | 61.0 | -2.3 |
| Ohio | | | |
| White | 61.9 | 64.4 | +2.4 |
| Black | 63.3 | 61.0 | -2.3 |
| Pennsylvania | | | |
| White | 62.5 | 63.3 | +.8 |
| Black | 65.2 | 63.2 | -2.0 |
| Wisconsin | | | |
| White | 75.0 | 74.0 | -1.0 |
| Black | 78.5 | 46.8 | -31.7 |
| Total | | | |
| White | 64.1 | 65.3 | +1.2 |
| Black | 66.2 | 59.1 | -7.1 |

U.S. Census. 2017. "Voting and Registration in the Election of November 2016." https://www.census.gov/data/tables/time-series/demo/voting-and-registration/p20-580.html
U.S. Census. 2013. "Voting and Registration in the Election of November 2012." https://www.census.gov/data/tables/2012/demo/voting-and-registration/p20-568.html

declined to 59.1 percent. In 2012, the black–white voter turnout gap was 2.1 percent in favor of black voters. The higher black voter turnout no doubt favored the election of Obama. In 2016, the black–white voter turnout gap was 6.2 percent in favor of the white vote. The higher white voter turnout favored Trump.

Midwestern swing states played a major role in electing Trump. Between 2012 and 2016, black voter turnout declined in every single swing state. White voter turnout increased in all but Michigan. However, the black-white voter turnout gap increased in every state, including Michigan. In Michigan, black voter turnout declined by 2.3 percentage points, compared to a 1.4 white voter turnout decline. Between 2012 and 2016, the decline of black voter turnout was substantial in Illinois and Wisconsin. In Illinois, the black voter turnout declined from 71.8 percent in 2012 to 58.7 percent in 2016, a decline of 13.1 percentage points. In Wisconsin, black voter turnout went from 78.5 percent in 2012 to 46.8 percent in 2016, a decline of 31.7 percent.

As will be demonstrated in a later chapter, substantial declines in the black vote are associated with deliberate efforts to suppress the black vote. An alternative to Gharbi's perspective is that the suppression of the black vote and the increase of the white vote better explains the shift of key swing states from blue to red.

## RACISM, SEXISM, AND XENOPHOBIA

Thomas Wood's research on the 2016 election focused on the issue of whether economic distress or symbolic racism motivated low-income voters to shift from the Democratic Party to the Republican Party in the 2016 election. He relied on data from the American National Election Study (ANES) surveys from 1948 to 2016. Although the majority of voters with incomes below $50,000 voted for Clinton as indicated in table 3.3, Wood's data indicated that a higher proportion of low-income white voters compared to high-income white voters favored Trump over Clinton. This trend was an anomaly. Wood noted that the 2016 election was the first time since 1948 that a higher percentage of low-income white voters favored the Republican Party compared to higher income white voters (Wood 2017). Clearly, after decades of voting against the Republican Party, in the 2016 election, a significant proportion of low-income white voter had shifted from the Democratic Party to the Republican Party and voted for Trump.

Wood's data illustrated the significant role played by low-income white voters in the election of Trump. However, the data did not explain whether economic distress or racial prejudice or both motivated low-income white voters to support Trump. Wood relied on the ANES symbolic racism scale to test the hypothesis that race motivated white voters. This scale is based on four questions:

1. Irish, Italian, Jewish, and many other minorities overcame prejudice and worked their way up. Blacks should do the same without any special favors;
2. Generations of slavery and discrimination have created conditions that make it difficult for black to work their way out of the lower class;
3. It's really just a matter of some people trying hard enough; if blacks would only try harder, they could be just as well off as whites; and
4. Over the past few years, blacks have gotten less that they deserve.

Wood demonstrated that throughout the 1980s and 1990s, the difference between the two parties on symbolic racism was trivial. However, this difference widened over the past four presidential elections. Although symbolic racism declined slightly between the 2012 and 2016 elections, the distance between the two parties increased. The Republican Party scored significantly higher on symbolic racism than the Democratic Party in 2016 compared to 2012. Wood's data indicated that there was a high level of authoritarianism among Republicans, a point demonstrated by other researchers (Hetherington and Weiler 2009). However, there was little change in the level of authoritarianism between 2000 and 2016.

Diana Mutz used a panel survey method involving multiple surveys and datasets accumulated between 2011 and 2016 to tract the same white voters from 2012 to 2016 to test two competing hypotheses: First, does being left behind with respect to personal financial wellbeing predict change in the direction of Republican support in 2016? Second, did issue positions reflecting perceived status threat, whether racial or global, increase the likelihood of shifting toward the Republican presidential candidate in 2016?

Mutz's research focused on explaining why white voters shifted from the Democratic Party in 2012 to the Republican Party in 2016. She examined whether panelists' feelings and votes shifted from the Democratic Party to the Republican Party and whether this shift to the Republican Party and to a vote for Trump was explained by economic hardship factors or perceived status threat factors. She measured economic hardship two ways: multiple survey questions administered over several years and economic data matched to each panelist's zip code. The survey questions included changes in job status, income, and family finances. The survey also included questions on whether trade had impacted individual or family economic or financial situation. Economic data included changes in levels of unemployment, manufacturing employment, and income within each panelist zip code.

Mutz identified two forms of status threat: racial status threat and global status threat. Drawing from socio-psychological literature on changes in racism, she hypothesized that white Americans are no longer plagued with old fashion white supremacy racism. They do not see blacks as intellectually inferior. However, despite multiculturalism's expressed commitment to inclusion and equality, many whites experienced multiculturalism in zero sum terms. That is, an increase in the proportion of non-whites or the enhancement of their social status was perceived as a threat to the dominance or social status of whites. The awareness of an impending loss of white majority or white dominant status is experienced as threatening to whites, particularly those who envision the United States as a white nation. This racial status threat was augmented by the election of a black president. Mutz used a social dominance orientation scale to measure racial status threat. This scale includes questions that measure preferences for hierarchy over equality. Mutz also hypothesized that the perceived decline of America and rise of China as a world power is perceived as a global status threat. Thus, she includes questions on China and immigrants as perceived threats to American jobs and security.

Mutz found that there was little association between the actual performance of the economy and vote choice in the 2016 election. Racial and global status threats were stronger predictors of a vote for Trump than perception of stagnant wages or job losses. The idea of China threatening America's dominance and attracting American manufacturing facilities and jobs, and immigrants taking jobs from Americans in their own country, and illegal immigrants and undeserving minorities getting social welfare benefits had become salient issues before Trump ran for president. Trump simply attracted white workers already concerned about these issues.

Mutz relied on hard economic data and actual changes in financial status rather than survey data on general perceptions of the performance of the economy and partisan vote choice. Although political scientists use actual changes in the economy, such as increases in GDP or decreases in unemployment to predict election outcomes, they rarely rely on partisan perceptions, which tend to be unreliable (Garber and Huber 2010). Mutz rejected the economic factor because it was contradicted by both survey data and actual economic data. She added that real economic trends challenged the left-behind economic argument because by 2015 and 2016, unemployment rates were down and the manufacturing sector was rebounding.

Like Mutz, Reny et al focused exclusively on white voters who switched party affiliation from the 2012 to the 2016 election. They noted that about 6 percent of white working-class voters switched from the Democratic Party to the Republican Party and voted for Trump in 2016. These researchers constructed several hypotheses to explain why these white working-class Democrats voted for Trump. Their hypotheses can be condensed into two perspectives: 1. Attitudes toward racial minorities and immigrants explain the switch and 2. Economic dislocation explains the switch.

They relied on several sources for data. They relied primarily on the 2016 Cooperative Congressional Election Studies Survey to examine vote choice and to test whether racial and immigration attitudes correlated with switches in vote choice. They used both survey and direct economic data to test the economy hypotheses. They relied on survey data to measure changes in individual personal financial and economic circumstances. They drew from county-level data covering a period of fourteen years to measure changes in the unemployment rates and changes in the number of manufacturing jobs. Like Munz, they found racial and immigration attitudes strongly associated with the likelihood of switching from Obama in 2012 to Trump in 2016. As the attitudes of white Democrats toward minorities and immigrants moved from positive to the negative, their likelihood of voting for Trump increased.

While working-class whites were more likely to switch their vote to Trump in 2016 than non-working-class whites, both working-class and non-working-class whites with strong racially conservative or punitive immigration views were more likely to switch than those with racially liberal or pro-immigration views.

In order to test whether Trump supporters were motivated by economic or cultural concerns or both, Jeff Manza and Ned Crowley relied on ANES surveys conducted in January 2016. The surveys included nine issue questions and a feeling thermometer scale measuring how strongly respondents supported Trump. The surveys allowed Manza and Crowley to determine the association between specific issues and the level of support for Trump. The surveys indicated that strong Trump supporters were concerned more about cultural and ethnonational issues than economic issues. Manza and Crowley concluded that there was little association between support for Trump and the belief that economic mobility is harder today than in the past and only a marginal association between support for Trump and opposition to free trade. The strongest attitudinal predictor of support for Trump was racial resentment and the belief that minorities were taking jobs from whites. The strongest policy issues that predicted support for Trump were opposition to allowing Syrian refugees into the United States and opposition to immigration (Manza and Crowley 2017).

Setzler and Yanus (2018) examined three sets of variables explaining the Trump vote: partisanship, demographics, and attitudes. They relied on data from the ANES survey. Partisan variables included Republican or not. Demographic variables included race, marital status, social class, education, religion, region, age, or gender.

Their attitudinal variables included authoritarian, racial resentment, and sexism. Their measure of authoritarianism consisted of choices among four sets of childrearing traits: respect for the elderly versus independence; obedience versus self-reliance; curiosity versus good manners; or being considerate of others versus being well-behaved. Their assessment of racial resentment consisted of the same four ANES survey questions used by Wood.

Their evaluation of sexism consisted of four questions:

1. How much discrimination is there in the United States today against women?
2. When women demand equality these days, how often are they actually seeking special favors?
3. When women complain about discrimination, how often do they cause more problems that they solve?
4. How important is it to get more women elected?

They used a multivariate regression model with vote for Trump as the dependent viable. This model allowed them to see how much each variable influences an individual's vote for Trump. Given the possibility of one variable masking or co-varying with another, this model allowed them to determine the dominant variable affecting the vote. For example, if younger people live in cities and order people live in rural areas, a multivariate regression model can determine whether age or residency is determining the vote choice. That is, rural people may be voting for Trump because people over 50 are more likely to vote for Trump and more likely to live in rural areas.

After accounting for most of the variables, the few independent demographic variables associated with the vote for Trump were white racial identity, evangelical protestant membership, married status, and party identification. People who identified as white, evangelical protestant, and married were highly and independently likely to vote for Trump. Racial resentment and sexism were the two strongest attitudinal variables associated with the vote for Trump. Moreover, the level of racial resentment or sexism was a stronger predictor of the vote for Trump than partisanship. White working-class status was a spurious variable. That is, racial resentment and anti-immigrant sentiment rather than working-class status predicted the vote for Trump.

Setzler and Yanus' most astonishing discovery was that, like men, women who voted for Trump were strongly motivated by racial resentment and sexism. They conclude:

> Our results challenge the popular wisdom that Republican middle-aged, working-class, not college-educated men and their loyal wives delivered victory to Donald Trump. Although many of Trump's female supporters shared these characteristics, it appears that attitudes hostile to gender and racial equality were more decisive motivators of vote choice in 2016. (Statzler and Yanus 2018, 526)

The research remains divided over the effect of economic discontent. The use of different categories, definitions, data bases, and surveys yielded slightly different results. Abramowitz and McCoy included the same demographics and measures of racial resentment and misogyny as other studies. Like other studies, they found that after controlling for racial/ethnic resentment, demographic variables—age, education gender, and family income—had little effect on the vote for President Trump. Racial resentment was the major factor associated with the vote for Trump. For example, for both voters with a college degree and voters without a college degree, the stronger the racial resentment, the more likely the voter would vote for Trump. However, unlike Mutz and others, they found that economic discontent had a modest impact. Contrary to Setzler and Yanus, they concluded that Republican Party identification had a stronger effect than racial resentment. Unlike other studies, Abramowitz and McCoy (2018) included ideology and economic conservatism.

Morgan and Lee's (2018) research is important because of their precise categorization of social classes and definition of the white working class. Whereas most studies of the white working class rely on either income or education, Morgan and Lee use occupational classifications. The problem with using education as a surrogate measure of the white working class is that wealthy business owners without a college degree would be misclassified as working class. The problem with income as a surrogate measure is that independent business owners or contractors with low income would be classified in the working-class category. Morgan and Lee relied on U.S. Census occupational data. They grouped hundreds of job categories into four different class groups: white-collar class, working class, intermediate class, and farmer-agricultural class. Whereas each class group consisted of between twenty and eighty different job classifications, this classification system provides a more precise picture of class divisions. The white-collar class group consists of highly educated and trained professionals such as doctors, nurses, lawyers, engineers, computer specialist, school teachers, and many other classifications. The working-class group includes manual and non-manual, skilled and unskilled laborers, janitors, dishwashers, retail salespersons, cashiers, assembly-line workers, plumbers, carpenters, etc. The intermediate class group contains non-professional self-employed workers, small contractors, managers, supervisors, construction managers, public safety workers, police, fire fighters, and others. The farmer-agricultural class group includes agricultural workers, farmers, ranchers, loggers, fishermen, and others.

Morgan and Lee's research provided a better picture of the role of the white working class and other white social classes in the election of Trump. Their research supported the general consensus that a marginal increase in the white working-class vote was associated with the election of Donald Trump. The decline in the black vote was also a significant factor in the election of

Trump. More importantly, they demonstrated that between the 2012 election and the 2016 election, the white working-class vote increased from 53.5
percent to 56.9 percent; whereas the farm-agricultural working-class vote
increased from 64.1 percent to 74.2 percent. Trump has a much stronger voting base of support in rural areas (Morgan and Lee 2018).

Morgan and Lee's study used survey questions to assess changes in three
sets of attitudes and opinions between 2006 and 2016: political efficacy,
social-economic policy choice, and racial attitudes. Political efficacy was
measured with two survey questions: (1) "People like me don't have any say
about what the government does," and (2) "I feel that I have a pretty good
understanding of important political issues facing our country." Compared to
white-collar and intermediate voters, white working-class voters feel powerless. Whereas about half of the white working-class voters feel they have a
good understanding of the issues, larger percentages of white-collar and intermediate class voters feel they understand the issues. Out of the four groups,
farm-agricultural works are the most likely to feel powerless. Compared to
the other three groups, including white workers.

Four major points arose from responses to these survey questions.
First, compared to the white-collar and the intermediate class groups, the
white working-class group is the most progressive on public policy issues.
Working-class whites compared to white-collar and intermediate class whites
are more likely to agree that the government has the responsibility to reduce
inequality between the rich and the poor, provide a job for everyone who
wants one, provide a decent standard of living for the unemployed, provide
health care for the sick, and provide decent housing for those who can't
afford it. Second, compared to the white-collar and the intermediate class
group, the white working-class group is more likely to favor the government
reducing inflation and assisting industries with the help they need to grow.
Third, all four groups have been overwhelmingly supportive of the government providing "a decent standard of living for the old." That is, for all four
groups, well over 80 percent believed that government had a responsibility
"to provide a decent standard of living for the old." This finding is consistent
with the view that Social Security enjoys substantial political support among
most political groups, including Trump supporters. Finally, opinions on these
policy issues have been remarkably stable between 2006 and 2016 among
white-collar, working class, and intermediate groups. The farmer-agricultural
group shifted between 2006 and 2016 and became more supportive of the
role of government in reducing inequality and providing a decent standard of
living for the unemployed. This shift in opinion may have been triggered by
the 2008–2010 recession (Morgan and Lee 2018).

Morgan and Lee's research offers a different perspective on racism and
white social classes. They found that compared to the intermediate class

and the farmer-agricultural class, the white working class was the least racist and the most tolerant of immigrants. This discovery was consistent with
other studies of class, region, and racial attitudes. Urban workers tend to be
more tolerant of immigrants, even though immigrant populations are higher
in urban areas. In contrast, farmers and workers in rural areas tend to be the
least tolerant of immigrants, even though there are fewer immigrants in rural
areas (Blanchflower 2021; Morgan and Lee 2018).

## REASSESSING THE WHITE WORKING CLASS

The white working class is not the racist class it is too often portrayed to
be. In fact, compared to the intermediate class and the farmer-agricultural
class, it is the least racist class. Morgan and Lee assessed racial attitudes
among the classes with four survey questions. They asked respondents
whether they were

1. Opposed to a close relative marrying a black person;
2. Opposed to a close relative marrying a Hispanic person; and
3. Against preferential hiring and promotion of blacks;
4. In favor of reductions in number of immigrants to America.

The attitudes were relatively stable between 2006 and 2016. Compared to
respondents from the intermediate and the farmer-agricultural class, white
worker respondents were more tolerant when it came to interracial marriage
and immigration. Respondents from the farmer-agricultural groups were the
most likely group to oppose interracial marriage in 2006, but became more
tolerate on interracial issues by 2016. In 2006, about 44 percent of the farmer-
agricultural class group opposed a close relative marrying a black person.
This figure had declined to about 30 percent by 2016. In contrast, this group
became more hostile to immigrants. In 2006, about 52 percent were in favor
of reducing the number of immigrants to American. By 2016, this figure had
increased close to 80 percent. This discovery is consistent with the research
that finds a strong association between anti-immigrant sentiments and the
vote from President Trump. It is also consistent with the higher voter turnout
and higher percentage of Trump voters in rural areas.

The intermediate group respondents became more intolerant as well. The
percentage opposed to a close relative marrying a black person increased
from about 25 percent to over 40 percent. The percentage oppose to immigration as increased marginally (Morgan and Lee 2018).

Morgan and Lee found no evidence of an increase in anti-immigration
sentiment among the white working class. In fact, there was a marginal

decline in working-class respondents who claimed they favored the reduction in the number of immigrants. This discovery seems to contradict the view that the working class played a pivotal role in electing Trump in the 2016 election.

## Reassessing the White Working Class and Trump Voters

White workers do not constitute a homogeneous group nor do they form a significant part of Trump's base. They are divided over Trump. Labor unions are divided. Unions have a long history of divisions over human rights and civil rights issues. Skilled trade unions have a past history of opposition to civil rights. Some have engaged in racial exclusion and racial segregation (Foner 1982). Police unions have a reputation for supporting racially conservative candidates. The union representing Immigration and Custom Enforcement (ICE) supported Trump.

In contrast, unions representing unskilled workers have a long history of strong support for civil rights and racial equality. Some of these unions include the American Federation of State County and Municipal Employees (AFSCME), International Longshore and Warehouse Union (ILWU), Service Employees Union International (SEUI), United Automobile Workers (UAW), United Mine Workers of America (UMW), and many others (Foner 1982).

Most unions have not supported Trump. However, many white union members broke from the union leadership and voted for Trump. For example, the UAW Union never endorsed Trump, but many white UAW members broke ranks with the union membership and supported him.

A number of case studies provide more detailed insights into Trump supporters and voters. Arlie Russell Hochschild's studied white Trump supporters in the Lake Charles, Louisiana area. These supporters were not poor white workers. Most were doing well economically, holding a range of different jobs and professions including real estate and skilled trade. The petroleum industry was a major employee. Despite the fact that the area suffered high cancer rates most likely tied to the petroleum industry, Hochschild describes a political culture deferential to this industry and hostile to the government and government regulations. She also described a pervasive anxiety associated with minorities, as if all the residents were in a long line to get to the top of the hill, with minorities unfairly taking cuts. Residents of this area believed that minorities were given benefits and opportunities that they did not deserve. They believed that Barack Obama was the biggest line cutter of all. For them, Trump symbolized the restoration of traditional white America.

Trump's strongest base of support is not in cities among unionized manufacturing workers, but in rural areas. Robert Wuthnow provides a detailed a vivid description of white residence of rural areas, most of which are Trump supporters. Many of them are farmers. He describes rural areas as complex and varied. He insists that rural areas are in economic distress. Some areas have recovered from the 2008–2009 recession. Most have not fully recovered. He describes areas that have a strong sense of community. These communities are isolated from the big cities. They are 85–90 percent white. Most residents see the promotion of diversity as undesirable intrusion from big government. They resent government. They strongly and enthusiastically support the slogan: drain the swamp, shrink the size of government, and shut down the government. They vehemently opposed President Obama largely on symbolic grounds: "The people we talked to held nothing back in criticizing what they did not like about Obama. They called him a socialist, a raving liberal, somebody from a different planet, a president who did not know how to get anything done and a person who made them physically sick" (Wuthnow 2018, 155).

Wuthnow explained that people living in rural areas lived in a political world largely created by Rush Limbaugh, Fox News, and Donald Trump. When pressed on substantive policy issues, they support Social Security, Medicare, and subsidies to farmers. They believed in cutting government benefits, except when they realize those benefits effected them.

Justin Gest provides an illuminating study of white working-class Trump supporters in Youngstown, Ohio, a declining steel city in the Rustbelt. Their attitudes toward immigrants and minorities were more complex than aggregate studies. These Trump supporters did not hate immigrants. Most were proud descendants of immigrants. Most respected today's immigrants "as hardworking members of society, chasing the American dream" (Gest 2016, 196). However, they were frustrated with what they perceived as a federal government overly leniency toward undocumented immigrants whom they believed took jobs from, and drove down the wages of, American workers. They believed this even though they came into contact with few immigrants. Many supported Social Security, Medicare, food stamps, disability, and unemployment benefits, as many were recipients of these programs. However, they opposed welfare programs, because they believed these programs gave benefits to cheating and undeserving immigrants and minorities. They believed that affirmative action was more pervasive than it really was and that it victimized white workers by denying them job opportunities reserved for blacks.

It wasn't that immigrants and affirmative action provoked a populist backlash that elected Trump. It was more like excessive inequality and economic distress precipitated frustration, resentment, and anger. Right-wing populist political leaders and media host stoked resentment and anger over immigrants and minorities. Trump was the most effective Republican candidate in exploiting identity politics and redirecting resentment and anger. Although Republicans elected Trump, he benefited from swing voters from areas marked by excessive inequality and economic distress. Hacker and Pierson added, "Trump did well in areas where unemployment was higher, job growth slower, earnings lower, and overall health poorer. One of the strongest county-level predictor of votes for Trump was the rate of premature death among white Americans" (Hacker and Pierson 2020, 139).

The point is that contrary to the aggregate data, economic stress played a role in producing rage. Although whites from all classes supported Trump, white rage fueled his base and fed a white nationalist movement. This was a mass movement that cut across social class lines. Although racial resentment, economic stress and inequality were factors contributing to this movement, it was by no stretch of the imagination a working class movement. Trump exploited and legitimized this movement. Moreover, four political movements, the realignment of the Republican Party, and an energized right-wing media propaganda ecosystem all came together to produce the perfect political storm which enabled the election of Trump. The next chapter investigates this perfect storm.

*Chapter 4*

# Perfect Storm

The preceding chapter examined Trump voters. This chapter investigates sets of political and historical events that formed Trump base of support, put him in the White House, and shaped his public policy agenda. Four sets of historical events created the perfect storm for a right-wing reactionary populist movement that threatened an equal opportunity, inclusive liberal democratic state. The first set of events involves four political movements that formed Trump's political base. These movements included the economic elite movement, the Christian right movement, the Tea Party movement, and the white nationalist movement. The second event was the unprecedented political dominance of economic elites in U.S. politics. The third event was the realignment of the Republican Party in ways that intensified polarized politics. The fourth event was the formation of a right-wing media propaganda machine. This investigation begins with the economic elite movement and the formation of unprecedented corporate power. Economic elites paved the way for the ascension of Trump and set most of his domestic policy agenda.

## UNPRECEDENTED ECONOMIC POWER

While economic elites have been active in American politics throughout history, the current period is different. Understanding this difference is important in understanding the ascension of Trump.

Economic elites dominated the constitutional convention in 1787, although there were strong differences between the southern land aristocracy, plantation owners with over a 1,000 acres of land and more than 100 slaves, and northern merchant, manufacturing and banking elites (Beard 2014/1913). Northern manufacturing elites preferred protective tariffs;

the southern aristocracy opposed tariffs. A general consensus among the economic elites, north and south, emerged in the early twentieth century. This consensus entailed an acceptance of the basic principles of limited government, laissez-faire capitalism, state's rights, and protection of private property.

This consensus broke down at the beginning of a new political and economic era that lasted roughly from 1933 until near the end of the century. Political scientists refer to this era as the period of interest group liberalism (Lowi 1969), pluralism, or pluralist democracy (Dahl 1989, 2005; Lindblom 1980). It was characterized by different sets of competing interest groups operating in different issue areas. Business elites were generally active primarily in issue areas that impacted their businesses. Political power was fragmented with multiple centers of power. Although business interest occupied a privilege position, it was not a controlling or dominating interest (Dahl 1989; Lindblom 1980).

As chapter 5 will demonstrate, economists refer to the period from 1940 to 1980 as the Great Compression. In terms of public policies, this was the era of progressive taxes, expanding federal powers, growing social welfare programs, declining inequality, increasing upward social mobility, and an expanding middle class. This era was anchored by the Franklin D. Roosevelt's New Deal and Lyndon B. Johnson's Great Society. This was the era of Keynesian economic theory, the ideology that justified the growth of the federal government. Economic elites were divided over this ideology and the New Deal. A faction of these elites mobilized in fierce opposition of both Keynesian theory and the New Deal.

Several corporate elites participated in Roosevelt's Business Advisory Council and the Industrial Advisory Board, established in 1933. Many, including the chair of the United States Chamber of Commerce, accepted Keynesian economic theory and supported Roosevelt (Phillips-Fein 2009). In his first 100 days, Roosevelt declared a bank holiday and recruited bank executives to assist in developing public policies to save the banking industry (Schlesinger 2003). Roosevelt rejected the advice of radical members of Congress who demanded that he nationalize the banks (Schlesinger 2003). He opposed socialism and ascribed to Keynesian economic theory. He was committed to saving capitalism and opposing socialism.

Nevertheless, a major faction of corporate leaders joined the opposition. These insurgent leaders engaged in an assault on the New Deal (Phillips-Fein 2009; Schlesinger 2003). Two organizations stand out in this assault: the National Association of Manufacturing and the American Liberty League. The National Association of Manufacturers (NAM) was established in 1895 to lobby for tariffs to protect the manufacturing sector from foreign competition and to crush labor unions. It emerged as a fierce opponent of the New

Deal legislation, incensed over policy protections for the rights of workers to organize in unions and engage in collective bargaining.

The American Liberty League was created in 1934 by some of the richest and most powerful families of this era: "the Morgans, the du Ponts, the Pews, the Harrimans, the Mellons, the Weirs, the Warburgs, the Rockefellers" (Steinberg and Hoefle 2009). The DuPont family played a central role in leading the organization. It was an offshoot of the National Security League, a league of bankers and industrialists, including Rockefeller, J.P. Morgan, Coleman du Pont, and H.H. Rodgers of Standard Oil, committed to increasing arms production for national defense and to getting the United States engaged in World War I. The League launched a relentless assault on the New Deal and Roosevelt. It lobbied to repeal New Deal legislation. It challenged the legality of New Deal programs in court. It got involved in elections, backing anti-New Deal candidates, mostly Republicans. It assisted other organizations fighting Roosevelt and the New Deal. These organizations included the American Taxpayers League, the Crusaders, the Sentinels of the Republic, the Southern Committee to Uphold the Constitution, and others. The Southern Committee to Uphold the Constitution was affiliated with Ku Klux Klan organizations (Colby 1984). It engaged in a fierce propaganda campaign against Roosevelt and the New Deal. It distributed millions of propaganda pamphlets. One pamphlet stated, "You can't recover prosperity by seizing the accumulation of the thrifty and distributing it to the thriftless and unlucky" (quoted in Phillips-Fein 2009, 11). Other pamphlets targeted Social Security claiming that it was unconstitutional, unworkable, an egregious violation of the rights of the states, and a fiscally unsound program that took the property of employers and employees without due process of law. The League sponsored anti-New Deal radio programs. It claimed that the New Deal was ineffective, wasteful, socialistic, communistic, totalitarian, and crazy. It considered taxes as thief and regulations as oppressive. It presented itself as a grassroots organization representing the common man. However, the chair of the Democratic Party referred to it as the "American Cellophane League," because it was clear that it was well financed by the owners of the Du Pont Chemical Company, the manufacturer of cellophane. Most of the money that supported the American Liberty League came from about twenty-four corporate executives (Phillips-Fein 2009, 12).

Despite fierce opposition to the New Deal and Roosevelt, insurgent corporate leaders failed. They failed to defeat Roosevelt at the polls. They failed to dismantle the New Deal. Roosevelt won re-election in 1936 and 1940 and by large margins.

Government programs continued to expand throughout the 1950s, 1960s, and 1970s. The 1950s was the era of federal interstate highways, federal guaranteed homeowner loans, and suburban development. The 1960s was the era of the Great Society, the War on Poverty, and civil rights. The 1970s saw the establishment of block grants, the Environmental Protection Agency, Occupational Safety and Health Administration, and other programs.

By the end of the 1970s, corporate leaders mobilized into another insurgency movement, initiating a new offensive against equal opportunity, inclusive state, the accumulation of New Deal, Great Society, anti-poverty, and protective regulatory programs. Several events provoked this mobilization: stagflation, stagnant economic growth, inflation and high unemployment, and the continual growth of government programs and regulatory policies under the Nixon administration. Moreover, radical left-wing political movements emerged in the late 1960s and early 1970s. These radical movements were anti-capitalist and hostile to multinational corporations. The passage of anti-business regulations as well as these radical political movements precipitated a backlash, a second corporate insurgency movement.

In 1971, before Nixon appointed him to the Supreme Court, Lewis Powell wrote a famous manifesto, a call to arms for corporate leaders. This manifesto, addressed to the U.S. Chamber of Commerce, stated that the entire U.S. free enterprise system was under attack. Powell argued that this attack was not coming from outside the United States or from a small left-wing extremist group. The attack was coming from multiple sources within the United States and the survival of the free enterprise system was at stake. Powell argued that all business leaders and the U.S. Chamber of Commerce must act to re-educate the nation and to save the system (Powell 1971).

Corporate political activism and political investments intensified in three areas. First, corporate leaders invested in an intellectual crusade to change the dominant political culture. Second, corporate leaders invested in the construction of an organizational infrastructure to enhance corporate political power and to promote the corporate political agenda. Third, they invested in changing campaign finance laws to increase corporate political influence of the economic elites. These investments increased corporate political power and pushed the United States out of the era of interest group liberalism or pluralism into a new era of corporate-dominated politics and policy making.

## POLITICAL CULTURE: NEOLIBERALISM
## AND NEO-CONSERVATISM

Since the New Deal era, corporate leaders had been investing in a crusade to change U.S. political culture: to get Americans to reject Keynesian economic theory, embrace laissez capitalism, accept free enterprise, and to join the campaign to cut taxes, roll back regulations, and shrink government. These investments resulted in the establishment of a long list of conservative think tanks such as the American Enterprise Institute, the Cato Institute, the Heartland Institute, the Mont Pelerin Society (MPS), and many more.

The American Enterprise Association was established in 1938 by executives from Eli Lilly, General Mills, Bristol-Myers, Chemical Bank, Chrysler, and Paine Webber. Its initial mission was "to defend the principles and improve the institutions of American freedom and democratic capitalism—limited government, private enterprise, individual liberty and responsibility" It was renamed the American Enterprise Institute (AEI) in 1962. Richard Mellon Scaife, heir to the Mellon fortune, contributed money to resuscitate this organization in the latter half of the twentieth century.

The Cato Institute was established by Charles Koch in 1976. This libertarian think tank has continued the attack on New Deal programs and has advocated the privatization of major social programs like Social Security. It has opposed the Affordable Care Act and argued for market solutions for health care.

The Heartland Institute was established in 1984. It was well-funded by the tobacco and petroleum industries (Conway and Oreskes 2010). It specializes in public relations campaigns designed to raise doubts about climate change.

In 1947, with money from executives representing the DuPont, B.F. Goodrich, and other corporations, Friedrich Hayek established the MPS. Prominent intellectual affiliated with the MPS, like Milton Friedman and many others, and formulated the ideas behind the neoliberal intellectual movement.

Two new ideologies emerged from these think tanks. They are important to understand because they form the ideological foundation for Trump's actual public policy agenda, minus the trade war. These two new ideologies are neoliberalism and new conservatism. The former is much like libertarianism as it advocates minimalist government and it is hostile to the New Deal. The latter, neo-conservatism, is much like traditional conservatism. It is hostile to Johnson's War on Poverty and Great Society programs. It blames poverty on the bad choices and moral failings of the poor and it advocates workfare programs to replace welfare programs. While elaborating on the details of these two ideologies goes well beyond the scope of this text, a brief statement on one intellectual representing each will suffice in defining these two ideologies.

Milton Friedman was a leading proponent of neoliberalism. This MPS scholar earned the Nobel Prize in Economics for his quantitative research on monetary policy. However, there was a normative aspect of Friedman's scholarship, particularly when he argued for the use of market mechanism, rather than government, to solve social problems. For example, in his book, *Capitalism and Freedom,* he insisted that there is no need for federal anti-discrimination laws because the free market would washout racial discrimination firms (Friedman 1992). When non-discriminating firms hire well-qualified minorities for much lower wages than racially discriminatory firms, these non-discriminating firms would run racially discriminating firms out of business. The reality of the severity and intransigence of the racial caste system in the south testifies to the naivety of Freidman's normative ideals.

Friedman advocated introducing market mechanism or privatization into the public sector to improve governmental services. He argued that competitive private enterprise is far more efficient than government, as governmental services are monopolies and lack consumer-driven incentives to provide higher quality services for a cheaper price. He introduced the ideal of vouchers in education. Giving vouchers to families to choose private schools over public schools would break up the public education monopoly and transform the education system into a market-driven enterprise (Friedman 1955). In his book, co-authored with his wife Rose, *Free to Choose*, he argued against both labor unions and minimum wages (1990). Both artificially raise wages, which have the effect of reducing jobs. Friedman insisted that what improves the living standards of workers is not unions nor higher minimum wages, but greater investment and increased productivity. Friedman is correct to claim that greater productivity increases wealth and income. He is incorrect to assume that income distribution would automatically be fair in the absence of unions or minimum wage policies. Friedman's hostility to unions and minimum wage enables an upward distribution of income. Neoliberalism is an ideology that legitimizes hostility to public policies that protect collective bargaining rights and the right to a decent and livable wage. Friedman rejected the idea of corporate responsibility. He argued that the only responsibility that corporate leaders have is to increase the profits of the corporation. In his book, *Democratic Theory*, C.B. Macpherson claimed that Friedman's concept of classical liberalism or neoliberalism is eerily similar to Herbert Spencer's concept of Social Darwinism, which advocates for minimalist government and the survival of the fittest.

Charles Murray was a leading intellectual representing neo-conservatism. He was a scholar-in-residence at the AEI. Three of his books deserve mention: *Losing Ground, The Bell Curve,* and *Coming Apart. Losing Ground* was published in 1984. It is a critique of the social programs of the 1960s. He claimed that welfare programs provided incentives for women to leave their husbands and teenage girls to have babies, contributing to the rapid disintegration of the black family, the rise of single-parent households and the dramatic increase in teen pregnancy. Murray attributes government liberalization of criminal justice policies to the increase in crime in black neighborhoods. Murray argues that government protection of the rights of criminals in the 1960s reduced the penalties for crime and thus provided incentives for the commission of more crimes. In *The Bell Curve* co-authored by Richard Herrnstein presented considerable statistical data to exhume a theory that had long been refuted, dead, and buried, that there is a correlations between intelligence and class position in society and that blacks were inherently less intelligent than whites. The two most offensive parts of this book identified by critics are these: First, the authors excluded well-known data that contradicted their racist assertion that blacks similarly situated as whites are endowed with a lower intelligence than whites. Second, the book claimed that black men, compared to white men, have larger penises and smaller brains. The book drew heavily from the Pioneer Institute, a think tank with a long reputation for racism and anti-Semitism.

## LOBBYING AND PUBLIC RELATIONS

Corporations put more resources into direct lobbying to influence members of Congress and shape the formation of public policies. Since 1980, both the number of active corporate lobbyist in Washington and the amount of corporate money spent on lobbying increased dramatically. The top 500 corporations have full-time lobbyist in Washington D.C. Lobbying is a multi-billion dollar industry, with over 80 percent of the spending done by major corporations. Less than 2 percent of lobbying money is represented by labor unions. The top two spenders of lobbying are the National Association of Realtors and the U.S. Chamber of Commerce, each spends over $82 million a year. The Business Round Table spends about $17 million a year (Open Secrets/ Center for Responsible Politics 2021).

The Business Roundtable was established in 1972 as a result of the merger of three organizations: the March Groups, the Construction Users Anti-Inflation Roundtable, and the Labor Study Group. Alcoa and General Electric were involved with the March Group, which focused on public policy issues of concern to the corporate sector. The Construction Users Anti-Inflation Roundtable involved with U.S. Steel. It was concerned with rising construction costs. The Labor Study Group involved corporate leaders involved with collective bargaining issues. The Business Roundtable played a major role in defeating pro-labor legislations under the Carter administration.

The National Federation of Independent Businesses is a much older organization. It was established in 1943. It represented small businesses and major franchises. As small businesses were impacted by the Affordable Care Act of 2010, this organization sued the U.S. Department of Health and Human Services in an attempt to challenge the constitutionality of this law.

## AGENDA SETTING AND POLICY MAKING

Several corporate-sponsored organizations now play a major role in setting the public policy agenda for state legislatures and Republican presidents. Although there are several corporate-sponsored agenda-setting and policy-making organizations, these three stand out: the Heritage Foundation, the Heritage Action for America, and the American Legislative Exchange Council.

The Heritage Foundation was established in 1973 by Paul Weyrich, Edwin Feulner, and Joseph Coors, largely with Coors' money. The goal of this organization was to do much more than what think tanks do, to go beyond writing position papers. Its goal was to set conservative policy agendas and to develop and enact conservative public policies. The Heritage Foundation set Reagan's agenda. In 1980, it produced a 1,093 page document entitled, "Mandate for Leadership." As president, this document became Reagan's public policy agenda.

The Heritage Foundation played a major role in selecting the top administrators and setting the policy agenda for Trump as well. Initially, Trump chose Chris Christie to head his transition team. However, with the intervention of Rebekah Mercer, the multi-billionaire Trump contributor who put Steve Bannon and Kelly Ann Conway at the head of Trump's campaign committee, the Heritage Foundation took over the selection process. Before the Republican Party nominated Trump to run for president, the Heritage Foundation had developed a 3,000 name data base of candidates to fill positions for the 2016 Republican president. Summarizing the role of Heritage, a *New York Times* article stated:

> Today it is clear that for all the chaos and churn of the current administration, Heritage has achieved a huge strategic victory. Those who worked on the project estimate that hundreds of the people the think tank put forward landed jobs, in just about every government agency. Heritage's recommendations included some of the most prominent members of Trump's cabinet: Scott Pruitt, Betsy DeVos (whose in-laws endowed Heritage's Richard and Helen DeVos Center for Religion and Civil Society), Mick Mulvaney, Rick Perry, Jeff Sessions and many more. (Mahler 2018)

The Heritage Foundation also produced a booklet entitled, "Blueprint for Impact." The booklet claimed that Trump had embraced 64 percent of the foundation's policy recommendations.

Heritage Action for America was founded in 2010, as an arm of the Heritage Foundation. It was established by the president of the Heritage

Foundation to harness grassroots energy to thwart the liberal agenda and to secure the passage of the Heritage agenda (Heritage Action for America Website 2021). Heritage Action lobbied to repeal the Affordable Care.

After Trump lost the 2020 election, Heritage Action exploited Trump's lies about voter fraud and a stolen election to get key swing states to enact more voter suppression laws.

Heritage Action worked with the Heritage Foundation, the Republican National Committee, and the Republican State Leadership Committee.

The largest, most productive of the new corporate-sponsored legislative-generating organizations is the American Legislative Exchange Council. Paul Weyrich co-founded this organization in 1973. It represented some of the most notable corporations in America. It brings conservative state legislators from all over the country together to seminars and workshops (Lafer 2017).

It operated as a factory to generate bills for Republican-dominated state legislatures. As a legislative mill, ALEC had a reputation for generating about 200 model bills a year. These bills covered a wide range of issues areas including criminal justice, education, gun regulations, health care, labor relations, voting regulations, and many others. ALEC played a role in developing minimum sentences, truth in sentencing, and three-strikes you are out laws (Elk and Sloan 2011). These were some of the most draconian criminal justice laws in the world.

The three-strikes you are out law mandated life sentences for non-violent felonies. In one case, a defendant was sentenced to life for stealing golf clubs (Johnson v California 2005). These laws reintroduced the practice of exploiting prison labor for private gain, as prisoners work for a little as 20 cents an hour (Elk and Sloan 2011). Education laws include charter schools and school vouchers, which have fundamentally changed public education, as a host of private corporations have emerged to compete with public schools. In the healthcare area, ALEC has opposed the individual mandate and has promoted free-market models. ALEC sponsored voter identification laws that civil rights groups claimed suppressed the minority vote. ALEC sponsored Florida's stand your ground policy.

Charles Koch has been active with ALEC and several other organizations, most notably, Americans for Prosperity and Freedom Works. Americans for Prosperity has played more of a lobbying and grassroots organizing role. Skocpol and Hertel-Fernandez (2016) demonstrate that the main factor explaining why a state rejected Medicaid expansion was the presence of a well-established Americans for Prosperity network in the state. This organization plays a powerful role in lobbying in state legislatures.

## THE FEDERALIST SOCIETY AND
## CORPORATE LEGAL THEORY

Corporate leaders put money into organizations to challenge liberal legal theory and promote conservative constitutional perspectives. The Federalist Society emerged as the premier conservative legal society. It was initially established in 1982 by students from Yale, Harvard, and University of Chicago Law Schools. This organization has been well-funded by the Olin Foundation, Scaife Foundation, and the Koch Family Foundation. It experienced phenomenal growth in the twenty-first century. Its budget grew from $3 million in 2002 to over $7 million by 2006 (Avery 2008). Today, it has a chapter at every accredited law school in the nation.

While a liberal legal theory dominated the Supreme Court during the last half of the 20th century, conservative legal theory promoted by the Federalist Society now dominates the Supreme Court. Indeed, today, all six conservative members of the Supreme Court are affiliated with the Federalist Society: Samuel Alito, Amy Barret, Neil Gorsuch, Brett Kavanaugh, John Roberts, and Clarence Thomas.

Several legal scholars insist that a conservative and business perspective now dominate Supreme Court decisions (Cohen 2020). Michael Avery claims that the court now protects corporations from laws favoring unions' rights, workers safety, and consumer interests (Avery 2008). Adam Cohen adds that with the replacement of Kennedy with Kavanaugh, an epochal shift has occurred from a court that had mediated competing interests to a court that now wages "an unrelenting war on the poor and the middle class and enthusiastically championed wealthy individuals and corporations" (Cohen 2020, 313).

## CAMPAIGN FINANCE

Corporate elites engaged in an assault on campaign finance laws. Campaign finance laws dominated the era of interest group liberalism, with the Tillman Act of 1907 prohibiting corporations from making direct contributions to candidates and political parties and the Taft–Hartley Act of 1947 banning unions from making similar contributions. The Tillman Act was enacted in response to corporate leaders dominating elections in the late nineteenth and early twentieth centuries in ways that threatened basic principles of democracy. These laws were strengthened with the passage of the Federal Election Campaign Act of 1971 and the Campaign Finance Reform Act of 1974. The 1971 act created the Federal Election Commission to enforce campaign finance laws. It also introduced disclosure and reporting requirements and set limits on individual donations to candidates and political parties. The 1974 act set limits on candidate expenditures. State governments also passed campaign finance laws.

Conservatives and economic elites assaulted campaign finance laws through the courts. The first assault came with the *Valeo v Buckley* (1976)decision. This decision upheld campaign contribution limits but struck down campaign expenditure limits. Because campaign contributions could have a corrupting effect, the court allowed them. The major change with this decision was that the court claimed that limits on expenditures violated free speech, protected by the First Amendment. In fact, it defined money as speech. It thus amplified the voices of those with the most money over those with the least money. This decision shifted political voice and power to those with the most money.

This distorting effect of money on political equality and democracy has become most evident after the *Citizens United v Federal Election Commission* (FEC) (2010). Writing for the majority, Justice Kennedy redefined the issue as more than a government attack on free speech, but a government suppression of the speech rights of corporations. He argued that the free speech right of corporations is indispensable to decision making in a democracy:

> Political speech is indispensable to decision making in a democracy, and this is no less true because the speech comes from a corporation rather than an individual. Bellotti, 435 U.S., at 77 . . . (the worth of speech "does not depend upon the identity of its source, whether corporation, association, union, or individual") Buckley, 424 U.S., at 48-49 ([T]he concept that government may restrict the speech of some elements of our society in order to enhance the relative voice of others is wholly foreign to the First Amendment. (Citizens United 2010)

This decision struck down major parts of the Bipartisan Campaign Reform Act (BCRA) of 2002 and the Federal Election Campaign Act (FECA) of 1971. It overturned a previous decisions (*Austin v Michigan Chamber of Commerce* 1990) that prohibited corporations and unions from directly funding "electioneering communications." In a blistering dissenting opinion, Justice Stevens argued that corporations have pumped billions of dollars into public relations firms and issue advertisements. These corporations dominate the airways. Corporate leaders put hundreds of millions of dollars into political action committees to promote issues and candidates, privileging corporate speech over all other speeches. Campaign finance laws placed restraints on the spending of money for promoting candidates and issues. The Supreme Court eliminated these restraints.

The *Speechnow.org v FEC* decision eliminated the limits of individual contributions to PACs. The decision along with Citizens United and others fundamentally changed America democracy. With a $5,000 limit on contributions to PACs, millions of millionaires dominated campaign spending.

Thomas Kuhner argues that in its misguided quest to protect the free speech rights of multi-billionaires to dominate the broadcast and cable media, the court invalidated all efforts of the government to protect the political voice and free speech rights of most Americans (Kuhner 2014). The court ignored the extent to which the voices of most Americans are excluded from the same airways. The evisceration of campaign finance laws amplifies the voices of the wealthy and allows the exclusion of the voices of all others.

Kuhner points out that in the case of super PACs and dark money, where these laws are weakest, "200 millionaires and billionaires (0.000063 percent of the population) stand behind roughly 80 percent of all money spent. In the end, 0.37 percent of the population supplies approximately 70 percent of all the money in politics" (Kuhner 2014). Prior to the liberalization of campaign finance laws, politicians relied on a large number of donations and the cost of getting elected was cheaper. Today, presidential elections have become multi-billion dollar enterprises, getting elected to the house costs well over a million dollars. Candidates are more dependent on major contributors than ever before.

In her book, *Dark Money*, Jane Mayer documents the corporate leaders behind the assault on campaign finance laws. She focuses largely on the role of the Devos and Koch families. She summarizes the tactic:

> The tactic was intentional. Clint Bolick, a pioneer in the conservative legal movement whose group, the Institute for Justice, had received start-up funds from Charles Koch, had argued that the Right needed to combat the Left by asserting appealing "counterrights" of its own. Thus Citizens United was cast as the right of corporations to exercise their free speech . . .

> While polls consistently showed that large majorities of the American public—both Republicans and Democrats—favored strict spending limits, the key challenges that led to dismantling the laws were initiated by an extraordinarily right minority: the Kochs and their clique of ultra-wealthy conservative activists. (Mayer 2016, 379)

## MULTI-BILLIONAIRE SUMMITS

The weakening of campaign laws and the emergence of multi-billionaire funding summits have changed both the role of political parties and the policy agenda-setting process in fundamental ways. Because of limits on contributions to political parties, candidates depend less on political parties. Candidates—representative, senator, and presidential hopefuls—flock to multi-billionaire summits in which the donors set candidates' agendas. Candidates reject the policy recommendations of donors at their own peril. Jane Mayer documents what happens when a leading presidential hopeful fails to accept donor advice at a Charles Koch sponsored summit:

> Rare was the Republican candidate who wouldn't toe the Kochs' line. John Kasich, the iconoclastic governor of Ohio, prompted an angry walkout by some twenty donors at the Kochs' April 2014 summit for criticizing the Koch network's position against Medicaid expansion. In answer to Randy Kendrick, who had questioned his pro-Medicaid position, Kasich retorted, "I don't know about you, lady. But when I get to the pearly gates, I'm going to have to answer for what I've done for the poor." He added, "I know this is going to upset a lot of you guys, but we have to use government to reach out to people living in the shadows." The Kochs never invited Kasich back again. (Mayer 2016, 596)

Ohio governor John Kasich ran for president in 2016 and fell to almost last place in a race with about sixteen candidates.

Gordon Lafer provides another example of the influence of super donors. This example involves the process in which Michigan, historically a strong labor union state anchored by the United Auto Workers and the United Mine Workers in the Upper Peninsula, became a right to work state. The campaign was led by Richard (Dick) DeVos, the CEO of Amway, a major contributor to the Republican Party and a major supporter of ALEC-affiliated Mackinac Center. DeVos was part of a network of billionaires that included casino tycoon Sheldon Adelson and Texas investor Harold Simmons. They hired a public relations firm to launch a series of aggressive commercials to promote a right to work law for the public sector. In the November 2012 election, Republican members of the Michigan State Legislature lost seats. That month, fearful that the campaign would fail if they waited until January 2013 and anxious because the Republican leader of the Michigan Senate pledged his opposition to the bill, DeVos and about a dozen other billionaires met privately with the Republican legislative leaders and told them that either they support the bill or face well-financed opponents in the next Republican primary. Shortly afterwards, the right to work bill was passed (Lafer 2017). This case illustrates how multi-billionaire donors use the threats of primary elections to circumvent party organizations and directly pressure Republican leaders to support right-wing extremist policies that they would not ordinarily support (Lafer 2017).

## THE KOCH EFFECT

Theda Skocpol and Alexander Hertel-Fernandez insist that since 2002, the U.S. political terrain and the Republican Party universe had shifted in important organizational ways missed by a focus on wealthy donors or mass politics. Indeed, wealthy donors and mass politics impact both parties. A focus on these organizational changes helps to explain how the Republican Party became "ideologically extreme; contemptuous of the inherited social and economic policy regime; scornful of compromise; unpersuaded by conventional understanding of facts, evidence and science; and dismissive of the legitimacy of its political opposition" (Mann and Ornstein 2012, xiv; quoted in Skocpol and Hertel-Fernandez 2016, 1). They argue that this organizational change involved more than simply the rise of multi-billionaire donors or networks of dark money. It involved the rise of numerous interconnected Koch Industries affiliated organizations serving multiple political functions that have hijacked the Republican Party and pushed the party and its leaders to the far right. These organizations include think tanks like the Cato Institute, Mercatus Center, Charles G. Koch Foundation, Heritage Foundation and other organizations tied into the mainstream media. They involve Koch seminars that bring multi-billionaires and business leaders together twice a year to be exposed to ultra-free-market ideas and to meet political leaders. Within the past five years, these seminars include over 500 participants, paying fees of $100,000. The Koch-affiliated organizations include politically active organizations like Americans for Prosperity, Freedom Works, American Energy Alliance, and Center to Protect Patient Rights. Americans for Prosperity and Center to Protect Patient Rights led the fight against the Affordable Care Act. These organizations entail the public policy production mill, American Legislative Exchange Council, and business advocacy organizations like Freedom Partners Chamber of Commerce. Whereas in 2002, 53 percent of Republican campaign money was spent by the Republican Party, this figure had declined to only 30 percent by 2014. About 52 percent of the campaign money was spent by non-party funders and constituency organizations. Koch-affiliated organizations did more to promote the dominant public philosophy and set the conservative policy agenda than the Republican Party. These organizations pushed the party to the far right.

## TRUMPISM AND THE CORPORATE
## INSURGENCY MOVEMENT

It is critically important to understand this complex history behind the corporate insurgency movement in order to understand the ascension of Trump.

The corporate insurgency movement did not intentionally make Trump president. This movement unintentionally enabled the ascension of Trump. This movement undercut the influence of the Republican Party, targeted moderate Republicans, pushed the Republican Party to the far right, polarized politics, engendered contempt for opponents, tolerated a disregard for facts, evidence, and science, and engaged in an assault on the equal opportunity and inclusive state. The Trump phenomenon was not a produce of any working-class movement. It was the product of a corporate insurgency movement. Working-class America did not set Trump's agenda nor assist in the selection of his top officials. The corporate insurgency movement paved the way for the rise of Trump, set the Trump agenda and handpicked Trump's top administrators. Other movements accelerated the ascension of Trump and formed his political base. These movements include the Tea Party, Christian right and white nationalist movements.

## TEA PARTY MOVEMENT

The Tea Party movement accelerated the ascension of Donald Trump to the White House. Most observers trace the origins of this movement back to Rich Santelli, a CNBC contributor and commodities broker, who delivered a passionate rant against President Obama's Homeowner Affordability and Stabilization Plan designed to provide assistance to millions of homeowners facing foreclosure. He claimed that the government was rewarding bad behavior with a big government, socialist like program. The Tea Party movement emerged out of the 2008–2009 recession. It ascended in opposition to the bank bailout and the stimulus bill. It shared some of the same goals as the corporate insurgency movement. Tea Party leaders advocated shrinking government, cutting taxes, and rolling back regulations. It was energized by the passage of the Affordable Care Act. The Tea Party movement grew in opposition to Obama and the ACA. Prominent conservative media personalities like Glenn Beck, Sean Hannity, and Laura Ingram provided assistance in publicizing Tea Party demonstrations. Freedom Works provided transportation for the April 15, 2009 Tax Day Rally.

The 2009 Tax Day Rally in Washington, DC, brought out the worse in Tea Party behavior as many Tea Party demonstrators verbally accosted U.S. Representatives, using profanity and racist language toward black representatives, spitting on them and using the "N" word. They even called Representative Barney Frank a "faggot."

Most Tea Party members were from the middle class. The Tea Party movement was a Republican insurgency movement. Most Tea Party members were Republicans driven by anger toward both Obama and the moderate and centrist Republicans willing to compromise with Obama. Indeed, Tea Party Republicans revolted against Republican Speaker of the House, John Boehner and other moderate Republicans, because they were willing to compromise with Obama. Trump's hostility toward Obama, his crusade against Obama's policies, and his intolerance for moderate Republicans resonated with this movement.

Researchers differ over two aspects of the Tea Part movement. They disagreed over whether the Tea Party was a grassroots movement or a front for an elitist, multi-billionaire movement and whether the movement was motivated by ideology or racial prejudice.

There were several branch Tea Party organizations. Some of the more visible and active branches are:

Tea Party Patriots
Tea Party Alliance
Tax Day Tea Party
State and Local Tea Parties

Some organizations are more local and decentralized. The State and Local Tea Parties tend to be more local.

The Tea Party Patriots is a more centralized organization. It is well connected to major contributors. The ideology of this organization favors multinational corporations over ordinary workers. It received substantial money and other forms of support from multiple organizations such as Let Freedom Ring, a Republican Party organization; Freedom Works, an organization financed by the Koch brothers of Koch Industries, Americans for Prosperity, another Koch financed organization; Americans for Tax Reform; the Council for National Policy and several others. Tea Party expert, Lee Fang adds,

> Let Freedom Ring was not the only group propping up the Tea party Patriots. Staffers from FreedomWorks, the front group led by Dick Armey, had managed the Tea Party Patriots' listserv. Corporate front groups like Americans for Prosperity and the Heartland Institute provided many of the talking points and speakers used by the Tea Party Patriots and its affiliates. Free training seminars and online tutorials for grassroots organization were provided to the Tea party Patriots by the Leadership Institute, which is funded by the billionaire Koch family as well as by other corporate interests, including Amway. Even the Tea party patriots' website was sponsored by a who's who of Republican front groups, including Regular Folks United Freedom Works and Americans for Tax Reform. (Lee 2014, 10–11)

Some Tea Party leaders had no problem with multinational corporations like Exxon Mobile not paying any corporate taxes at all and Google paying only a 2 percent corporate tax. The rationale was that these corporations are job generators. Although leaders were hostile to immigrants, some leaders were business and corporate friendly, "On national television, Tea Party leaders declared that they sought an outright elimination of Social Security, a repeal of the Seventeenth Amendment, and even mass deportation of undocumented immigrants" (Lee 2014, 12).

Vanessa Williamson and Theda Skocpol paint a complex picture of the Tea Party movement. They acknowledge the connection between multi-billionaires like Charles and the late David Koch and conservative media personalities like Glenn Beck. They even document the role of Freedom Works in paying for the buses to transport members from all over the country to Washington, D.C. for Tea Party protests and demonstrations. They summarize the ideology of party leaders that favor multinational corporations and denounce big government, taxes, excessive government spending, and liberal constitutionalism. However, they present demographics of rank-and-file members who tend to be older, 45 plus, better-off, and better educated than most Americans. However, their ideology does not necessarily match the ideology of the leaders. The Tea Party movement overlaps with the Christian right movement. About 40 percent of Tea Party members are evangelical Christians (Skocpol and Williams 2012, 35). These rank-and-file members want more government to go after undocumented immigrants. They strongly support Social Security and Medicare (Skocpol and Williamson 2012). However, at the same time, they are likely to take extreme and uncompromising positions. They are more likely to oppose same-sex marriage, gays in the military, and immigration reform. They are particularly hostile to programs initiated by the Obama administration. They a prone to conspiracy theories and more likely to believe Obama is a Muslim and foreigner. They are more likely to support the birther movement. The Tea Party movement and Tea Party-affiliated Republicans in Congress played a central role in shutting down the government in their effort to repeal the Affordable Care Act. According to Skocpol and Williamson, these extremist actions precipitated opposition from the U.S. Chamber of Commerce and the NAM, as both of these organizations were most concerned with the impact of the shutdown on the country's credit rating.

Christopher Parker and Matt Barreto also noted inconsistency between the ideology of Tea Party leaders and the beliefs and attitudes of Tea Party supporters. While leaders were more likely to be motivated by neoconservative and libertarian ideology, rank-and-file members were more likely to be motivated by hostility to Obama, resentment of blacks, fear of Muslims, and hostility to immigrations (Parker and Barreto 2013).

Strong Tea Party supporters compared to non-supporters were more likely to harbor racial stereotypes. Compared to non-supporters, strong Tea Party supporters were more likely to perceive blacks as lazy and Latinos as untrustworthy. These supporters were more likely to believe that the United States went too far in pushing for equal rights (Parker and Barreto 2013).

The Tea Party movement was a right-wing Republican insurgency movement. It was hostile to liberal elites and to the Washington establishment. Not only was it precipitated by the passage of the stimulus bill and Affordable Care Act, Tea Party activists were enraged and energized by moderate Republicans willing to compromise with Obama. This movement targeted both moderate and centrists Republicans. In the House, this movement targeted Republican leaders, including the Republican Speaker of the House, John Boehner and the Republican Majority Leader, Eric Cantor. The movement pressured Boehner to retire early in 2015. Local Tea Party activists in the State of Virginia mobilized to defeat Cantor in the 2014 primary election. The Tea Party was a right-wing insurgency movement that pushed the Republican Party to the far right. Out of all of the Republicans running in the Republican Party primary, Donald Trump resonated the most with the Tea Party's rank-and-file.

## THE CHRISTIAN RIGHT

The Christian right or extreme conservative Christians, not to be confused with the Christian left or liberal Christians, played a major role in shaping political culture, politics, and public policies throughout U.S. history and has recently emerged as a reactionary political movement. The Christian right tends to be conservative, moralistic, and authoritarian. In contrast, the Christian left tends to be liberal, humanistic, and tolerant. Many conservative Christians are evangelicals. Most evangelicals voted for Trump. However, some evangelicals ascribe to the Social Gospels—the teachings of Jesus that emphasize compassion for the poor, love for one's enemy, and help for the stranger or the immigrant. These more liberal evangelicals were less likely to vote for Trump. The more extreme conservative Christians have tended to be less welcoming to minorities and foreigners and hostile to gays and lesbians. White conservative southern Christians played a major role in promoting slavery before the Civil War and defending racial segregation in the first two-thirds of the twentieth century. Indeed, the Southern Baptist Convention was formed over the issue of slavery, as Northern Baptists believed slavery was morally wrong and Southern Baptist insisted that slavery was ordained and sanctified by God. Even after Congress passed the Civil Rights Act of 1964 to prohibit racial segregation in schools and universities, many conservative Christians continued to struggle to maintain segregated school.

Over the past 150 years, conservative Christians were successful in establishing conservative public policies. They played a key role in passing laws to outlaw abortion, birth control, sex education, evolutionary theory, recreational drugs, homosexuality, and communism. During the twentieth century, southern conservative Christians supported laws that mandate racial segregation and that outlawed miscegenation.

The 1960s and 1970s had been devastating and humiliating to conservative Christians. Liberals had attacked and killed almost every law promoted by conservative Christians. The courts and Congress trashed public policies in their most cherished policy areas: race, sexuality, religious observance, and religious beliefs. In the area of race, the courts and Congress shot down racial segregation, promoted integration, and allowed interracial marriage. In the area of sexuality, the courts decriminalized homosexuality and allowed same-sex marriage. In the areas of religious observances, the courts hinder teacher-led prayer in schools and prohibited the public display of the Ten Commandments and other exclusively Christian décor. In the area of beliefs, the courts legalized the teaching of evolution and snubbed creationism and intelligent design.

The Christian right reactionary movement accelerated after the Brown v Board of Education decision (1954/55). Indeed, the founder of the Moral Majority, Jerry Falwell, was passionate in his support for racial segregation and his opposition to civil rights. Falwell referred to civil rights as civil wrong, called Martin Luther King a communist, and claimed that integration would destroy the white race. In a sermon entitle, "Segregation or Integration? Which," delivered in respond to the Brown decision, Falwell said: "If Chief Justice Warren and his associates had known God's word and had desired to do the Lord's will, I am quite confident that the 1954 decision would never have been made . . . . The true Negro does not want integration. He realizes his potential is far better among his own race" (Falwell quoted by Blumenthal 2007).

Falwell was not the only extreme conservative Christian who passionately defended segregation during the 1960s. W. A. Criswell the president of the Southern Baptist Convention shared Falwell views. In response to the pressure to desegregate schools, a number of conservative Christians established what some journalist referred to as segregated academies. Indeed, Falwell created the Lynchburg Christian Academy, which was later renamed Liberty University. The Lynchburg News referred to the school as "a private school for white students" (quoted in Blumenthal 2007). These schools were forced to cease their *de facto* segregation and allow non-whites to enroll or lose their tax exempt status. The Christian right emerged as a political movement by the end of the 1970s and beginning of the 1980s. Evangelicals who had supported one of their own, Jimmy Carter, for president in 1976 but switched in 1980 and supported Ronald Reagan. Although, the Southern Criswell and the SBC took a moderate position on abortion in 1971, scholars are divided over whether this switch was precipitated by Carter's refusal to oppose *Roe v Wade* or his refusal to tolerate deliberately segregated all-white Christian schools.

The number of conservative Christian organizations increased dramatically in the late 1970s and early 1980s. Organizations like Focus on the Family, the Family Research Council, and the Traditional Values Coalition were established during this time period. Paul Weyrich, one of the founders of the Heritage Foundation, urged Falwell to establish the Moral Majority. By the early 1980s, a well-established organizational infrastructure formed a solid foundation for the Christian right movement. These foundational organizations included the Christian Broadcasting Network, founded by Pat Robertson in 1960, Trinity Broadcasting Network (1973).

The abortion issue attracted more support and traction than the racial integration issue. Other anti-abortion organizations sprung up and joined the Christian right movement. Indeed, by the end of the twentieth century and the beginning of the twenty-first century, the anti-abortion movement became a major attraction to the Republican Party. Indeed, the Value Voters Summit was established in 2006. Issues like abortion and LGBT rights attracted a much larger segment of the population to the Christian right movement. This intensified as it lost ground. As the court enabled same-sex marriage, as the military accepted LGBT service men and women, and as civil rights were extended to LGBT individuals, the Christian right perceived itself as under continual attack.

Today, conservative evangelicals see themselves as victims. They are involved in politics to defend their religious rights and to take back their nation from what they believe are liberals, socialists, and anti-Christians who have allowed the teaching of evolution, who have banned prayer in school, who tolerate the mass murder of unborn children, who have outlawed Christmas, who bar the Ten Commandments from public view, who allow gays and lesbians in the military, and who violate the conscience and basic freedoms of Christians.

The movement has long since modified its position on race. In 1995, the Southern Baptist Convention issued a statement apologizing for supporting slavery and racial segregation. It shifted its focus from race to abortion and LGBT rights. The Christian right movement has attracted more black ministers. Indeed, Martin Luther King Jr.'s niece, Alveda King, joined the movement and endorsed Trump in 2016 and again in 2020 (King 2020; Lemon 2019).

Trump appealed directly to the Christian right movement. In his appeal, he promised to promote their agenda: to protect religious freedom, to appoint anti-abortion judges to the Supreme Court, to oppose abortion policy, to repeal policies that promoted the rights of individuals who happen to be gay, lesbian, and transgender, and to restrict the immigration of non-Christians into the United States. To conservative evangelicals, religious freedom meant the right to one's religious belief that homosexuality was a sin and an abomination before God. It meant the freedom of devout conservative Christians to refuse to serve customers or hire candidates who were gay, lesbian, or transgender.

Several evangelical leaders considered President Trump their liberator from the oppression of liberals. These evangelical leaders compared Trump to Cyrus, the Persian King who liberated the Hebrews from the Babylonians. For them, God chose Trump to save them from liberal oppression (Strang 2020; Wallnau 2016). Trump appealed directly to evangelical fundamentalist ministers. Not only did he earn their support. He meets with evangelical fundamentalist ministers regularly. Trump has maintained strong ties with, and support from, some of the most influential televangelists and evangelical leaders, including John Hagee. He maintained support from Pat Robertson up until the fall of 2019. He lost this support after John Bolton testified against Trump in Congress and published his book, *The Room Where it Happened* (Bolton 2020).

Trump's ties with conservative evangelicals explain his commitment to appoint anti-abortion judges to the Supreme Court, his promotion of a form of religious freedom that allows discrimination against gays and lesbians, his defense of prayer in school, and his urgency to reopen churches during the covid-19 pandemic.


## WHITE NATIONALIST MOVEMENT


Like evangelicals, white nationalist movements have been a major feature of American history and politics. A number of scholars have documented an association between economic crises and the rise and fall of these movements (Diamond 1989; Dryer 1997; Gallaher). The movement flared up in the 1990s following the farm crisis and the foreclosures of millions of family farms. Leaders of organizations like the Posse Comitatus, the Patriots, and the militia exploited the crisis, blaming it on scapegoats: immigrants, minorities, Jewish bankers, and the government. Timothy McVeigh, the 1995 Oklahoma Federal Building bomber, was affiliated with the Michigan militia (Dyer 1997). The movement receded under the George W. Bush administration, but flared up again after the 2008–2009 recession and the election of

Obama. New organizations emerged. Movement leaders attempted to rebrand and expand the movement, creating the so-called alt-right movement. This white nationalist movement was fragmented. It flared up on the internet like a California wildfire after a hot, dry summer. Most of the organizations associated with the alt-right are online "blogs, podcasts, forums and webzines that discuss cultural and political ideas—examples of these include Radix, The Right Stuff, Counter-Currents, American Renaissance and many others" (Hawley 2017, 19). It also includes *Taki Magazine*, Stormer 4-chan, and others. The term alt-right was popularized by Richard Spencer, who emerged as one of its most prominent leaders. Spencer was the executive editor of *Taki Magazine* and the founder of Alternative Right.com. He served as president of the National Policy Institute, a white nationalist think tank. He organized 2017 "United the Right" protest in Charlottesville, Virginia. Steve Bannon provided a platform for the alt-right movement. Allum Bokhari and Milo Yiannopoulos published an article on Breitbart's website defining the movement and distinguishing it from white supremacist movements. The article labeled the Skinheads as ignorant thugs with low IQs and defined the alt-right movement as an intellectual movement grounding in a well-established anti-egalitarian, anti-liberal, and anti-democracy literature, which included fascist writers, such as Julius Evola. It maintains that Western civilization and white communities were under attack by liberals. It claimed that liberals stand for racial equality, while promoting discrimination and violence against whites. It advocates for the establishment of homogeneous white communities and insists that mass immigration of non-whites is a threat to whites. The article endorsed Trump as the only Republican candidate who share the alt-right perspective. The movement spawned the formation of other groups, such as the Proud Boys, established in 2016.

Almost all groups affiliated with the white nationalist movement—the more intellectual alt-right, more traditional white supremacists, such as the KKK, neo-Nazi, and Skinheads, and others like the Posse Commitatus—traffic in some form of the white genocide or white replacement conspiracy theory. This theory promotes the belief that there is a deliberate conspiracy or multiple unrelated plots to intentionally dilute, replace, or exterminate white Western culture and the white race. Groups and leaders differ on the culprits responsible, the methods used, and the proper way of responding to white genocide. Culprits include globalists, Jewish elites, white liberals, socialists, communists, blacks, and others. Methods include the promotion of liberal, egalitarian, democratic, anti-discrimination, permissive immigration, and pro-diversity policies. More extreme methods include the removal or elimination of non-whites. Extreme methods have led to mass shootings. For example, the 2016 mass shooting in a church in a Charleston, South Carolina church was motivated by the white genocide conspiracy theory. Dylann Roof claimed that blacks had to be stopped, because they were killing whites. Another example includes the 2019 mass shooting in El Paso, Texas. The shooter, Patrick Crucius, was provoked by this theory. He made his position clear in a manifesto. He stated to the police, "I am simply defending my country from cultural and ethnic replacement brought on by an invasion" (Quoted by Kennedy 2020).

Trump was strongly supported by the white nationalist movement. As noted in chapter 2, former KKK leader, David Duke endorsed Trump, along with most other white nationalist leaders, including Richard Spencer. However, Trump supporters claim that Trump support from the racist right does not mean that Trump endorsed the racist right. Indeed, Trump has stated that he did not support white supremacists. Nevertheless, there is considerable evidence that Trump not only interacted with white genocide conspiracy theorists but courted their support (Kharakh and Primack 2016). In the 2016 campaign, Trump frequently re-tweeted messages from supporters promoting the white genocide conspiracy theory. He re-tweeted fake statistics grossly inflating the number of whites murdered by blacks, and he accepted invitations to appear on Alex Jones, InfoWars program (Wendling 2018, 193–196; Kharakh and Primack 2016). Trump was not just supported by the racist right. He emboldened the racist right (Neiwert 2018). Illustrating this connection, David Neiwert offers these observations:

The American radical right—the violent, paranoid, racist, hateful radical right—was back with a vengeance. Actually, it had never really gone away. And now it had a presidential candidate;

Hopefully, he's going to sit there and say, "When I become elected president, what we're going to do is we're going to make the border a vacation spot, it's going to cost you twenty-five dollars for a permit, and then you get fifty dollars for every confirmed kill."

—Supporter of Donald Trump, interviewed in the *New York Times*.

"This robocall goes out to all millennials and others who are honest in all their dealings . . . The white race is being replaced by other peoples in America and in all white countries. Donald Trump stands strong as a nationalist."

—William White (a white nationalist), pro-Trump robocall to Massachusetts voters.

"The march to victory will not be won by Donald Trump in 2016, but this could be the steppingstone we need to then radicalize millions of White working and middle class families to the call to truly begin a struggle for Faith, family and folk."

—Matthew Heimbach, cofounder of the neo-Nazi Traditionalist Youth Network, at

"Get all of these monkeys the hell out of our country—now! Heil Donald Trump
—-THE ULTIMATE SAVIOR."
>—Tweet from the Daily Stormer, a neo-Nazi website.

"Donald Trump was right, all these illegals need to be deported."
>—White man in Boston who with another man beat a homeless Latino to within an inch of his life with a metal pole and then urinated on him.

"People who are following me are very passionate. They love this country and they want this country to be great again. They are passionate."
>—Donald Trump, when asked about the Boston hate crime
>(Neiwert 2018, 1–2).

President Trump's administration had several direct ties with white nationalists: Stephen Miller and Steve Bannon. Stephen Miller, the author of the president's inauguration speech and the architect of the president's immigration policy to cage children to send a message to asylum seeker, had worked with Richard Spencer at Duke University. Spencer considered Miller a mentee. They shared a similar vision of America as a white nation.

Steve Bannon co-chaired the president's election committee with Kelly Ann Conway. Joshua Green insists that Bannon helped deliver the alt-right for Trump. As the manager of the Breitbart news website, Bannon was well connected to both the alt-right and the right-wing news sources. Indeed, Robert Spencer was often a guest columnist for Breitbart (Green 2018, 125). Of course, Bannon did not survive one year in the Trump administration.

Trump's demand to close the border, build a wall, and keep immigrants out appealed to a broad segment of Americans fearful of immigrants taking their jobs. However, his characterization of Mexicans as rapist and murders, his open hostility to the Black Lives Matter movement, and his flirtation with racists resonated most with the alt-right and white nationalist movements.

These four movements overlapped and intersected. Although the Tea Party movement emerged as a grassroots revolt against the bailout, stimulus, and Obama, this movement received considerable support from Koch brothers sponsored organizations such as Freedom Works and Americans for Prosperity. Although most Tea Party supporters were unaware of this connection, many of the organizers of local Tea Party groups were former leaders of the racist right movement—Posse Comitatus, Patriots, and militia groups. Indeed, the rise of the Tea Party movement enabled the racist right to move into mainstream politics. The conservative evangelical movement has always had strong connections with the economic elite movement.

The Council for National Policy, established in 1981, acted as a hub connecting multi-billionaire families like the Koch family, the DeVos family, and many others to a wide range of conservative organizations and causes, including the Christian television and radio networks, Focus on the Family, the Values Summit, the campaign to outlaw same-sex marriage, campaigns for governors, congress persons, and presidents. Although some donors are libertarians and support same-sex marriage, they see their donations as a bargain:

> Donors know their contributions went to a list of approved causes, and they received a tax write-off in return.

> The result was a merry-go-round of reciprocal funding. The Koch network and CNP donors—especially the DeVos family—grew ever closer, despite their religious differences. The DeVoses joined the Kochs' Seminar Network, and Charles Koch attended CNP meetings. (Nelson 2019, 127)

As a result of this hub and network of donations, both multi-billionaires and conservative Christian leaders influence not just the outcome of elections. They set the policy agenda inside government. Indeed, both Tony Perkins, president of the Family Research Council and Charles Koch played a key role in setting President Trump's agenda (Nelson 2019, 260–202).

Trump's policy agenda was a function of what Skocpol referred to as "an uneasy marriage of free-market plutocrats and populist ethno-nationalists" (Skocpol 2020, 22). Multi-billionaire donors were uneasy with some of Trump's anti-immigration policy, flirtation with white supremacist groups, and trade wars. These policies appeal to Trump's movement base: Tea Party members, white nationalists, and conservative evangelicals. Trump's promise to appoint anti-abortion and pro-gun judges, his hostility to the Black Lives Matter movement, and his draconian anti-immigration policies resonated with this movement base. However, multi-billionaire donors supported Trump with enthusiasm, because he delivered the public policies that mattered most to them: tax cuts, deregulation, and pro-business judges appointed to the courts. They see Trump's larger policy agenda as their policy agenda: repealing of the Affordable Care Act, cutting taxes, terminating the Clean Energy Plan, ending the Paris Agreement, assaulting labor unions, expanding school choice, stopping the student loan forgiveness programs, and hacking away at social welfare programs for the poor. They enjoyed Trump's quiet opposition to raising the minimum wage, his inconspicuous roll back of regulations that protected the rights of workers to organize in unions and engage in collective bargaining, and his invisible assault on workplace health and safety regulations.

These four insurgency movements collectively contributed to the formation of a right-wing mass populist movement. Whereas the corporate insurgency movement was an economic elitist movement, the Tea Party, Christian right and white nationalist movements joined the corporate elite to provide the foundation for a massive right wing movement. The emergence of a right-wing media eco-system acted as an accelerate to the right wing populist flames, creating a perfect storm.

## THE RIGHT-WING MEDIA ECOSYSTEM

The type of media system that complemented the pluralist system of the twentieth century had metamorphosed into a more polarizing system, with the rise of a right-wing media ecosystem.

The transformation of the media started with the rise of right-wing radio and the ascension of Rush Limbaugh. Three factors contributed to the rise of Rush. First, the elimination of the fairness doctrine played a role. The fairness doctrine operated under the assumption that air space occupied by radio and television waves was public space and companies obtaining a license to operate on public space had an obligation to the public to provide the news as a public service. The Federal Communications Commission required licensed radio and television stations to devote some of their air time to controversial issues of importance to the public and to present the issue in an honest, equitable, and balanced way. Stations were required to give equal time to representatives of both sides of an issue or equal time to candidates running for a political office. Whenever the honesty, character, or integrity of a private individual was attacked, stations are required to give that individual a reasonable opportunity to respond (*Red Lion Broadcasting Company v FCC* 1969). The fairness doctrine was repealed in 1987 under the Reagan administration. The repeal of this doctrine enabled the transformation of broadcast news from a public service dedicated to informing the public to profit-making entertainment. It also allowed for broadcast stations to air offensive one-sided editorializing, promote misinformation, and engage in unanswerable and malicious personal attacks.

Second, Rush exploded on the AM radio scene at a time when AM radio stations were losing money and going out of business, because FM music dominated radio. There was a hungry market for right-wing conservative talk radio. Conservatives who believed that television news suffered from a liberal bias were attracted to radio stations that engaged in constant and unrestrained attacks on liberals.

Rush Limbaugh was articulate, talented, entertaining, and effective. He was gifted in the use of language, creative in telling stories, and imaginative in creating caricatures of liberals. He opened up an entire industry for right-wing talk radio hosts. He was joined by a long list of other talented hosts that provided the foundation for a major part of the right-wing media ecosystem:

Right-wing talk radio hosts played a major role in moving the Republican Party to the extreme rights and promoting a toxic political climate, hostile to liberals, and tainted with racists overtones. Rory O'Connor's book *Shock Jocks: Hate Speech and Talk Radio* provide a good summary of this anti-liberal hostility and anti-black and Hispanic bias. O'Connor cites Rush Limbaugh referring to environmentalists as "wackos" and claiming that carbon monoxide is not a toxic pollutant and the "Antarctica ice is actually increasing" (O'Connor 2008). Referring to the devastation Hurricane Katrina inflicted on New Orleans, he said, "Once whites leave town, all you got is overwhelming lawlessness . . . it's a proven demonstrable fact" (quoted in O'Connor 2008, 56). In reference to Hispanics on the television show, "Survivors," he claimed that Hispanics will win, because they "have shown a remarkable ability to cross borders" and "they will do things other people won't do" (quoted in O'Connor 208, 57).

O'Connor cites Michael Savage's bizarre argument that gays are threatening religious freedom: "The radical homosexual agenda will not stop until religion is outlawed in this country . . . They threaten your very survival . . . Gay marriage is just the tip of the iceberg" (quoted in O'Connor 2008, 70). More recently, the Southern Poverty Law Center placed Savage on its Hatewatch list for promoting a white supremacist conspiracy theory of non-whites and white race traitors plotting to exterminate whites. In a February 2018 radio program, he attacked Nancy Pelosi for criticizing President Trump's anti-immigration policy for trying to "make America white again." Savage claimed that Pelosi's statement was not only racist but part of a plot to exterminate whites and white culture. The Center quoted Savage:

> Do you have any idea how sick and vile this racist statement is? . . . She's basically unhitched herself from her own people, her own culture, her own heritage in order to appease the masses who keep her in power . . . Unless we stand up to the racists and the genocidal maniacs who are attacking, attacking, attacking, "there will be nothing left to protect, there will be nothing left to save. Everything of our culture will be gone. (Quoted in Janik 2018)

In *Talk Radio's America: How an Industry Took Over a Political Party That Took Over the United States*, Brian Rosenwald explained how in the 1990s, Rush Limbaugh and other talk radio hosts helped key Republican leaders raise money, get elected, and promote a conservative policy agenda. Unable to defeat the Lobbying Disclosure Act of 1994, Tom Delay and Newt Gingrich elicited the assistance of hundreds of talk radio hosts, as well as the Christian Coalition and the National Rifle Association. Gingrich faxed Limbaugh talking points. Limbaugh precipitated strong opposition by promoting misinformation about the act.

Rosenwald noted that by the twenty-first century, Limbaugh and other talk radio hosts were able to expand their audience by becoming more provocative and taking more extreme position. Rush Limbaugh, Mark Levin, Michael Savage, and others played a major role in the defeating of the Comprehensive Immigration Reform Act of 2007. According to a study of the role of the media and the defeat of this bill, conservative talk radio devoted more time to this bill and attacked it with more vitriol than any other news sources:

> Conservative talkers Rush Limbaugh, Sean Hannity and Michel Savage were highly critical in their coverage of the immigration bill. Rush Limbaugh on May 18 accused democrats of trying to destroy America. He also was highly critical of Trent Lott for supporting the immigration bill and his [Lott's] attack on talk radio saying, "Talk radio is running America, we have to deal with that problem . . .

> Michael Savage, the wildcard among conservative talkers, was more explosive in his coverage of the immigration bill. On May 17, he called Bush a traitor and a sellout for his stance on immigration and he likened the wave of immigration to the Alamo proclaiming, "We are not giving away the sovereignty of America." (Akdenizli 2007)

After the election of Obama, Limbaugh and others began to target the Republican leadership in the House of Representatives. They attacked the Speaker of the House, John Boehner. They, most notably, Laura Ingram, played a key role in defeating the House Republican majority leader, Eric Cantor. Rosenwald demonstrated how control over the Republican Party shifted from the party leaders to the right-wing conservative radio hosts. This change pushed the Republican Party further to the far right and enabled the election of Donald Trump. At the same time, they normalized and promoted anti-immigrant sentiments and racial resentment.

The right-wing media ecosystem started to form in the late 20th century with the rise of right-wing radio. This ecosystem expanded enormously with the formation of cable television and the internet. Cable news was led by Fox News, established by multi-billionaire Rupert Murdoch, who hired the late Roger Ailes as CEO to produce Fox news. Ailes began his career as an executive producer in the early 1960s but worked on framing national campaign issues for Richard Nixon and Ronald Reagan. He also assisted Donald Trump in preparing for the debate with Hillary Clinton. Ailes centralized Fox's news reporting, providing scripted conservative talking points for news reporters and turning the news station into the propaganda arm of the Republican Party (Brock 2005; Brock and Rabin-Havt 2012).

Right-wing online news has been dominated by Breitbart News Network, established by Andrew Breitbart and Larry Solov with considerable funding from the Mercer family. After the death of Andrew Breitbart, Steve Bannon managed the site and aligned it with the alt-right, featuring stories from neo-Nazi and white supremacists. There are other websites more extreme than Breitbart in promoting conspiracy theories and white supremacy. As noted in chapter 2, these sites include Radix, The Right Stuff, Counter-Currents, American Renaissance, and Infowars. The combination of these websites, talk radio, and Fox News constitutes an alternative media ecosystem. It has changed fundamentally the infrastructure of public policy making in the United States. Whereas in the twentieth century, policy makers and most American acquired their news from similar sources, with comparable information, today, the right-wing media ecosystem functions as a propaganda machine for the far right, allows conservatives to operate in a different media universe, intensifies polarized politics, and encourages an assault on progressive public policies (Jamieson and Cappella 2008).

Although interest groups continue to shape the formation of public policies, the framework for policy-making process has changed from the twentieth to the twenty-first century. Four major factors have changed the privileged position of the business and corporate sector to a dominant position, polarized politics, and encouraged an assault on progressive public policies. These factors include the shift in the two-party system, the mobilization of the corporate sector, the ascension of a conservative public philosophy, and the formation of a right-wing media ecosystem.

The two-party system shifted from one that encouraged bargaining and compromise to one that was polarized. Racist Southern Democrats migrated to the Republican Party and extreme conservative Republicans targeted moderate Republicans for expulsion from the party, moving the Republican Party further to the right and creating a right-wing, white identity party.

Corporate leaders mobilized to assault and destroy labor unions, to assault and delegitimize liberal ideology, to assault and dismantle campaign finance laws, and to liberalize constitutional theory. These corporate leaders organized propaganda think thanks and public policy-making mass production mills. They mobilized individually and collectively to prevent the enactment of laws unfavorable to corporations and to secure the passage of laws that favored and enriched corporations.

Conservative intellectuals, many of which were fellows in conservative think tanks, produced a new dominant conservative public philosophy. This philosophy rejected Keynesian economics, promoted supply-side economics, opposed labor unions, minimum wage legislation, and other progressive policies. It advocated tax cuts, deregulation, privatization, and minimum government. It included neoliberalism, neoconservatism, and right-wing libertarianism.

The right-wing propaganda media ecosystem emerged independent of corporations. It emerged, because there was much money to be made trafficking in prejudice and right-wing extremism. This media ecosystem spewed out misleading and false information in ways that have distorted the policy-making process and exacerbated polarized politics.

These four changes were reinforced by the Tea Party, conservative evangelical, and white nationalist movements. The combination of these changes and movements enabled assaults on the progressive public policies that emerged out between 1935 and 1975 and undermined efforts to address the problems of the twenty-first century, especially problems impacting the working class and minorities. As will be demonstrated in the next chapter, these changes are associated with the growth of extreme inequality, the erosion of organized labor, the shrinkage of the middle class, and the decline of the life changes of the working class. These movements provided the fertile ground for the growth of Trumpism.

## THE RISE OF ASYMMETRIC
## POLARIZED PARTY POLITICS

By 2016, an asymmetric polarized party system had emerged. Three major changes characterize the ascension of this new party system. First, studies indicate that since 1994, conservative, authoritarian, racially resentful, xenophobic, and homophobic voters had been self-selecting into the Republican Party (Abramowitz 2018; Feagin 2012; Grossman and Hopkins 2016; Hetherington and Weiter 2010). This self-selection made Republican voters more authoritarian, racially resentful, xenophobic, and homophobic than other voters.

Second, the Republican Party has emerged as the ideologically conservative party. Whereas the party of Nixon appealed to the center to broaden its base of support, the current Republican Party is now anchored by a far right populist movement. It adhers to and promotes a far right eclectic ideology. Indeed, in *Asymmetric Politics: Ideological Republicans and Group Interest Democrats*, Matt Grossmann and David Hopkins demonstrate that the Republican Party's policy agenda is driven by conservative ideology, whereas the Democrat Party's agenda is driven by response to interest groups (Grossmann and Hopkins 2016).

The consequence of these two changes is that the Republican Party has emerged with a reputation as the white conservative party. The Democratic Party has emerged as the party of diversity, which caters to identity interests: blacks, women, Hispanics, and so on.

Third, the new party system is not only a polarized system, but a new phenomenon has emerged: negative partisanship. Negative partisanship is characterized by the political behavior of Republicans opposing public policy proposals, not because they are against the proposal, but because the policy was proposed by a Democrat. Negative partisanship is more than just hyper-partisanship. It involves intense hostilities between Democrats and Republicans. Whereas in 1964, people were more likely to object to their daughters marrying someone from a different race, today they are more likely to object to their daughters marrying someone from a different political party.

This realignment of the two-party system shook the foundation of interest group liberalism and enabled the election of Donald Trump. The new Republican Party was more racially resentful, more xenophobic, and more authoritarian than the old Republican Party. Instead of appealing to the center of public opinion, this realigned party moved the policy-making process further to the right. Other external factors, most notably multiple political movements, accelerated both the erosion of interest group liberalism and the assault on the New Deal and Great Society programs. This new Republican Party headed by Donald Trump was committed to a full scale assault on the equal opportunity state.

# Chapter 5

# Inequality

Chapter 4 underscored the importance of understanding the corporate insurgency or economic elite movement in any analysis of Trumpism and public policy. Unwittingly, this movement along with the Christian right, Tea Party, and white nationalist movements paved the way for the emergence of Trump. The political organizations associated with these movements formed both the coalition of the Republican Party and the base of political support for Trump. Moreover, the economic elite movement promoted a public policy agenda that favored the elites and the corporate sector, assaulted the equal opportunity, inclusive state, and contributed to the rise of excessive inequality.

Understanding public policy changes associated with the ascension and consequences of excessive inequality is essential in understanding the irony and tragedy of the Trump administration. As will be demonstrated throughout this chapter and succeeding chapters in the second part of this text, the irony and tragedy of the Trump administration is this: in response to the excessive inequality that devastated the working class, Trump promised to rescue this class while he pursued a similar public policy agenda that devastated this class in the first place. Trump's policy agenda included his commitment to repealing labor regulations that had protected and empowered the working class, his opposition to raising the minimum wage, his campaign to terminate the Affordable Care Act, his proposals to shred the social safety net, his promotion of a more regressive federal tax system, his refusal to assist communities devastated by plant closings, and his shifting of the blame for the relocation of U.S. manufacturing facilities to Southeast Asia from corporate leaders to China.

This chapter focuses on the rise of excessive inequality. It reviews different methods of measuring inequality. It examines the shift from the compression period—an era of declining inequality and a plus sum society—to the current divergence period—an era of increasing inequality and a zero sum economy. While it acknowledges that the factors contributing to excessive inequality are complex, it argues that a hyper-conservative policy agenda played a major role in increasing inequality. It demonstrates that excessive inequality has had a devastating impact on white workers, especially those with less than a college education. It challenges the neoliberal view that excessive inequality does not matter and the neoconservative view that the growth of inequality is associated with changes in moral values and individual choices.

## MEASURING INEQUALITY

There are several ways of measuring inequality. One way involves looking at the percentage of a nation's total income going to the top income earners: the top 1 percent, 5 percent, 10 percent, or 20 percent of income earners. Most studies of inequality divide groups into deciles or quintiles. The deciles approach divides income earners into ten groups ranked from the top 10 percent to the bottom 10 percent. The quintile approach divides income earners into five groups ranked from the top 20 percent to the bottom 20 percent. The other way is through the use of the Gini coefficient, expressed either as a decimal or a percentage, a continuum between 0 and 1, or 0 and 100, where 0 indicates perfect equality and 1 or 100 indicates that all income goes to one rich person. In studying the growth in inequality, scholars have identified two major era: the Great Compression (roughly 1941–1979) and the Great Divergence (roughly 1979-today). These two time periods have been distinguished by examining percentage of income going to the top decile, the Gini coefficient and by two other measures: the percentage change in the average income of each quintile and the change in the gap between the average annual salaries of chief executive officers and workers.

## COMPRESSION AND DIVERGENCE

Piketty and Saez examined fluctuations in income inequality in the United States from 1900 through 2010 (Piketty and Saez 2014). They used the percentage of total earned (pre-taxed) income going to the top decile or 10 percent of income earners. In 1900, about 40 percent of total income went to the top decile of income earners. By the end of World War I, this figure came close to 45 percent. It fluctuated throughout the 1920s. It peaked at 45 percent in 1929. When Piketty and Saez added capital gain income to earned (pre-taxed) income, this percentage of total income peaked at just below 50 percent (Piketty and Saez 2013). In other words, by 1929, the top 10 percent of income earners received close to half of all income. This figure dropped down to about 43 percent just after the stock market crash in 1929. It fluctuated up and down until about 1941, afterward it declined. By around 1944, the percentage total (including capital gain) income going to the top decile plummeted down to about 32 percent for both earned income and earned income plus capital gains income. These two figures remained below 35 percent between 1949 and 1981. Piketty and Saez categorized the time period, 1941–1979, the Great Compression (Piketty and Saez 2013, 2014). The gap between high incomes and low incomes compressed. Excessive inequality—occurring when 45 percent or more of total income goes to the top 10 decile—receded.

The Great Compression ended by 1979. Piketty and Saez categorized the period between 1979 and the present as the Great Divergence. This current era is the period of diverging incomes and increasing inequality. Between 1980 and 1992, the percentage of total income, including capital gain income, going to the top decile increased from about 35 percent to about 40 percent. This figure increased throughout the 1990s and into the first decade of the twenty-first century. By 2007, this percent (including capital gain income) was just under 50 percent. In other words, the top 10 percent of income earners were getting about half of all income earned, including capital gain income. Excluding capital gain income it was just above 45 percent.

Table 5.1 examines changes in the incomes of select groups of families, separated into quintiles, between 1947 and 1979 and between 1979 and 2009. Quintiles rank groups families into five income groups, from the highest 20 percent of family incomes to the lowest 20 percent.

Table 5.1 Percentage Change in Real Family Income, 1947–1979 and 1979–2009 (by quintile and top 5 percent)

| Quintile | % Change 1947–1979 | % Change 1979–2009 |
|---|---|---|
| Top 5% ($200,000+) | +86 | +72.7 |
| Top 20% ($112,540+) | +99 | +49.0 |
| 4th Top 20% ($73,338–$112,540) | +114 | +2.7 |
| Middle 20% ($47,914–$73,338) | +111 | +11.3 |
| 2nd Top 20% $26,934–$47,914) | +100 | +3.8 |
| Bottom 20% (Less than $26,934) | +116 | −7.4 |

*Sources:* Composite from two separate tables compiled by Economic Policy Institute, US Census Bureau, Historical Income Tables Families, Table F-3 (for income changes) and Table F-1 (for income ranges for 1979–2009);{ and analysis of US Census Bureau data in Economic Policy Institute, *The State of Working America 1994–95* (New York: M. E. Sharpe, 1994), p. 37.

This table indicates that during the Great Compression, the United States experienced a plus sum economy. In other words, as the economy expanded, all income groups experienced increases in income. Indeed, the bottom quintile experienced the greatest increase, 116 percent.

The top quintile experienced an increase of about 99 percent. Middle income families—those making between $73,338 and $112,540 and those making between $47,914 and $73,338—enjoyed a 114 percent and 111 percent increase, respectively. Table 5.1 indicates that the top five percent of income earners enjoyed the lowest increase, 86 percent.

Table 5.1 offers a striking contrast between the Great Compression and the Great Divergence. During the Great Divergence, the income of the top 5 percent of income earners increased by 72.7 percent. The average income of the top 20 percent increased by 49 percent. In contrast, the average income of middle quintile groups stagnated. The average income of the second from top and the second from the bottom quintiles experienced a lethargic 2.7 and 3.8 percent increase, respectively. The third quintile did slightly better with an 11.3 percent increase. The bottom quintile suffered a loss, a 7.4 percent decline in income.

To put these two time periods in perspective, during the Great Compression, a thirty year period between 1947 and 1979, all five quintiles experienced an increase in income of about 100 percent or more. During the 30-year period between 1979 and 2009, the top quintile enjoyed a 49 percent increase income, while the bottom quintile suffered a 7.4 percent loss of income.

The Great Compression was a plus sum period, in which all families enjoyed substantial increases in income, the lowest income group enjoyed the greatest increase in income. More income was redistributed downward. In contrast, the Great Divergence was a zero sum period, in which the rich got richer, while the poor became poorer. More income was redistributed upward to the wealthy.

Piketty and Saez also examined inequality of wealth over a 150 year period. They demonstrated that inequality of wealth increased sharply in the United States between 1870 and 1920, the Gilded Age. During this time period, the share of the nation's wealth held by the top decile increased from about 70 percent to 80 percent. It hovered just below 80 percent for several years, but dropped down to around 65 percent where it remained between 1941 to about 1975, the Great Compression era. The amount of wealth held by the top decile increased to just below 70 by 1990. It creeped up to slightly above 70 percent by 2010. While the concentration of wealth increased during the Great Divergence period, it did not reach the level it was at during the Gilded Age (Piketty and Saez 2014, 839).

Another way of measuring inequality is to compare the annual average salaries of chief executive officers (CEOs) to the annual average salaries of workers. Mishel and Wolfe examined changes in the ratios of the annual average salaries of CEOs to the salaries of the workers of the top 350 corporations from the mid-1960s to the current period. During the period from 1960 to 1978, the ratio of average CEO annual salary to the average worker salary was less than 30 to 1. During the 1960s, the ratio was around 20 to 1. In other words, the average CEO salary was twenty times the average worker salary. This ratio increased dramatically during the Great Divergence era. It went from 29.1 to 1 in 1978, to 58.1 to 1 in 1989. In 2007, it had reached 345.9 to 1. This ratio declined sharply after the 2008 recession, down to 195.3 to 1 by 2009. By 2016, it had climbed up to 262 to 1. In other words, during the 1960s, CEOs were paid twenty times what workers were paid. By 2016, CEOs were paid 262 times what workers were paid (Mishel and Wolfe 2019). Mishel and Wolfe added, "From 1978 to 2018, CEO compensation grew by 1,007.5 percent . . . far outstripping S&P stock market growth (706.7) and the wage...In contrast, wages for the typical worker grew by just 11.9 percent" (Mishel and Wolfe 2019). This trend of the accelerated growth of CEO salaries and the slow growth of worker salaries continued throughout the Trump administration. Indeed, in a 2021 article, Mishel and Wolfe reported that the CEO-to-worker compensation ratio jumped from 276.2 in 2016, to 307.3 in 2020 (Mishel and Kandra 2019).

A final way of assessing the rise of excessive inequality is to examine changes in the Gini coefficient. Table 5.2 summarizes changes in Gini coefficients from 1950 to 2019, in increments of every five years. This coefficient declined from .379 in 1950 to .364 in 1960. By 1965, it had reached an historic low of .356. By 1980, it had increased to .365. It continued to increase throughout the Great Divergence. It climbed to .421 by 1995 and reached .433 by 2000. It continued to increase throughout both the Obama and Trump administration. By 2019, it had reached an all-time high of .454.

## INEQUALITY AND PUBLIC POLICY

The literature explaining the rise of excessive inequality offers a long list of plausible suspects, including the natural dynamics of market capitalism, new technology, globalization, meritocracy, a mismatch between high levels of skills and education required for high paying knowledge-intensive high tech jobs and the low level of skills and less than a college degree among most occupants of the working class. In recent times, many of these theories have declined in their explanatory power. There is no question that the United States passed through a period prior to 1960 of a great migration of workers from low-income rural areas to higher income manufacturing urban area jobs, increasing the middle class and reducing inequality; a period after the 1970s

Table 5.2    Gini Index of Family Income Inequality for Select Years, 1960–2019

| Year | Index |
|------|-------|
| 1950 | .379 |
| 1960 | .364 |
| 1965 | .356 |
| 1970 | .357 |
| 1975 | .357 |
| 1980 | .365 |
| 1985 | .389 |
| 1990 | .396 |
| 1995 | .421 |
| 2000 | .433 |
| 2005 | .440 |
| 2010 | .440 |
| 2015 | .448 |
| 2016 | .452 |
| 2017 | .449 |
| 2018 | .452 |
| 2019 | .454 |

*Source*: U.S. Census Bureau historical Table F-4. Gini Indexes for Families by Race and Hispanic Origins of Households: 1947–2019 (All Households/All Races).
https://www.census.gov/data/tables/time-series/demo/income-poverty/hostorical-income-inequality.html.

of deindustrialization in which many production facilities packed up and moved out of the United States and relocated to another country were wages were low and unions were non-existent, contributing to greater inequality. There is no question that the mining industry, especially coal mining, has been impacted by new technology, fracking, and the rise of the cheaper and cleaner natural gas. Most scholars acknowledge these trends. However, because other countries have experienced similar trends in globalization and new technology as the United States without suffering dramatic increases in inequality, the globalization and new technology theories are not as persuasive as they once were. Because education levels increased as inequality increased and because some high education professions like teachers and computer specialists experienced wage stagnation, the knowledge–skills mismatch thesis had fallen in popularity (Blanchflower 2021).

A number of economists have given less weight to many of these earlier explanations and more weight to perspectives emphasizing the role of politics and public policies in explaining the rise of excessive inequality (Hacker and Pierson 2010, 2016; Katznelson 2006, 2013; Krugman 1994, 2009, 2021; Reich 2007, 2012, 2016, 2020; Stiglitz 2012, 2019). Acemoglu and Robinson have identified a strong association between plutocratic regimes, regimes dominated by economic elites, and excessive inequality. They argued that robust expansions of the right to vote, especially among working class and low-income voters, have "led to unprecedented redistributive programs"

(Acemoglu and Robinson 2000, 1167). These programs included substantial investments in education, progressive taxes, labor regulations protecting collective bargaining rights, and a minimum wage comparable to a living wage. Acemoglu and Robinson caution that democracies are fragile and vulnerable to economic crises (Acemoglu and Robinson 2001, 939). Piketty intimated that both a hyper-capitalistic public policy agenda and a political culture that tolerates inequality contributed to extreme inequality.

For about two decades, economists and political scientists have been promoting the perspective that public policy changes have been contributing to the rise of extreme inequality. A number of Nobel Prize–winning economists have contributed to this perspective, including Angus Deaton (2020), Paul Krugman (1994, 2009, 2021), Amartya Sen (1992), and Joseph Stiglitz (2012, 2019). Former labor secretary Robert Reich (2007, 2012, 2016) has emphasized the corporate insurgency movement and the dramatic decline of labor unions contributing to the failure to raise the minimum wage, the decline in public investment in education, the shrinkage of the social safety net, and many other public policy changes.

In 2004, the American Political Science Association (APSA) convened a taskforce to examine inequality and American democracy, headed by Lawrence Jacobs and Theda Skocpol. Although the task force emphasized market forces contributing to inequality, it concluded that excessive inequality has distorted American politics and public policy making in favor of economic elites, exacerbating inequality (Jacobs and Skocpol 2007).

After noting the impact of technological change, globalization, and demographic shifts, Larry Bartel concluded that public policy shifts played a major role in generating inequality. He adds, "I find that partisan politics and the ideological convictions of political elites have had a substantial impact on the American economy, especially on the economic fortunes of middle-class and poor people. Economic inequality is in substantial part, a political phenomenon" (Bartel 2008). He also noted a partisan bias in politics and public policy associated with inequality, "On average, the real incomes of middle-class families have grown twice as fast under Democrats as they have under Republicans, while the real incomes of working poor families have grown six times as fast under Democrats as they have under Republicans" (Bartel 2008, 3). He focused on changes in tax, minimum wage, and labor policies.

In his study, *The Vanishing Middle Class: Prejudice and Power in a Dual Economy*, Peter Temin identified a dual economy, split between the high wage sector, which included finance, technology, and electronics and constitutes 20 percent of the labor force and the low wage sector, which constitutes the bottom 80 percent. Temin documented the decline of the middle class and attributed this decline to failure of public policy: the failure to maintain a minimum wage; the failure to protect contract workers in the new so-called gig economy (Uber, custodial, and other workers); the failure to protect fair labor and the rights of workers to organize and engage in collective bargaining; the failure to invest robustly in public education and health care; and the failure to enforce anti-trust laws (Temin 2017).

Adam Cohen examined changes in constitutional law that favors corporation and the top 1 percent over the bottom 99 percent. He noted Supreme Court cases that restrict the voice of the poor, denying grassroots and neighborhood organizations the right to post public interest or campaign posters on public places like telephone posts but allows corporate money to dominate the airways. He illustrated how welfare recipients lost due process rights when claims to public benefits were denied (Cohen 2020).

Jacob Hacker and Paul Pierson provided a comprehensive contrast of the public policies of the compression period with public policies of the current divergence period. They demonstrated that the cumulative effects of multiple public policies enabled the rapid expansion of the middle class after World War II. These policies involved more than just a progressive income tax and social welfare. They involved massive investments in multiple areas: research and development, infrastructure, education, housing, and many others. They included rules of the market and regulatory policies designed to insure a fair market system. Inequality was enabled by relentless assaults on these policies (Hacker and Pierson 2016).

In his book, *Who Stole the American Dream*, Hedrick Smith provided a detailed narrative of public policy changes that eroded the middle class and stole the American dream. He began with the Powell Memorandum. He documented the assaults on labor unions. He noted the deregulation frenzy and its devastating consequences. He highlighted changes in bankruptcy laws favoring Wall Street and hurting workers (Smith 2012).

Smith provided several cases involving the rise of Wal-Mart as a super retail store, powerful enough to dictate to manufacturing firms and to behave in ways that have contributed to the destruction of mom and pop businesses in small towns. The case of the Rubbermaid manufacturing firm provided a good example. Rubbermaid was founded in 1959 in Wooster, Ohio. By the 1990s, it had contracts to sell its products to Wal-Mart and several other major retail outlets, including Target and Kmart. Because of an increase in the costs of raw material used to make Rubbermaid products, the company was forced to increase its prices. Wal-Mart insisted that Rubbermaid close down its U.S. production facility and move to China, where wages and the costs of production are much lower. This relocation would enable Rubbermaid to continue to produce its product for low costs. Because of the size of the Wal-Mart contract, Rubbermaid could not afford to lose the Wal-Mart contract. Indeed, over 25 percent of its products were sold at Wal-Mart.

The case of Wal-Mart illustrated several points about the change from compression to divergence. First, it demonstrated the weakness of anti-trust laws that allowed for the emergence of mega retail giant like Wal-Mart able to coerce manufacturing firms to close down U.S. facilities and relocate abroad (Smith 2012, 245). Second, it revealed a change in corporate culture encouraged by neoliberal ideology from a culture that once valued social responsibilities and communities to a culture that places a premium on profits, regardless of consequences. Third, it underscored the problem with a tax structure that provides incentives for relocating production facilities abroad.

The Wal-Mart case unveiled the major problem of an unrestrained commitment to reducing labor costs. During the 1980s, many U.S. manufacturing facilities relocated in countries with non-existing unions and low labor costs. Wal-Mart not only pressured manufacturing facilities to move to reduce labor costs, Wal-Mart itself had exerted strong pressures to keep its own labor costs down. As one of the largest employers in the nation, with over 1.2 million employees, its efforts to keep wages low and benefits non-existent has done a great deal to shrink the middle class and to increase inequality.

When wages constitute a large part of the costs of running a business, reducing wages does much to increase profits and the wealth of corporate owners. Since 1982, the wealth of the Waltons of Wal-Mart grew by more than 6,000 percent, adjusting for the cost of living (Reich 2020, 141). Robert Reich added, "Over the same period, the typical household's wealth dropped 3 percent. The Wal-Mart heirs alone have more wealth than the bottom 42 percent of Americans combined. Today, the Wal-Mart family fortune grows by $70,000 per minute, $4 million per hour, $100 million per day" (Reich 2020, 141). As complex as this literature is, the short and simple explanation is that the change in corporate culture, corporate political power, and corporate initiated public policy are the major culprits contributing to extreme inequality in the United States.

## INCREASED CORPORATE POLITICAL POWER

Corporate political influence increased at the end of the compression period and accelerated during the divergence era. Chapter 3 illustrates this point as well as outlines the growth of corporate power. This increase of power resulted from the combination of the ascension of a dominant corporate ideology, an effective right-wing ecosystem to promote this ideology, the formation of networks of corporate policy making organizations, and the greater political mobilization of the corporate section.

Corporate power was also enhanced by the dramatic decline of countervailing powers. Political groups that checked corporate power, especially during the 1960s and 1970s, have declined. These groups included labor unions, welfare rights, community action, legal aid, consumer interest, and many others. Today, welfare rights and community action organizations are gone. Most died from attrition. One large active grass root organization, Association of Community Organization for Reform Now (ACORN), was targeted by Breitbart. Even as late as 2005, ACORN had a membership around 175,000 members. In 2009, Breitbart sent two journalists posing as a pimp and prostitute to seek assistance from ACORN. In a plot to destroy the organization, they doctored the video to make it appear that the organization illegally agreed to assists pimps and prostitutes. The negative publicity destroyed the organization.

Labor power, as measured by union density or the proportion of the labor force unionized, declined dramatically between 1945 and today. In 1945, the proportion of the labor force unionized was around 35 percent. It hovered around 25 percent the next couple of decades. By 1983, it had declined to 20.1 percent. It continued to decline throughout the late twentieth and early twenty-first century. By 2010, it was at 11.9 percent. It continued to decline throughout the Obama and Trump administrations. By 2019, only about 10.3 percent of U.S. workers were unionized (U.S. Bureau of Labor Statistics Reports 2021).

As noted in the previous chapter, this decline was the result of a deliberate campaign by U.S. corporate and business leaders to suppress union movements (Reich 2016, 2020; Hacker and Pierson 2016; Stiglitz 2012). It not only weakened the political power of unions, it contributed directly to stagnant wages and diminished the economic vitality of the working class. Putting this decline into perspective, Robert Reich says, "The pressure to crush unions hasn't come from globalization or automation. Other developed nations, facing the same international competition and with access to the same technologies have maintained far higher levels of unionization along with high wages and benefits" (Reich 2020, 119). Weak enforcement of National Labor Relation Board regulations enabled this assault.

Today, corporate contributions to elections and lobbying dwarf union and public interest contributions. Illustrating the extent to which corporate power overwhelms the power of both unions and public interest organizations, Robert Reich offers this observation:

> The disappearance of labor's countervailing power can readily be seen in the 2015–16 election cycle, when corporations and Wall Street contributed $34 to candidates from both parties for every $1 donated by labor unions and all public interest organizations combined. Business outspent labor $3.4 billion to $213 million. All of the nation's unions together spend about $48 million annually on lobbying in Washington. Corporate America spends $3 billion. (Reich 2020, 56)

Reich demonstrates how corporate political spending is not charity but investments. For example, major oil companies spend about $150 million a year on supporting the election campaigns of political candidates. Reich claims that this spending was like an investment that netted the oil companies $2.5 billion in government benefits. For another example, JP Morgan's contributions to the Republican Party in 2016 yield "about $20 billion in tax savings over five years" (Reich 2020, 57). He adds, "Pfizer, whose donations to the GOP in 2016 totaled $16 million, would reap $39 billion in tax savings. GE contributed $20 million and will get back $16 billion in tax savings. Chevron donated $13 million and received $9 billion. Not even a sizzling economy can deliver anything close to the returns on political investments" (Reich 2020, 57).

The Bankruptcy Abuse Prevention and Consumer Protection Act of 2005, promoted by credit card companies, provided strong protections for creditors and weak protections for debtors. This law made it more difficult for middle-class families to declare bankruptcy and attain debt forgiveness. This law allowed banks to charge high interest rates for student loans because of the risks of students defaulting on loans. At the same time, it prevented students from declaring bankruptcy over student loans. The new bankruptcy law gave bank debts priority over union contracts and pension funds. Indeed, several airline companies used the threat of bankruptcy to squeeze billions of dollars in concessions from workers. For example, in 2003, American Airlines used the threat of bankruptcy to "wring almost $2 billion of concessions from American's major unions" (Reich 2016, 61).

## ANTI-TRUST AND RURAL AMERICA

Rural America has been the hit hard by changes in the U.S. economy. This area has a long history of prosperity in the manufacturing, mining, retail, farming, and leisure sectors of the economy. Manufacturing has been hit hard by plant closings. Mining has been hit by new technology, particularly natural gas supplies expanded by fracking and the push for renewable energy. Small mom and pop retail stores have been put out of business by Wal-Mart. The failure to enforce anti-trust laws has had its most devastating impact on farmers.

In her book, *Foodopoly: The Battle Over the Future of Food and Farming in America*, Wenonah Hauter documented the deliberate abandonment of anti-trust policy in the agricultural area, beginning in the Reagan administration and continuing into the twenty-first century (Hauter 2012). This abandonment has enabled the rise of near monopolies or oligopolies in agriculture, large multi-national corporations that have shifted market power from the farmers to the corporations. This shift enables the super exploitation of farmers. For example, she points out that chicken farmers producing chicken for Kentucky Fried Chicken make about 25 cents on a bucket of chicken that sells for $20 dollars.

For another example, the Tyson chicken company turns chicken farmers into serfs, with little control over their labor. The company supplies all of the equipment, including the eggs, and detailed instructions for raising the chickens. As the company dominates the market, it is able to dictate the terms and price of production, and keep the earnings of the farmers low and the profits of the company high. Tyson family chicken farmers make on average about $15,000 a year.

The Tyson chicken processing plants are like sweathouses, with low pay, long hours, hard work, and deplorable conditions. Hauter added:

> A 2000 survey of poultry companies by the Department of Labor (DOL) found that over 60 percent of plants violate basic wage and hour laws. A majority of poultry plants illegally force employees to work off the clock by not compensating workers for job-related tasks before and after their shifts, not compensating workers for job-related tasks before and after their shifts, and for brief breaks during the workday. The DOL survey also confirmed that over half of poultry plants, mainly nonunion plants, illegally force workers to pay for their own safety equipment by deducting the costs of required gear from workers' paycheck. (Hauter 2012, 205)

She also documents how changes in intellectual property laws not only favor multinational corporations, but give these corporations considerable power over famers. The prime example is Monsanto that has trademarks for a wide variety of seeds that are herbicide resistant. Once the farmer buys the seed, the law prohibits farmers from using the seeds from the plant, even though the seeds were produced by the farmers. These rules forced the farmers to continue to buy Monsanto seeds and herbicides.

## THE CONSEQUENCE OF EXTREME INEQUALITY

In 1970, this nation had a robust middle class, as 62 percent of the aggregate share of household income went to this class. Only 29 percent went to the upper class. The share going to the middle class declined steadily throughout the 1980s, 1990s, and the first decade of the twenty-first century. By 2014, only 43 percent went to the middle class. Close to 50 percent went to the upper class. The lower class lost income between 1990 and 2000 (Temin 2017).

Rising levels of inequality are not only associated with declines in the middle class. They are associated with declines in upward social mobility.

Several studies have reinforced this point. In their book, *The Spirit Level*, Richard Wilkerson and Kate Pickett demonstrated a strong inverse linear association between inequality and upward social mobility. Nations with high levels of inequality have low levels of upward social mobility. The United States with its higher level of inequality has a much lower level of upward social mobility (Wilkerson and Pickett 2010).

Another study summarized by the Brookings Institute, examined the probability that a child born in the bottom quintile of the income distribution would emerge to the top quintile.

This probability was the lowest in the United States at 7.5 percent compared to a probability of 9 percent for the UK, 11.7 percent for Denmark, and 13.5 percent for Canada (Reese and Krause 2018).

High levels of inequality and economic stress are associated with higher levels of morbidity and mortality. Wilkinson and Pickett examined the association between inequality and life expectancy and morbidity rates (Wilkinson and Pickett 2010). They demonstrated the clear association between rising inequality and declining life expectancy. They associated higher levels of inequality with lower levels of life expectancy. Wilkinson and Pickett also demonstrate that increasing levels of inequality are associated with higher morbidity rates—obesity, diabetes, hypertension, cancer, lung disease, and hearth disease. Countries with high levels of inequality are more likely to experience higher levels of these physical ailments and suffer higher rates of homicides, suicides, and drug overdoses.

Anne Case and Angus Deaton examined life expectancy and mortality rates among men 50 to 54 from the United States and six select countries: Australia, Canada, France, Germany, and the United Kingdom. Between 1990 and 2017, most of the countries experienced increases in life expectancy and declines in mortality rates. They discovered that while men in the other countries experienced increased life expectancy rates and decreased mortality rates, white men in the United States without a college degree and between the ages of 50 and 54 suffered declining life expectancy and increased death rates (Case and Deaton 2017). They labeled the increased mortality rates as deaths of despair. Deaths of despair are associated with suicides, alcoholism, and opioid and other drug overdoses. In their book, *Deaths of Despair and the Future of Capitalism*, Case and Deaton provided a more detailed analysis of the determinants of deaths of despair. They show that between 2000 and 2015, deaths of despair had increased sharply in the United States among both black and white men with less than a bachelor's degree. They attribute the rising rates of deaths of despair to more than just inequality and economic stress. For them, American's lack of a robust safety net and universal health care are also major factors (Case and Deaton 2020).

*In Dying of Whiteness: How the Politics of Racial Resentment is Killing America's Heartland,* Jonathan Metzl found an association between the politics of racial resentment and self-destructive behavior among white males. He illustrated connections between growing racial fears and increasing rates of handgun-related suicides and accidental deaths. Aggregate data indicated that gun-related suicides increased between 2009 and 2015 among white males (Metzl 2019). The most striking case in Metzl's study is the self-destructive opposition to the Affordable Care Act. The Medicaid expansion program under the Affordable Care Act saved lives. States that accepted ACA Medicaid expansion experienced declining white male morbidity and mortality rates. States that refused to accept the Medicaid expansion suffered increased white male morbidity and mortality rates (Sheppard 2020).

In a vivid illustration of self-destructive opposition to the ACA, Metzl featured the case of a white male, Trevor. Trevor, who lived in Tennessee, a few miles from the Kentucky border, was dying from a treatable liver disease, hepatitis C. In Tennessee, Trevor had no health insurance and was likely to die of his disease. However, if he lived in Kentucky he would have access to health insurance and survive his disease. Nevertheless, Trevor was adamant in his opposition to the ACA. Metzl offers this observation:

> Even on death's doorstep, Trevor wasn't angry. In fact, he staunchly supported the stance promoted by his elected officials. "Ain't no way I would ever support Obamacare or sign up for it," he told me. "I would rather die." When I asked him why he felt this way even as he faced severe illness, he explained, "We don't need any more government in our lives. And in any case, no way I want my tax dollars paying for Mexicans or welfare queens. (Metzl 2019, 3)

## CRITIQUE OF NEOCONSERVATIVE
## AND NEOLIBERAL PERSPECTIVE

Neoconservatives and neoliberals reject the view that assaults on progressive public policies contribute to inequality. Neoconservative, Charles Murray, espoused the opposite perspective. He argued that welfare programs created incentives for teenagers to have babies out of wedlock and become dependent on welfare. He insisted that expanding these programs created more dependency and more poverty. Thus, cutting these programs, according to Murray, would reduce both welfare dependency and poverty (Murray 1984). As will be demonstrated in chapter 8, Trump followed the ideas of this perspective.

Rejecting the idea that inequality of a problem, neoliberal Michael Tanner of the Cato Institute published an article, "Five Myths about Economic Inequality in America." These myths are (1) inequality has never been worse;

(2) the rich didn't earn their money; (3) the rich stay rich and the poor stay poor; (4) more inequality means more poverty; and (5) inequality distorts the political process. He presents considerable data and evidence supporting his argument that all five statements are myths. In short, Tanner is arguing that inequality is not a problem, the rich deserve their money, upward social mobility persists, more inequality is not associated with more poverty, and greater inequality does not distort the political process. The preponderance of the evidence contradicts all five arguments, except number four. The increase in inequality does not produce an increase in poverty. Indeed, the economic expansion under the Trump administration reduced poverty, but at the same time, increased inequality.

Contrary to Tanner, inequality is a problem and it is worse than ever before. At first glance, it appears that Tanner is correct to reject the statement that "inequality has never been worse," as a myth. Tanner identifies three major problems with Piketty's data. First, Piketty's own data supported Tanner's point. A higher percentage of income was concentrated among the top decile during the 1920s than today. However, in his book, *America's Inequality Trap*, Nathan Kelly demonstrated that when focusing on the top .01 percent of income earners instead of the top decile, the statement is true. Just before the stock market crashed, the top .01 percent received a little more than 4 percent of total income. Today, the top .01 percent of income earners receive more than 5 percent of total income (Kelly 2019). When looking at the top .01 percent, income is more concentrated than ever before.

Second, Piketty used before-tax rather than after-tax data. When using after-tax data, Gini coefficients decline by about one- or two-hundredths of a decimal point. The use of after-tax data reduces inequality, but not enough to conclude that it does not matter.

Third, Piketty does not account for transfer payments and welfare benefits. Accounting for transfer payments and welfare benefits do make a difference for families receiving these payments and benefits, which primarily include families whose incomes fall below the poverty line and workers who lost their jobs and became unemployed. Unlike welfare benefits which go to families whose incomes fall below the poverty line, Social Security benefits are distributed to individuals over 65 in all five quintiles, thus minimizing its equalizing effect. Because TANF benefits have been substantially cut over the past 20 years, these benefits have less of an equalizing effect than Tanner claims.

Contrary to Tanner, it is difficult to justify excessive income earned by CEOs. Tanner argues that inequality is justifiable because most wealth and income are earned. It is not inherited. While the data support Tanner's argument about earned rather than inherited wealth and income, he ignored the 1,000 percent increase in CEO salaries and the extreme disparity between

CEO income and worker income. This increase in CEO salaries and the extreme disparity between CEO and worker salaries are difficult to justify.

While Tanner is correct to argue that the rich do not stay rich and the poor do not stay poor and that upward social mobility persists, he ignores the data that demonstrate the association between increasing levels of inequality and decreasing levels of social mobility.

The bottom line is that, contrary to Tanner, excessive inequality matters. Excessively high levels of inequality, extreme disparities between the super-rich and everyone else intensifies social stress. Rising extreme levels inequality are associated with declining rates of life expectancy and higher rates of deaths of despair. Extreme inequality has its most devastating impact on the working class.

Extreme inequality distorts politics. Tanner suggests that the multi-billionaire influence of libertarian Charles Koch is balanced by the multi-billionaire influence of George Soros and Warren Buffet. The problem is not just the dramatic increase in the income and wealth of the top .01 percent. The problem is the organization of the top .01 percent into Koch networks of multi-billionaires committed to affecting both the outcome of elections—for president, U.S. senators, U.S. Representatives, governors, and state representatives—and the formation of public policies. These networks function as plutocratic political institutions. The problem is not just the mobilization of the business and corporate sector—the mobilization of the U.S. Chamber of Commerce, the National Association of Manufacturers, the National Federation of Independent Businesses, and many other corporate and business organizations. The problem is the ability of these organizations to promote a policy agenda that eclipses most other organizations and that dominates the policy-making process.

The economic literature on inequality raised the question whether Trump was a product of a working-class revolt tainted by nationalism and racism or a plutocratic revolt that exploited nationalism and racism. Piketty suggested the latter. Indeed, the multi-billionaire real estate tycoon, Donald Trump, is a plutocrat himself.

## SUMMARY

In his 2017 inaugural address, Donald Trump acknowledged the economic devastation the nation was experiencing. He spoke directly to workers who had lost their jobs and women and children who were living in poverty in inner cities because of factory closings. He provided a vivid image of "rusted out factories scattered like tombstones across the landscape of our nation" (Trump 2017). He identified the alleged culprits: the Washington establishment, "a small group in our nation's capital" who reaped the rewards of government "while the people have borne the costs" and foreign nations. He added, "We must protect our borders from the ravages of other countries making our products, stealing our companies, and destroying our jobs" (Trump 2017). Trump claimed that with his inauguration, power was transferred from Washington, DC back to the people. He promised that every decision made on taxes, immigration, trade, and foreign affairs "will be made to benefit American workers and American families" (Trump 2017).

His speech was eloquent, powerful, and unifying. It was clean, wholesome, therapeutic, curative, and completely devoid of any hint of xenophobia or racist innuendos. Nevertheless, it identified typical right-wing populist targets: the federal government and foreign nations. It provided the perfect misdirection. It shifted responsibility and blame from U.S. corporate leaders to foreign nations. It was ironic because the problem was never other countries stealing American jobs. The problem was American corporate leaders closing down factories and relocating in other countries to reduce labor costs and undercut labor power. Trump's inaugural speech was ironic because economic elites had been engaged in an assault on federal programs designed to improve the quality of the lives of low-income workers and poor mothers living in inner cities. It was ironic because corporate greed and the corporate policy agenda had contributed to the inequality and economic distress. It was ironic because Donald Trump had just empowered those same corporate leaders and had adopted a corporate policy agenda. These ironies will become evident in an investigation of Trump's public policies, beginning with his labor policy agenda.

*Part II*

# SELECT DOMESTIC PUBLIC POLICIES OF THE TRUMP ADMINISTRATION

# Chapter 6

# Labor Policy

This chapter examines labor issues and the major labor policy changes of the Trump administration. It begins by commenting on Trump's choice of administrators to lead the U.S. Department of Labor and the National Labor Relations Board. It proceeds to examine three labor issue areas: wages and working hours, workplace health and safety, and unions and collective bargaining. A careful review of both Trump's choice of labor policy administrators and his actual public policy changes demonstrates a clear pattern. Whereas Trump claims to favor workers over corporations, he follows a labor policy agenda set by the U.S. Chamber of Commerce. While Trump boasted loudly about being a friend of labor, his personnel decisions and his actual public policy choices demonstrated a profound bias in favor of employers and corporations and an extreme prejudice against workers, especially low-income workers. Indeed, Trump's labor policy agenda represented an all-out assault on progressive labor policies that had historically empowered and protected workers. This assault targets wage and working hours, unionization and collective bargaining, and health and safety protections

## CHOICE OF ADMINISTRATIVE LEADERS

President Trump's first nominee to become secretary of the U.S. Department of Labor (DOL) was Andy Puzder, CEO of the conglomerate that owns Hardees and Carl's Jr. He withdrew under rumors that he had physically assaulted his ex-wife, admitted to hiring an undocumented immigrant as a housekeeper, had abused his own workers, and was hostile to policies that favored labor (Wheeler 2017).

After Puzder withdrew, Alexander Acosta became secretary of the DOL. Acosta was a former state attorney general, a former National Labor Relations Board (NLRB) member, and a former director of the Civil Rights Division of the Justice Department. He had a mixed record as the head of the Civil Rights Division. He supported the rights of Muslim public school girls to wear the hijab. However, he sided with the State of Ohio over its voter suppression issue. The most troubling aspect of the appointment of Acosta is the fact that he was closely affiliated with the American Legislative Exchange Council, the corporate-dominated, anti-labor legislative mill (Wittner 2018). He served as labor secretary from April 2017 to July 2019, under the cloud of the Jeffry Epstein scandal.

Acosta was replaced by Eugene Scalia, son of the late Supreme Court Justice, Antonin Scalia. As a nominee for secretary of labor, Eugene Scalia was strongly supported by the U.S. Chamber of Commerce. Indeed as a corporate attorney, he represented the Chamber of Commerce in opposing ergonomic regulations. He represented Sea World against OSHA over charges that Sea World had violated labor regulations by failing to provide a safe environment for Orca trainers. Scalia had authored a law review article arguing that employers should not be liable for workplace sexual harassment, including cases in which supervisors grope subordinates on business trips or threaten to fire them for refusing to submit to sexual advances (Vogtman 2019). Senator Patty Murray of Washington State expressed strong opposition to Scalia:

> I opposed Eugene Scalia's nomination to the Labor Department in 2001 because of his hostility toward workplace protections and his position on workplace harassment and workers' health and safety . . . After spending the last 18 years defending corporations who have trampled on the rights of their workers he is still the wrong choice and President Trump needs to choose another nominee for Secretary of Labor. (quoted by Bocchetti 2019)

Trump made two more anti-labor appointments to the DOL worth mentioning. Trump nominated Patrick Pizzella for deputy secretary of the DOL and David Zategalo for assistant secretary of Mine Safety and Health Administration. Both nominees have disturbing anti-labor records.

Pizzella was a former employee of the anti-union organization, the National Right to Work Committee (Wittner 2018). He was also part of Jack Abramoff's team at Preston, Gales Ellis & Rouvelas LLP from 1996 to 2001. This organization fought against efforts to impose basic wage, workplace safety, and anti-sweatshop regulations on the Northern Mariana Islands. The Islands, located in the Southwest Pacific Ocean, became part of the U.S. commonwealth in 1975 and under U.S. sovereignty in 1986, with a non-voting representative in the House of Representatives. Whereas it has serious problem with apparel industry sweatshops, it is able to produce goods with the "made in the USA" labels, but without U.S. wage and workplace safety regulations (Arria 2017). In a 2006 National Public Radio interview, anti-sweatshop activist, Wendy Doromal, described the working conditions surrounding the Island garment factories:

> The barbed wire around the factories faces inward so that the [workers] couldn't get out. They had quotas that were impossible for these people to reach and if they didn't reach them, they'd have to stay until they finished the quota and they wouldn't be paid for that work. They were hot, the barracks were horrible. A lot of the females were told you work during the day in the garment factories and then at night you go and work in a club and they'd force them into prostitution at night. (Arria 2017)

Pizzella claimed that he was not aware of the working conditions on the Island and that Abramoff had gone to jail (Arria 2017).

David Zatezato began his career as a United Mine Worker laborer but quickly rose to become a mine manager, superintendent, and general manager. In response to a 2010 mine explosion that killed twenty-nine coal miners and to a report that concluded that the explosion resulted from criminal negligence, as the company deliberately disregarded safety regulations, the Mine Safety and Health Administration (MSHA) increased inspections and enforcement of safety regulations. As chairman of Rhio Resources Coal Company, Zatezato fought against the inspections and clashed with MSHA regulators. The company was cited for multiple serious mine safety violations. Zategalo served as Trump's assistant secretary of MSHA.

The point here is that there was a clear and definite pattern in President Trump's appointments to the DOL. Trump appointed officials who had reputations for supporting management over labor. The deputy secretary of labor had a reputation for his indifference or hostility to the rights and wellbeing of American workers. The assistant secretary of MSHA had a reputation for his opposition to mine safety regulations. Trump's DOL officials were supportive of management and hostile to labor.

Trump nominated William Emanuel, Marvin Kaplan, and John Ring to the NLRB and Peter Robb as NLRB General Council. All four were nominated with enthusiasm and strong support by the U.S. Chamber of Commerce. William Emanuel was an attorney for the Littler Mendelson PC law firm. He specialized in representing major corporations against unions. He had a reputation as a union busting attorney. He represented Uber in its successful effort to fight off a unionization drive. Senator Warren referred to him as the nation's most ruthless union buster (Lanard 2017).

Marvin Kaplan had worked with the Republican leadership in the House Education and Labor Committee to draft legislation to overturn the progressive labor policies of the Obama administration. John Ring, the chair of the National Labor Relations Board, had worked for Morgan Lewis & Bockius, a law firm that advised Trump before he was elected president. Morgan Lewis & Bockius was recognized as an outstanding corporate law firm by the Chambers & Partners' 2016 book, *Chambers' European Guide*. The law firm was also the recipient of the 2016 the "Russia Law Firm of the Year" award (Gajanar 2017). These three board members were approved by the Senate along strict party lines. These appointments gave the NLRB a solid conservative Republican majority. The current NLRB members are:

| | |
|---|---|
| John Ring, Chair | 2017 Trump Appointee |
| William Emanuel | 2017 Trump Appointee |
| Marvin Kaplan | 2017 Trump Appointee |
| Lauren McFerran | 2014 Obama Appointee |

Peter Rob, the General Council (GC) of the NLRB, expressed a commitment to advancing labor policy proposals promoted by the U.S. Chamber of Commerce. Indeed, just after he was appointed GC, he publicly announced that he would move to reverse many of Obama era decisions and promote the Chamber agenda. McNicholas, Poydock and Rhinehart (2019) document the connection between the Trump administration's labor policy agenda and choice of candidates for the NLRB. They suggest that the Trump agenda and candidate list are mirror images of the preferences for the U.S. Chamber of Commerce.

## WAGES AND WORKING HOURS

One of the most contentious labor issues is the federal minimum wage law. This issue distinguishes between New Deal liberals and neoliberals. Franklin Delano Roosevelt was passionate and uncompromising in his support for a federal minimum wage law. After considerable debate, this law was enacted in 1938. Roosevelt had strong language in support of federal laws regulating wages and working hours. He said, "All but the hopelessly reactionary will agree that to conserve our primary resources of man power government must have some control over maximum hours, minimum wages, the evil of child labor and the exploitation of unorganized labor" (quoted in Baum 2015). He added, "No business which depends for existence on paying less than living wages to its workers has any right to continue in this country" (quoted in Baum 2015).

President Trump's view on minimum wage is antithetical to Roosevelt's view. Although his view seemed to vacillate, he persistently opposed raising the federal minimum wage. He expressed concern for workers earning the minimum wage. He said the minimum wage should be higher. However, he insisted that state governments, not the federal government should be responsible for raising the minimum wage. He assumed that wages would automatically increase when the economy expanded and when unemployment rates declined (See Lee 2016; Yuhas 2016). He intimated that increasing the minimum wage would hurt both businesses and workers. He laid out his perspective on the minimum wage in a May 8, 2016 "Meet the Press" interview with Chuck Todd:

Donald Trump:

I have seen what's going on. And I don't know how people make it on $7.25 an hour. Now, with that being said, I would like to see an increase of some magnitude. But I'd rather leave it to the states. Let the states decide. Because don't forget, the states have to compete with each other. So you may have a governor—

Chuck Todd:

Right. You want the fed—but should the federal government set a floor, and then you let the states—

Donald Trump:

No, I'd rather have the states go out and do what they have to do. And the states compete with each other, not only other countries, but they compete with each other, Chuck. So I like the idea of let the states decide. But I think people should get more. I think they're out there. They're working. It is a very low number. You know with what's happening to the economy, with what's happening to the cost. I mean, it's just—I don't know how you live on $7.25 an hour. But I would say let the states decide. (Todd and Trump 2016)

During the 2020 presidential campaign debate, Trump doubled down on his position that raising the minimum wage would hurt both businesses and their employees. He said, "How are you helping your small businesses when you're forcing wages?" He added, "What's going to happen and what's been proven to happen when you do that, these small businesses fire many of their employees" (quoted by Yglesias 2020).

Trump's statement that his position on the minimum wage has been proven is inaccurate. It misrepresents the academic literature on the minimum wage. This literature is vast. It spans more than a century and it includes thousands of book and articles. There is much disagreement in the literature, attributable to the use of different theories, models, methodologies, and variables. Despite these differences, there is a general agreement that a wage floor is necessary to prevent sweatshops and the excessive exploitation of low-income workers. The old literature suggested that raising the minimum wage would create pressures to reduce the workforce and to invest in labor-saving machinery. In other words, raising the minimum wage would kill jobs.

More recent research challenges the old research. In 1981, the U.S. Minimum Wage Study Commission published a report summarizing the research on the minimum wage. The report found that a 10 percent increase in the minimum wage reduced teenage employment by 1 to 3 percent. The employment effect on young adults (20–24 years old) was negative, but much less than the effect on teenagers. The overall effect on adults was contested, but likely positive. A recent Congressional Report on the probable impact of the proposed Raise the Wage Act of 2021 suggested that raising the minimum wage up to $15 would possibly produce a 0.9 percent increase in the unemployment rate (Congressional Budget Office 2021). Other studies have indicated that the impact of raising the minimum wage may vary depending on how much and how fast the minimum wage is raised.

A number of studies have demonstrated that raising the minimum wage reduces poverty, with negligible impacts on employment. In a study of raising the minimum wage in New Jersey compared to not raising the minimum wage in Pennsylvania, Card and Kruger concluded, "We find no indication that the rise in the minimum wage reduced employment" (Card and Kruger 1994). Studies of the actual impacts of increasing the minimum wage suggest that these increases actually reduce poverty rates and stimulate local economies, with more money in circulation (Card and Kruger 1995; CBO 2014; Reich et al. 2016). A press release from the Council of Economic Advisers announcing the Congressional Budget Office 2014 report on the minimum wage states:

> Seven Nobel Prize winners, eight former Presidents of the American Economic Association and over 600 other economists recently summarized the literature on the employment effect of the minimum wage in this way: "In recent years there have been important developments in the academic literature on the effect of increases in the minimum wage on employment with the weight of the evidence now showing that increase in the minimum wage have had little or no negative effect on the employment of minimum wage workers, even during times of weakness in the labor market." (White House Office 2014)

Trump's idea that raising the minimum wage will cause small businesses to fire their employees is just not supported by the literature. The idea that raising the minimum wage will reduce poverty is supported by the literature.

There is some validity to Trump's assertion that an expanded economy will reduce poverty and increase wages, without an increase in the minimum wage. Indeed, as the economy expanded from 2017 through 2019, poverty and unemployment rates declined. Under ordinary circumstances, wages should rise. However, contrary to the claims of Trump and his supporters, real wages stagnated (U.S. Department of Labor 2019). That is, the nominal value of wages increased, while the real value of wages, as determined by its purchasing power, declined.

Low-income wages stagnated despite the expanded economy and historic low unemployment rates for three major reasons. First, Trump's trade war precipitated increased consumer prices, which decreased the real value of labor. Second, labor power declined, that is, the power of workers to negotiate for higher wages evaporated. This decline in labor power is associated with the decline in union density, the percentage of workers who belong to a labor union. Third, while employment expanded, underemployment persisted. Underemployment has to do with workers working in undesirable low-income jobs. Underemployment mask low unemployment rates and distorts the labor market. Ordinarily, when the labor market is tight, that is when employers are begging for workers because unemployment is at an all-time low, employers are constrained to raise wages to attract employees. David Blanchflower demonstrates that the United States is experiencing stagnant wages under near full employment conditions, because the employment rate masks the underemployment rate (Blanchflower 2021).

## Subminimum Wage and Tipping Wars

In addition to having a minimum wage issue, the United States has a subminimum wage problem. Often overlooked in these issues is the relationship between wages and profits. Business owners are able to increase profits by reducing wages. The idea behind a government enforced minimum wage is to prevent wages from falling to far below subsistence levels, that is, the level required to work full time and to sustain life. Lowering wages below this level is a form of exploitation. Government has historically played a role in mediating this exploitation. However, the government's role has varied with the political influence of business owners and corporate leaders. Owners of restaurant and bar businesses have lobbied for a subminimum wage, a wage that is about half the minimum wage, to be supplemented by tips.

In 1991, the subminimum wage was decoupled from the minimum wage and was raised to $2.13 an hour, where it has remained. In 1991, the subminimum wage was about 50 percent of the minimum wage. Today, it is less than 30 percent of the minimum wage. Because of the low subminimum wage, workers in restaurants and bars are struggling. Compared to workers in other sectors of the economy, waiters, waitresses, and bartenders suffer higher rates of poverty and job insecurity. The rationale behind paying the subminimum wage is that the wages of these workers are subsidized by tips. However, an easy way of increasing the rate of exploiting these workers is to either confiscate their tips, expand their time on non-tip work, or classify non-tip workers as tip workers. To prevent this exploitation, the Department of Labor had established rules whereby employers were prohibited from confiscating tips. It added the 20/80 rule, which required tip workers to spend at least 80 percent of their work engaged in tip-related tasks; that is, serving customers. They could not spend more than 20 percent of their time on tasks unrelated to tip services, such as cleaning off and setting tables. These DOL rules are necessary because if owners are allowed to confiscate tips and share the tips with non-tip workers, without the 80 percent rule, these owners could classify cooks and dishwashers as tip workers and pay them a subminimum wage or they could use waiters and waitresses mostly as cooks and custodians and pay them subminimum wages. In early March 2018, the Restaurant Industry Association sued the Department of Labor to repeal the 80 percent rule (Brecher and Adler-Paindiris 2018). Shortly afterwards, the Trump administration proposed eliminating the 80/20 percent rule (U.S. Department of Labor, Notice of Proposed Rulemaking 2018). The administration claimed that the rule was too burdensome for the restaurant industry. In January 2019, Attorney Generals representing eighteen states sent a letter to the secretary of labor requesting that the proposal to eliminate the 80/20 rule be dropped because there was no evidence that the 80/20 rule was too burdensome (Romeo 2021). The next month, the secretary of labor sent out a memo to its Wage and Hour division stating that the department will no longer enforce the 80/20 rule. At the same time, the DOL dropped its proposal to allow owners to confiscate tips. The non-enforcement of the 80/20 rule would allow managers to super exploit all of their workers by paying them a subminimum wage (Koerner 2018; Shierholz and Cooper 2019). The point here is that the Trump administration was committed to changing labor rules in ways that shifted power to restaurant owners, enabling them to super exploit their workers.

## Overtime Regulations

In addition to the subminimum wage, overtime is another issue that involved the exploitation of workers. In the spring of 2016, the U.S. Department of Labor under the Obama administration issued new regulations under the Fair Labor Standards Act (FLSA). These new regulations raised the threshold of the salary of workers exempt from overtime pay. This threshold was raised from $23,660 to $47,476. In other words, under the old $23,660 threshold rule, anyone making more that $23,660 would be ineligible for overtime pay. With over 4 million workers making between $23,660 and $47,476, this change alone increased by over 4 million the number of workers eligible for overtime pay.

The Obama Labor Department noted that in 1975 about 60 percent of the workforce was eligible for overtime pay. However, by 2016, less than 10 percent of the workforce was eligible for overtime pay. The number of people ineligible for overtime pay declined because the threshold was never indexed to the cost of living.

The Trump administration initially attempted to kill the overtime rule change made under the Obama administration. However, the Trump administration reached a compromise rule, "raising the 'standard salary level' from the currently enforced level of $455 to $684 per week (equivalent to $35,568 per year for a full-year worker)" (U.S. Department of Labor 2019). Although this Trump rule is above the $23,660 threshold, it is still below the Obama $47,476 threshold.

## UNIONIZATION AND COLLECTIVE BARGAINING

Trump's labor policy agenda targeted unionization and collective bargaining. Unionization and collective bargaining rights are protected by the NLRB, established in 1935. All workers are not covered by the NLRB. The NLRB covers only private sector workers. Public service workers and independent contractors are not covered by the NLRB. Public service workers are covered either by state employment relations agencies or the Federal Labor Relations Authority. Independent contract workers were excluded, because they were considered independent businesses, rather than a sector of the labor force. However, a new category of workers have emerged, gig workers.

The gig sector is a function of two fundamental historical changes in the labor market: a structural and a technological change. The structural change occurred decades ago when corporations decided to cut costs by closing down an entire division of their workforce and replacing it with a small independent business or individual contract workers (Bluestone and Harrison 1990). A corporation would eliminate its custodial division, which paid janitors a decent salary with benefits, and contract out the custodial services with a private business that employed workers with lower wages and no benefits. The technological change involved the ascension of the internet, the formation of digital platforms, and the mass production and mass use of cell phones.

The line between gig workers and independent contractors has become blurred. Most gig workers are employed by a large corporation, but they enjoy some of the same independence as private contractors. Many work for taxi, home health aide, or delivery service companies. As independent contractors, they are not protected by the NLRB. As workers for a large business, they are protected by the NLRB. The Obama administration NLRB established an economic dependency test to determine whether a gig worker was covered under federal law. The economic dependency test classified workers as employees if their work depended on their employer. This test would allow gig workers to organize into unions and engage in collective bargaining for higher wages and benefits.

In January 2019, the Trump NLRB repealed an Obama administration's economic dependency test. The repeal re-established the old common law agency test. Under this test, workers could be classified as an independent contractor if they had opportunities for economic gain or risks of loss; if they had discretion to determine when or how long to work; or if they set their own schedules (NLRB, Velox Express, Inc. 2019). The economic dependency test was much stricter. If the workers depended on the employer for work, then they were not independent contractors. Under the Obama administration's test, fewer workers would qualify as independent contractors. Under the Trump administration test, millions more workers would qualify as independent contractors. A number of cases illustrate the implications of this test for collective bargaining.

Using the common law test, the NLRB ruled that Dallas-Fort Worth International Airport Super Shuttle drivers were independent contractors. As independent contractors, they did not have the right to unionize (Madland et al. 2019).

In another case, the NLRB used the Taft–Hartley Act to issue a ruling allowing an employer to fire custodial workers for engaging in informational picketing. In San Francisco, employees of Ortiz Janitorial Services (OJS) worked in a building managed by Harvest Properties. Preferred Building Services Incorporated (PBSI) provided janitorial services for Harvest and subcontracted with OJS. The OJS workers claimed that they were underpaid and subjected to abusive, unsafe, and sexually harassing working conditions. Seeking ways to resolving these problems, a few employees contacted San Francisco Living Wage Coalition (the Coalition). The Coalition directed them to the Service Employees International Union (SEIU). The SEIU recommended that the employees engage in informational picketing and negotiate with Harvest. In an attempt to help resolve the problems, Harvest contacted PBSI. PBSI cancelled its contract with OJS. OJS fired the employees involved with the informational picketing. SEIU filed a suit. OJS argued that the employees were engaged in secondary picketing in violation of the Taft–Hartley Act. The administrative law judge ruled against OJS and in favor of SEIU and the fired employees on grounds that case law allows for exceptions where both the primary and secondary employer are located in the same place, where picketing is limited to that location and picketers disclose clearly that the dispute is with the primary employer. The Trump NLRB reversed the administrative law judge's ruling and upheld the firing. This NLRB ruling weakened the power of labor unions and severely restricted the options of subcontracted custodial workers seeking redress of deplorable working conditions (Rosen and Bloom 2018).

In May 2019, the Center for Medicare and Medicaid Services issued a rule that prohibits unions representing home healthcare workers paid by Medicare or Medicaid from taking automatic payments from the paychecks of its members. This rule affects over 350,000 unionized home healthcare workers, 8,500 in the state of Connecticut alone, who are represented by the SEIU (VanBooven 2019). This rule is designed to cripple home healthcare unions. It is part of a larger movement to destroy public service unions.

There are other implications for the independent contractor status of gig workers.

For example, gig workers include Uber and Lyft drivers (Standing 2011, 2017). While they make a substantial income when they have fares, they lose money waiting for customers. They are responsible for purchasing their own gas and maintenance for their own cars. Not only are they ineligible to unionize, they are not entitled to benefits, and the company does not have to pay into social security or unemployment for them. The point is that labor rule changes under the Trump administration favored businesses and corporations to the detriment of American workers.

### *Janus v AFSCME*

The most devastating blow to collective bargaining rights since before the New Deal occurred in the 2018 *Janus v AFSCME* decision. In this decision, the Supreme Court struck down mandatory agency fees for public service unions. Agency fees are not union dues. Most unions charge for union dues and agency fees. Workers who are opposed to the union have a right not to pay union dues. However, the agency fee is a charge for services rendered by the union for the benefit of all workers covered by the collective bargaining contract. It is the costs that a union incurs in the process of negotiating, monitoring, and implementing a contract. Through this process, unions often employ the services of accountants to review budgets, especially when employers claim that they cannot afford to offer raises. Also, unions employ the services of attorneys, chief negotiators, secretaries, and grievance officers to assist in this process. The agency fee is the charge for these services. This fee is mandatory in order to prevent free-riders, workers who benefit from the services, but refuse to pay for them. A common strategy to destroy labor unions is to outlaw the mandatory agency fee. Without these fees, unions cannot afford the costs of negotiating contracts.

The *Janus v AFSCME* challenged the constitutionality of mandatory agency fees for public service workers. In 1977, the Supreme Court settled this issue in the *Abood v Detroit Board of Education* decision. The Detroit Board of Education deducted the agency fee from the salaries of teachers. Abood argued that he opposed public service collective bargaining and the political activities of the union. The Supreme Court ruled that Abood did not have to pay the union dues, but he had to pay the agency fee. For forty-one years, the mandatory payment of the agency fee was settled by law. For forty-one years, it was understood that supporting the rights of workers to engage in collective bargaining required the mandatory payment of the agency fee. This settled law was overturned by the *Janus v AFSCME* decision.

Mark Janus challenged the agency fee on grounds that it violated his first amendment right to freedom of speech. He insisted that public sector contracts were different from private sector contracts because the public sector contract impacted public spending. Agency fees in the public sector are political statements and constituted a form of political speech that he opposed. The Supreme Court ruled in his favor. The significance of this decision is that it immediately put all public sector agency fees and contracts at risks. In so far as right to work laws, which are hostile to labor unions, prohibit agency fees, this decision nationalizes right to work laws in the public sector. It has the potential to severely cripple public sector unions.

While the Obama administration opposed right to work laws and the assault on agency fees, the Trump administration submitted an amicus curiae brief in support of Janus. Public service unions and private sector unions condemned this decision because of its threat to labor unions in general. In this case, the Trump administration had joined forces with a multi-million dollar campaign in support of the Janus ruling and a protracted war against labor unions (see Urevich 2017; Bottari 2018).

The war on public service unions is critically important. Today only 10.5 percent of the total American workforce is unionized. Only 6.4 percent of the private workforce is unionized. Among public sector workers, 33.9 percent are unionized. About 40 percent of local-level public sector workers are unionized. The public sector and the service sector are the last bastions of unionization in America. President Trump is leading the assault on public service labor unions. The Janus decision has dealt a severe blow to public sector unions.

## Assault on the Rights of Federal Employees

While Trump campaigned on a promise to be a friend of labor and to support labor rights, his most savage assault was on the rights of federal employees. In the second year of his term, he issued three executive orders (E.O. 13836, 13837, and 13839) that targeted federal employees. These orders were designed to end progressive discipline; reduce due process to make it easier to fire workers; prohibit grievances for disputing poor evaluations, merit pay, or terminations; restrict to 25 percent the time that grievance officers or union workers could devote federal work hours to union business, such as pursuing grievances, protecting whistle blowers, or filing EEOC complaints; prohibit the use of federal space and resources for union business; and centralized the collective bargaining process to restrict the range of negotiable items. Several federal unions filed suit against the president and his executive orders: the American Federation of Government Employees the National Association of Government Employees, and the National Treasury Employee Union. U.S. District Judge Ketanji Brown Jackson struck down major parts of these orders, arguing that although the president has the authority to issue executive orders with respect to federal labor regulations, he does not have the authority to violate federal law. She added, "The Collective Bargaining process is not a cutthroat death match" (quoted by Rein 2018). Federal laws, particularly the Civil Service Reform Act of 1978, protected the rights and prerogatives of federal labor unions. President Trump's executive orders were designed to eliminate many of these rights, as they stood in the way of the president's power to reward and punish, promote and fire federal employees at will.

## WORKPLACE HEALTH AND SAFETY

President Trump promised to roll back regulations to stimulate the economy but at the same time to preserve regulations that protected the health and safety of workers. By December 2017, the president boasted of having achieved the "most far-reaching regulatory reform in history" (Trump 2017). He claimed to have cancelled or delayed about 1,500 regulations. He preached that deregulation creates jobs and stimulates the economy.

The problem with Trump's claim is four fold. First there is little evidence that regulations killed jobs (Irons and Shapiro 2011). Second, government reports indicate that while there are costs with regulations, the benefits greatly outweigh the costs (Office of Management and Budget 2016). Third, the rush to deregulate jeopardizes the health and safety of American workers. Finally,

Trump reneged on his promise not to kill regulations that protected the health and safety of workers.

There is considerable evidence that many of the regulations the Trump administration proposed to eliminate are likely to hurt workers; expose them to toxic substances and unsafe and unhealthy work conditions. Trump's Occupation Safety Health Administration (OSHA) proposed to rescind regulations that required shipyard and construction employers to monitor the workplace and periodically test workers in order to reduce worker exposure to beryllium, a toxic chemical associated with increased risk of lung cancer and other lung diseases. Trump's EPA proposed rescinding regulations that require employers to post warning signs around pesticide-treated areas and provide pesticide-handling safety training to reduce pesticide poisoning among farm laborers. Trump's MSHA proposed weakening mine safety inspections by eliminating anytime inspections, especially inspections while mines are operating. Since inspectors are more likely to observe hazardous conditions or violations while the mine is in operation, this change substantially weakens protections for mine workers and increases their chances of exposure to dangerous working conditions. Trump's U.S. Department of Agriculture has proposed rescinding the regulation that limits the line speed for processing poultry to only 140 birds per minute. This regulation was set because of evidence that increasing the line speed beyond this rate significantly increases the number of work-related injuries and illnesses. Eliminating this regulation would allow the excessive exploitation of poultry workers and increase their risk of serious workplace injuries. The Trump administration's efforts to roll back regulations has strong support from the corporate community, but it exhibits a callous and willful disregard for the lives and wellbeing of workers, especially agricultural and mine workers (McNicholars et al. 2018).

## CDC, OSHA, and Covid-19

Trump's deregulation campaign emasculated OSHA and crippled its ability to protect workers during the Covid-19 pandemic. Both the Centers for Disease Control and Prevention (CDC) and the OSHA are responsible for protecting the health and safety of American workers. These two federal agencies have a well-established reputation for upholding this responsibility. The CDC establishes guidelines. OSHA issues regulations to enforce them. Indeed, during the height of the HIV/AIDS epidemic in the 1990s, OSHA issued a series of regulations, some mandating special equipment to protect health care and emergency responder workers from exposure to blood-borne pathogens. These OSHA regulations saved lives and decreased HIV infection rates (Gary and Scholz 1993; Weissburg 1992; Ramsey et al. 1996). They decreased the annual work-related cases of hepatitis-B infections from 12,000 to just a handful (Michaels 2020).

OSHA and the Trump administration have the power to issue emergency regulations to protect workers from exposure to the Covid-19 virus (Michaels 2020). In April 2020, when Covid-19 cases were surging, Trump issued an executive order evoking the Defense Production Act of 1950 to keep meat-packing facilities open. The order acknowledged increasing cases of workers infected with the virus and of public health officials closing down facilities because of mass infections. However, the order claimed that the "closures threatened the national meat and poultry supply chain" (EO13917). Whereas the CDC and OSHA provided guidelines for improving safety, the guidelines were weak and tentative. For example, a guideline stated, "Configure communal work environments so that workers are spaced at least six feet apart, if possible" (quoted in Davis 2020). All of the guidelines were suggestions. They were not regulations. The result of this executive order is that without regulatory protections, over 40,000 meat and poultry packing workers were infected and several hundred died from the virus (McNicholas et al. 2020). Throughout his entire term in office, Trump exhibited a profound bias in favor of expanding the economy and against protecting the health and safety of workers.

## TRUMP'S LABOR POLICY IN A NUTSHELL

The cases reviewed in this chapter demonstrate clearly that Donald Trump was not a friend of the working class. His top labor officials were handpicked by corporate-sponsored organizations like the Heritage Foundation. They followed the labor policy agenda of the U.S. Chamber of Commerce. The Trump administration had become part of corporate America's assault on the rights of American workers. While Trump promised to listen to American workers, he followed the dictates of America's corporate leaders. While Trump claimed loudly and openly to listen to working-class Americans, he operated as a right-wing populist who listened to America's plutocrats. The Trump administration had joined the corporate movement's assault on the rights of American workers, all the while claiming to be their friends.

*Chapter 7*

# Healthcare Policy

This chapter reviews the healthcare policies of the Trump administration. It focuses on the Patient Protection and Affordable Care Act of 2010 (ACA). It examines the problems addressed by this policy: costs escalating out of control, people with inadequate or no health insurance, and health insurance companies denying people with preexisting conditions healthcare coverage. It exposes the conservative origin of this policy. It documents the successes and failures of this policy. It makes it clear that Trump promised to make this policy better, but instead led an all-out assault on this policy.

## THE COST PROBLEM

By most measures, healthcare costs were escalating out of control. In terms of per capita spending, these costs doubled between 1960 and 1970 and then tripled between 1970 and 1980. There was a substantial increase every decade, except the 1990s, the decade in which the federal government used diagnostic related groups to control Medicare and Medicaid costs. Healthcare costs as a percentage of GDP increased from 13.4 percent in 2000 to about 17.3 percent by 2010. In other words, healthcare costs as a percentage of GDP approached 20 percent of the economy (Centers for Medicare and Medicaid Services 2021).

## THE ACCESS PROBLEM

Escalating costs contributed to the access problem. Initially, public policy makers had dismissed the access problem because they assumed that health risks were functions of individual choices and life styles, not access to health care. That is, poor diet, obesity, lack of exercise, tobacco smoking, alcohol and drug use, and other forms of individual behavior are associated with the risk of premature death, not the lack of health insurance. Also, they assumed that even without health insurance, individuals had access to community health clinics and emergency hospital services.

Considerable medical research demonstrated that while individual choices do matter, the lack of access to health insurance had an independent and significant effect on health outcomes. Several studies published throughout the 1990s and 2000s demonstrated that even controlling for behavioral factors (exercise, consumption, etc.) and demographic factors (age, race, gender, disability, etc.), adults without health insurance had higher death risks than those with health insurance. Indeed, a 1993 study published in the *Journal of the American Medical Association* found that uninsured adults have a 25 percent greater risk of death than insured adults (Frank et al. 1993). A more recent follow-up study published in the *American Journal of Public Health* in 2009 just before the enactment of the ACA reported that over 46 million Americans lacked health insurance and that "lack of health insurance is associated with as many as 44,789 deaths per year in the United States" (Wilper et al. 2009). The study accounted for demographics ( age, race, and gender), and behavior (poor exercise and poor consumption habits):

> Unmeasured characteristics (i.e., that individuals who place less value on health eschew both health insurance and healthy behaviors) might offer an alternative explanation for our findings. However, our analysis controlled for tobacco and alcohol use, along with obesity and exercise habits. In addition, research has found that more than 90% of nonelderly adults without insurance cite cost or lack of employer-sponsored coverage as reasons for being uninsured, whereas only 1 percent report not needing insurance. (Wilper et al. 2009, 2293)

This study identified specific mechanisms of health insurance that affected death rates. The most important mechanism was access to preventive care. Access to preventive care increased the likelihood of the early detection of life-threatening diseases. It enabled consistent and long-term treatment of chronic ailments. This access improved health outcomes and reduced death rates. It also reduced costs by reducing the likelihood of needing expensive emergency care.

Prior to ACA, the access problem was generated by several factors: occupations or sectors of the job market without health insurance, the shift of jobs from the industrial sector to the service sector, the recession of 2008–2009, the decline of unionized jobs, and holes in the social safety net.

Vicente Navarro provided a comprehensive study of the problems with access to health care associated with the decline of the steel industry in Baltimore, Maryland, during the early 1990s. Thousands of steel workers lost both their jobs and their health insurance. Most were able to get jobs in the service sector. Some had multiple jobs, but no health insurance. Navarro documents several cases in which the lack of adequate health insurance contributed to the early death of workers (Navarro 1993).

Most people without health insurance have jobs. Indeed, about 75 percent of people without health insurance had jobs (Freund and McGuire 1999, 295). They just happened to work in occupations or jobs that provide no insurance such as the service, fast-food, retail, small businesses, or self-employed sectors.

The recession of 2008–2009, which occurred prior to the passage of the ACA, contributed to a dramatic increase in the uninsured, as a large number of people lost both their jobs and their health insurance. People without health insurance simply could not afford insurance and did not qualify for any public programs.

## THE PREEXISTING CONDITION PROBLEM

The practice of increasing premiums or denying coverage for preexisting conditions had been a persisting problem. The U.S. House of Representatives Subcommittee exposed this problem in public hearings. Several individuals and former health insurance employees testified and documented a pattern in which insurance customers were denied life-saving treatments because of preexisting conditions. The testimony was captured in the subcommittee's formal report. "Terminations of Individual Health Policies by Insurance Companies." The case of Robin Beaton stood out:

My name is Robin Beaton, and I am 59 years old. I was a registered nurse for 30 years. I worked in a hospital, had insurance, and was in good health. I retired from nursing and started a small business. I got an individual policy with Blue Cross and Blue Shield . . . in December 2007.

In May 2008, I went to the dermatologist for acne. A word was written on my chart and interpreted incorrectly as meaning pre-cancerous. Shortly thereafter, I was diagnosed with Invasive HER-2 Genetic Breast Cancer, a very aggressive form of breast cancer. I was told I needed a double mastectomy. When the surgeons scheduled my surgery I was pre-certified for my two days hospitalization. The Friday before the Monday I was scheduled to have my double mastectomy, Blue Cross red flagged my chart due to the dermatologist report.

The dermatologist called Blue Cross directly to report that I only had acne and please not hold up my coming surgery. Blue Cross called me to inform me that they were launching a 5-year medical investigation into my medical history and that this would take approximately 3 months.

I was frantic. I did not know what to do or where to turn . . .

Next, I found out that my insurance was completely cancelled; this was devastating . . . Cancer is expensive . . . This is America and we deserve good health care.

Earlier in my life off and on I had a fast beating of my heart which was not a current problem, just something that happened when I was upset . . . [Blue Cross considered the fast-beating heart a preexisting condition that justified cancelling her insurance] . . . Blue Cross will do anything to get out of paying for cancer. (Beaton 2009)

Former employees of health insurance companies provided supporting testimony. Many of these employees had quit because they believed the practices of denying insurance to customers' life-saving treatment because of preexisting conditions was immoral.

## THE CONSERVATIVE ORIGINS OF THE ACA

Skyrocketing healthcare costs precipitated other problems: lack of access to affordable healthcare coverage, healthcare-related bankruptcies, excessively high insurance premiums, and insurance companies' refusal to cover people with preexisting conditions. Because it was adamantly opposed to a nationally funded universal healthcare program, the neoliberal policy oriented think tank, the Heritage Foundation, came up with a comprehensive proposal that would minimize government involvement and maximize the role of the private sector. The proposal was presented in a manuscript entitled, "National Health System for America." This proposal was designed to address the dual problems of access and costs. It criticized the government dominated healthcare policies of Canada and European nations.

A neoliberal scholar noted for his promotion of the privatization of government programs, Stuart Butler, wrote a short pamphlet promoting the Heritage plan. He claimed that the Heritage plan offered a more viable option than the Canadian and European plans. It minimized government involvement and maximized consumer choice. To improve the quality of health care for the elderly, it expanded Medicare services. To eliminate the stigma of welfare, it required decoupling Medicaid from the Aid to Families with Dependent Children program. To expand access to health care, it allowed lower middle class families whose income was just above the poverty line but who could not afford health insurance to qualify for Medicaid. To reduce overall health-care costs, it mandated that all families have insurance. Explaining the logic behind the mandate Butler adds,

> Many states now require passengers in automobiles to wear seatbelts for their own protection. Many others require anybody driving a car to have liability insurance. But neither the federal government nor any state requires all households to protect themselves from the potentially catastrophic costs of a serious accident or illness. Under the Heritage plan there would be such a requirement. (Butler 1989, 2)

In 2006, while serving as governor of Massachusetts, Mitt Romney signed into law a state healthcare policy modeled after the Heritage Foundation proposal. This law mandates that all residents of the State of Massachusetts must obtain health insurance.

## THE AFFORDABLE CARE ACT

Initially, Obama favored the public option proposal of healthcare reform. However, after Democrats lost control of the House of Representatives in the 2010 Congressional election, Obama backed off the public option and opted for the more conservative Heritage plan Romney had established in Massachusetts.

The ACA was a massive piece of legislation, consisting of about a thousand pagers. It directly addressed a range of problems in the healthcare system: access, costs, perverse incentives, and others. Most of the major provisions of the ACA addressed these issues:

1. mandated all states to raise the eligibility standards to expand Medicaid for families with incomes just above the poverty line (although the Supreme Court struck down this mandate, making Medicaid expansion voluntary for the states);
2. allocated money to states to cover the initial costs of the Medicaid expansion;
3. required insurance companies to raise the age limit for children on family insurance plans from 18 to 26;
4. mandated all individuals to acquire healthcare insurance or pay a fine;
5. required all employers with fifty or more employees to provide health-care benefits by 2014;

6. encouraged states to create healthcare exchanges and pushed private, competitive health insurance markets to reduce the costs of insurance to individuals;
7. provided tax breaks and subsidies to reduce the insurance premiums of low-income individuals who do not qualify for Medicare or Medicaid;
8. provided subsidies to insurance companies to reduce the co-pay for their clients;
9. offered tax credits and subsidies to small businesses with less than twenty-five employees to offset the costs of providing health insurance;
10. prohibited companies from terminating insurance because of the high costs of medical treatment;
11. prohibited companies from terminating insurance when medical costs reach a milliondollars;
12. required insurance companies to provide adequate and essential medical services which include preventive care, mental health, drug treatment, maternity care, hospitalization, pharmaceutical drugs, and ambulatory services;
13. prohibited insurance companies from denying coverage for necessary medical procedures because of preexisting conditions;
14. required hospitals and medical clinics to establish electronic record-keeping.

## Benefits of ACA

The ACA has many accomplishments. Since its enactment, the number of uninsured Americans declined from a high of 48.6 million in 2010 to about 28.6 million by 2016, a decline of about 20 million (see table 7.1). In addition to reducing the number of uninsured Americans, the ACA addressed the preexisting condition problem. Today about 135 million Americans with preexisting conditions have some legal protection from insurance companies increasing their premiums or terminating their coverage.

The ACA Medicaid expansion saved thousands of lives in many ways. One study found that the expansion prevented thousands of premature deaths among low-income adults. Among states that expanded Medicaid under the ACA, the lives of over 19,000 adults aged 55–64 were saved from premature deaths. In states that refused the ACA Medicaid expansion, 15,000 adults aged 55–64 died prematurely (Rapfogel et al. 2020; Broaddus and Avon-Dive 2019; Miller et al. 2019).

ACA Medicaid expansion was particularly beneficial to rural areas. Most concentrated poverty Census Tracts (tracts with poverty rates of over 40 percent) are located in rural areas. About 22.5 percent of rural Americans have Medicaid coverage, including nearly half of all rural children (Rapfogel

Table 7.1 The Number and Percentage of Americans without Health Insurance: 2008–2019

| Year | Number in Millions | Percentage |
|---|---|---|
| 2005 | 41.2 | 14.2 |
| 2008 | 43.8 | 14.7 |
| 2009 | 46.3 | 15.4 |
| 2010 | 48.6 | 16.0 |
| 2011 | 46.3 | 15.1 |
| 2012 | 44.5 | 14.7 |
| 2013 | 44.8 | 14.7 |
| 2014 | 36.0 | 11.5 |
| 2015 | 28.6 | 9.1 |
| 2016 | 28.6 | 9.0 |
| 2017 | 29.3 | 9.1 |
| 2018 | 30.4 | 9.4 |
| 2019 | 33.2 | 10.3 |

Center for Disease Control and Prevention, National Center for Health Statistics, National Health Insurance Survey
http://www.cdc.gov/nchs/nhis/healthinsurancecoverage.htm

et al. 2020). Many rural hospitals lost money because of a high rate of emergency patients unable to pay their bills. Medicaid expansion reduced hospital losses from uncompensated emergency care. In states that participated in ACA Medicaid expansion, Medicaid increased the financial viability of rural hospitals. In contrast, states that refused to expand Medicaid under the ACA suffered much higher rates of rural hospital closures (Ropfogel et al. 2020).

ACA Medicaid expansion brought needed assistance to rural areas hit hard by the opioid crisis. A number of researchers have compared Kentucky, a state that expanded Medicaid under the ACA and Tennessee that refused to expand Medicaid. Compared to Kentucky, Tennessee suffered significantly more cases of opioid addictions, overdoses, and deaths attributable to overdoses. Researchers attribute the higher addiction and death rates in Tennessee to its failure to expand Medicaid (Metzl 2019; Sheperd 2020). As Medicaid covered treatment for drug addiction and mental health issues, adult Kentuckians received medical treatment. Tennesseans did not. Consequently, they suffered higher addiction and death rates.

## Problems with the ACA

The ACA had many problems, but none of them were as severe and as intractable as the right-wing media, the president, and other Republicans claimed. Contrary to Rush Limbaugh, there never were any death panels. The navigator server for the federal healthcare exchange market did crash, primarily because of inadequate initial investment (Emanuel 2014). Once the server was fixed, it provided access to health insurance for millions of Americans.

Costs were a persistent problem, but not as devastating as critics claimed. President Trump's press secretary, Kayleigh McEnany, provided several anecdotal cases of devastating increases in healthcare costs, which she attributes to Obamacare. A close inspection of one of her cases, which was showcased in the Oval Office by President Trump, illustrates this point. This case involved Stan Summers and his son, Talan, who suffered from a rare and painful disease, which involved the hardening of his lung tissues and was expensive to treat. In her book applauding the Trump administration, McEnany described catastrophic increases in out-of-pocket insurance costs, which she attributed to Obamacare:

> Stan's insurance cost him $240 with a $1,000 out-of-pocket maximum. But everything would change in the post-Obamacare world.

> Stan received coverage through the Box Elder County Commission, where he served as a part-time commissioner. Even though he was not on an Obamacare exchange plan, the new law caused Stan's healthcare costs to skyrocket. Stan's deductible initially soared to a $5,000 out-of-pocket maximum and then to $7,500 before hitting a whopping $9,000 in 2017. "I've been married twenty-nine years, and I've met my out-of-pocket maximum deductible twenty-six out of the twenty-nine years," Stan recalled. That meant that Stan had to pay a full $9,000 before his healthcare coverage would even kick in!

> An almost double-digit deductible is a devastating blow to the hardworking school bus driver and part-time commissioner. In 2016 alone, Stan spent $35,000 on health care—the equivalent of some people's salaries. (McEnany 2018, 192)

This case and many cases like it dramatized catastrophic increases in healthcare costs. They provided powerful headline news supporting Trump's claim that Obamacare was a disaster. However, what McEnany and Trump failed to mention is that his case occurred in the State of Utah, a state that refused to expand Medicaid. In other words, this case did not occur because of Obamacare. It occurred because the Republican-dominated state government refused to expand Medicaid under Obamacare. Although McEnany was honest enough to mention that Stan Summer's insurance was not part of the ACA healthcare market exchange, she failed to mention that these catastrophic increases in out-of-pocket costs rarely occur in policies within these exchanges.

The research on the impact of the ACA on the cost of insurance premiums varied wildly. A March 2017 *Forbes Magazine* article claimed that post-ACA insurance premiums increased by as much as 46.4 percent for Health Maintenance Organizations and as much as 66.2 percent for Point of Service insurance plans (Book 2017). Other studies reported more modest increases. The National Conference of State Legislatures' website stated, "In 2018 the average annual premium for employer-based family coverage rose 5% to $19,616, for single coverage, premiums rose 3% to $6,896" (NCSL 2020). An article summarizing research from the McKinsey Center for U.S. Health System Reform, the Henry J. Kaiser Family Foundation, and the *New York Times* found that premiums varied among the states and among the types of insurance. *The New York Times* reported that premiums increase by 8.4 percent in one year among the most popular plans, but only by 1 percent within the healthcare exchanges (Kurt 2019).

The Government Accountability Office reviewed the literature on insurance costs and interviewed select health insurance companies. It concluded that from 2014 through 2016 insurance claim costs increased between 6 and 10 percent. It attributed the higher costs to several factors. First and most significant, insurance companies expected mandatory health insurance to increase the number of low-cost young people bringing in revenue. This event was calculated to reduce premiums. Instead, these companies reported a much higher than expected number of new insurers with expensive conditions such as HIV infections, diabetes, hypertension, and others. Another factor was the overall increases in the costs of health care and pharmaceutical drugs. Other factors included the mandatory expansion of family insurance to cover children from 18 to 26; the mandate to cover essential medical services, such as preventive care, mental health, hospitalization, and others; the elimination of the million dollar cap on the cost of necessary medical services; and the prohibition against cancelling coverage for preexisting conditions or raising premiums because of occupation or gender (GAO 2019).

## The Assault on the ACA

The assault on the ACA began immediately after its passage. In The Dysfunctional Politics of the Affordable Care Act, Greg Shaw summarizes early battles:

> Literally within minutes of President Obama signing the bill into law, Virginia's Attorney General Ken Cuccinelli filed a law suit in federal district court arguing that Congress lacked the authority to compel Virginians to obtain health insurance. Virginia's legislature—as well as Idaho's—had recently passed laws prohibiting their residents from being required to purchase health insurance.

Lawmakers in at least 30 other states introduced similar measures, following a piece of model legislation created by the conservative American Legislative Exchange Council. (Shaw 2017, 33)

He added,

The refusal by many states to cooperate with the unfolding federal effort and, following the 2012 election in which the GOP retained congressional control, dozens of efforts to repeal the law would form two other fronts of attack. For many Republican office holders, the implementation of the ACA portended a new level of government intrusion into one of the largest sectors of the economy, and the prospects of this new status quo gaining a broad constituency unhinged them with fear and anger. (Shaw 2017, 33)

Fierce opposition came from multiple sources. As Shaw noted, it came primarily from the Republican Party, Republican state attorney generals, and Republican governors and state legislatures. Several states refused to accept the Medicaid expansion.

Opposition came from small businesses. Small businesses with more than fifty employees were required to provide insurance for their employees. This requirement would go into effect by 2014. It would automatically impact these businesses financially, even with subsidies and tax breaks. A major organization representing small businesses, the National Federation of Independent Businesses (NFIB), filed a major lawsuit again the ACA. Several state attorney generals joined the lawsuit.

In the *NFIB v Sebelius* decision, the Supreme Court struck down the provision mandating the state expansion of Medicaid. This ruling allowed states to opt out of this provision and not expand Medicaid. The court rejected the argument that the federal government had the power to impose the individual mandate under the commerce clause, but upheld this provision under the taxing clause of the constitution. Justice Ginsburg wrote a blistering dissenting opinion explaining how the individual mandate is designed to bring down health insurance costs and why the healthcare economy is part of the national economy and national commerce and therefore should be upheld under the commerce clause.

Congressional Republicans immediately mobilized against the ACA. In 2011, House Republicans passed the Repealing the Job Killing Health Care Law Act and several other bills to repeal the ACA, which did not get through the Democrat-controlled Senate. In 2013, House Republicans threatened to shut the government down over the budget unless the ACA was repealed. The Republican congressional campaigned against the ACA was relentless. Close to seventy repeal bill had been introduced by 2015. One passed in 2016, but was vetoed by Obama.

The Tea Party movement played a major role in the fight against the ACA. The Freedom Caucus, dominated by Tea Party enthusiasts, played a major role in promoting the repeal of the ACA.

The right-wing media joined the war against the ACA. Rush Limbaugh promoted the myth that the ACA created death panels, a government controlled panel that would decide whose grandmothers would live or die. Most conservative hosts attacked the bill claiming that it would hurt small businesses, kill jobs, dramatically increase insurance premiums, take away the right to choose a doctor, cut Medicare spending, and bankrupt the federal government.

The right-wing media ecosystem engaged in a relentless and incessant propaganda assault on the ACA. Conservative television and radio talk show hosts presented a seemingly endless parade of anti-Obamacare testimonies. Individual testimonies concentrated on excessive, unreasonable, and financially disruptive increases in premiums and medical-related bankruptcy. Death panel hysteria persisted.

These conservative hosts were loath to mention a single benefit of the ACA. They were oblivious of the Harvard and other academic research documenting the thousands of lives saved and premature deaths avoided by the law. Not one mentioned the federal subsidies and tax cuts provided to mitigate the costs of the ACA to small businesses. Not a single host challenged the veracity of the death panels or accuracy of a direct causal links between the ACA and the financial disasters. Not one explained that there was nothing in the actual ACA bill that would prevent anyone from choosing their own doctor. Not one mentioned the hundred million American with preexisting conditions protected by this bill.

The ACA discussions by the right-wing media was presented as news. Rush Limbaugh was billed as the doctor of democracy. However, presentations were neither news-worthy nor informative. They were dishonest and calculated to misinform the public and to provoke fear and hysteria. They succeeded in their mission. However, in doing so, they distorted the public policy-making process. Rather than producing an informed public engaged in a serious and enlightened discussion to solve a serious problem, they produced a profoundly misinformed and polarized public and a dysfunctional form of politics, skewed against the common American worker.

Conservative think tanks, corporate policy-making machines, and multi-billionaire campaign networks joined the fight. Research demonstrated that conservative organizations like Koch dominated Americans for Prosperity, Freedom Works, and the American Legislative Exchange Council played prominent roles in attacking and undermining this law. Indeed, there was a strong association between the state involvement of Americans for Prosperity and state opposition to Medicaid expansion. With the election of Donald Trump, the war against the ACA intensified.

## Race, Ideology, and the ACA

There are many different explanations for opposition to the ACA. Opponents claim that they oppose the ACA because it drives up premiums, kills jobs, and violates conservative principles. Some scholars suggest that partisan politics have been a strong factor explaining opposition. That is, the main motivating factor has been opposition to Obama and the Democrats. Indeed, opposition to the ACA falls along partisan lines. Republicans oppose it; Democrats support it. Indeed, a couple of scholars suggested that some Republican leaders opposed the ACA precisely, because they did not want the Democrats to get credit for it (Abramowitz 2018; Shaw 2017).

Other studies suggest that other factors provide a stronger explanation for opposition than concerns about insurance premiums, jobs, or ideology. Moreover, general public opinion surveys illustrate a profound, but revealing contradiction among opponents. Most Americans had opposed Obamacare. At the same time, these same Americans supported the major provisions of the ACA. Indeed, a Stanford University survey found that most opposition to the ACA is based on false or misinformation about the policy. For example, according to the survey only about 16.8 percent of those surveyed believed with a high degree of certainty that the law did not create death panels. The study concluded, "If the public had perfect understanding of elements that we examined, the proportion of Americans who favor the bill might increase from the current level of 32 % to 70%" (Gross et al. 2012).

The right-wing media ecosystem played a major role in promoting misinformation about the ACA. Some people who opposed the ACA believed that it actually created death panels. About 56 percent believed undocumented immigrants were eligible for ACA tax subsidies (Shaw 2017). This misinformation precipitated rage against the policy.

Michael Tesler shows that a great deal of the opposition to the ACA arose because of its association with President Obama (Tesler 2012). Using the National Election Study survey of attitudes toward the ACA, Tesler was able to control for ideology, partisanship, and concern for medical costs, while examining the effects of racial animus. He concluded that racial animus increased opposition to the act, independent of ideology, partisanship, and anxiety about healthcare costs. He also examined whether opposition to Obama affected opposition to the act. His data indicate that racial animus became a stronger predictor of opposition to the act as the president became more involved in campaigning for it. Both political leaders and right-wing radio hosts played a role in using racial cues to trigger opposition to both Obama and the ACA. For example, in the 2012 primary Newt Gingrich called Obama "the Food Stamp president." On national television on the MSNBC Morning Show with Joe Scarbough, Glenn Beck stated that Obama hated white people. Political and conservative opinion leaders conflated blackness with Obama and the ACA. They racialized the policy and exploited racial animus to generate opposition to both Obama and the ACA. Public opinion surveys demonstrated that conservative principles played only a small part of the opposition to the ACA. The research demonstrates that opposition to the ACA was driven more by racial prejudices than by conservative ideology (Shen and La Borff 2016; Michener 2020).

The ACA acquired a double stigma. It was stigmatized because of its association with Obama and was stigmatized because it was seen as a program that provided benefits to blacks, Hispanics, and immigrants. It was despised not because it taxed people. It was despised because it taxed white people and allegedly gave benefits to undeserving and undesirable people of color. The stigma was so bad that social workers would not mention its name for fear that white people who really needed the program would refuse to accept its benefits:

A person tasked with helping Kentuckians shop for insurance shared a story with a journalist about how he typically avoided talking about the ACA when helping others use the commonwealth's exchange, called Kynect. In the spring of 2015, he noted that "I don't ever mention the ACA [when helping people.] . . . I had one guy say, "I'm so glad I found you and didn't have to go through that Obamacare stuff." (Shaw 2017, 102)

## Trump ACA Changes

Changes in healthcare policy in the Trump administration must be understood from the context of polarized and racialized politics. Class politics also played a role. Right-wing billionaires and business and corporate organizations, such as the American Legislative Exchange Council, Americans for Prosperity, and the NFIB, played major roles in the campaign against the ACA. Working-class America had the most to lose from the repeal of this policy.

Trump was the quintessential reactionary populist. He identified with the working-class while promoting policy changes that would benefit insurance corporations and hurt ordinary working-class Americans. While Trump promised to repeal the ACA and replace it with something better, his idea of something better is none other than the unworkable market model. He makes this point clear in his book, *Crippled America: How to Make America Great Again*:

There's no question. Obamacare is a catastrophe, and it has to be repealed and replaced. And it was only approved because President Obama lied 28 times saying you could keep your doctor and your plan—a fraud and the Republicans should have sued—and meant it. As the different provisions kick in over the next few years, individual deductibles are going to continue to rise. People will have to get hit by a truck to be eligible for coverage because those deductibles are going to be so high.

Medical people hate it.

Doctors are quitting all over the place.

I have a friend who is one of the best doctors in the country. You would know the names of many of his patients. He told me, "Donald, I've never seen anything like this. I can't practice medicine the way I want anymore. I have more accountants and computer programmers working for me than I have nurses." He's right. There are no more than 100 codes for doctors to get reimbursements from insurance companies. (Trump 2015, 71)

Aside from providing gross lies and incredible exaggerations, Trump rarely comments on the healthcare access problem. Beyond pledging to repeal and replace Obamacare, Trump never offered any details for his policy proposal. In his book, he offered this solution, "Obamacare needs to be repealed and replaced with a sensible health care system that creates a competitive marketplace, which will reduce costs while providing for the medical needs of all Americans" (Trump 2015, 165).

Like other conservatives, he offered to solve the problems of health care by creating a competitive marketplace. He seems unaware of problems arising from the competitive market place. Although he made statements about preserving the prohibition against denying coverage to those with preexisting condition, his administration was committed to eliminate this provision and every other provision.

## LEGISLATIVE ASSAULTS UNDER TRUMP

With Republicans in control of Congress and the White House, the party moved quickly to repeal and replace the ACA. In 2017, several major healthcare bills were introduced; a few came extremely close to passage—the Health Care Freedom Act, the Better Care Reconciliation Act, and the American Health Care Act. One was passed—the Tax Cuts and Jobs Act. The Health Care Freedom Act was proposed in the Senate and it died in the Senate. It would have repealed the individual and employee mandates. The Better Care Reconciliation Act would have ended the individual mandate, reduced funding for Medicaid, and slowly phased out the Medicaid expansion. This was the bill that Senator McCain killed with a thumbs-down vote. The Health Care Freedom Act would have repealed the individual and employers mandate. It too died in the Senate. The House passed the American Health Care Act (AHCA).

The AHCA proposed several modifications to the ACA. It proposed eliminating the federal individual mandate, but allowing states to choose whether to keep the mandate or not. While the ACA provided subsidies to low-income insurers, the AHCA would provide the subsidies to the insurance companies. While the ACA limited how much insurers were allowed to charge older clients to no more than three times the charge for younger clients, the AHCA increased this limit to five times the charge for younger clients. While the ACA increased spending for Medicaid, the AHCA would decrease Medicaid spending and turn Medicaid into a block grant; thus, preventing Medicaid from expanding when the number of children who fall into poverty and need health insurance increases. The House passed the AHCA. The Senate voted it down.

None of these failed proposals would have addressed the problems of access or costs. Most provided benefits to health insurance companies, while taking benefits away from low-income families. All of these proposals were supported by Trump. Eventually, the Tax Cuts and Jobs Act eliminated the individual mandate. The elimination of the mandate precipitated court challenges to the validity of the entire ACA.

## Trump's Assault on the ACA

President Trump's agenda for healthcare policy consisted of only one goal: to use every power of the presidency to get rid of Obamacare. He used every weapon in his executive arsenal to undermine and destroy the ACA: executive orders, administrative rules, legislation, budgets, court decisions, and propaganda. He targeted the main pillars of the ACA: individual mandate, Medicaid expansion, consumer protection, and subsidies.

President Trump's first executive order (EO13765) targeted the ACA. It stated that it was the policy of this administration to repeal the ACA. The order required the U.S. Department of Health and Human Services to obstruct the implementation of the ACA through the use of deferrals, delays, waivers, exemptions, or grants. This executive order established the battle plans for the war against the ACA. The order made it clear that the Trump administration was committed to the development of a "free and open market" in health care.

The administration immediately targeted the individual mandate, the insurance subsidies, and the market place enrollment process. The administration made it clear that it was not going to enforce the individual mandate. Both HHS and the Internal Revenue Service (IRS) indicated that they were not enforcing the individual mandate.

In a May 2017 press conference, President Trump announced that he wanted to end the cost-sharing reduction program. In this program, the federal government provided subsidies to insurance companies that reduced out-of-pocket or co-payment costs for their customers. These subsides benefited workers by keeping both premiums and out-of-pocket or copayments low. The low payments would encourage people to participate in preventive care in order to prevent more expensive costs in the future. While the president did not have the authority to immediately end the program, Trump proposed to slash spending for the program by about 50 percent (Center for Budget Priorities 2020).

HHS engaged in a disinformation campaign against the ACA. It removed information explaining the benefits of the ACA, including the provision that young people can stay on their parents' insurance until they are 26 years old. It posted twenty-three videos featuring individuals who claimed that the ACA hurt them. The videos were reinforced by other anti-ACA messaging.

The Department of HHS cut funding for outreach advertisement and assistance for the healthcare exchanges. Outreach advertisement included radio and television commercials. The advertisement informed people of their eligibility for insurance, availability of subsidies, enrollment dates, and enrollment instructions. This advertisement was a major reason for the initial success of the ACA in reducing the number of people without health insurance. The Trump administration cut ties with medical, neighborhood, and faith-based groups that assisted with ACA advertisement.

## MEDICAID WAIVERS AND WORK REQUIREMENTS

In January 2018, the American Legislative Exchange Council posted an article on its website supporting the Department of HHS call for waivers to allow states to mandate work requirements for Medicaid. The author, Brooks Roberts, argued that these waivers would give power back to the states, reduce state budgets, and help people to be productive again and to cycle off Medicaid. Moreover, the waivers would improve the health outcomes of Medicaid recipients because "unemployed individuals have worse health outcomes than individuals who are employed" (Roberts 2018).

HHS granted its first waiver to Arkansas in June of 2018. The research on the consequences of these waivers has been disturbing.

A study of Arkansas indicates that the waiver produced worse health outcomes. Between October 2018 and December 2018, about 17,000 Arkansas adults were removed from the Medicaid rolls. The percentage of Arkansas residents between the ages of 30 and 49 with employer-sponsored health increased from 10.5 percent to 14.5 percent. However, the percentage of the same age group with Medicaid or marketplace coverage declined from 70.5 percent to 63.7 percent. The overall percentage of those uninsured increased significantly. Health outcomes declined as a result of the decline of the insured. The waiver had little or no effect on overall income or employment (Sommers et al. 2019).

Those individuals who lost Medicaid coverage because of their work requirement suffered both adverse financial and health consequences. Almost half of those aged 30–49 who lost coverage faced serious financial difficulties related to health expenses. The median debt for those who lost coverage was about a thousand dollars compared to zero debt among those who kept their services. Well over half of those who lost Medicaid coverage delayed their needed medical attention because of the costs. About two-thirds put off taking need medicine because of the costs.

HHS approved work waivers for several other states. Kentucky and Wisconsin have work and premium payment requirements. Wisconsin required Medicaid recipients to work and pay an $8 a month premium. Wisconsin became the first state to target people whose incomes fall below 50 percent of the poverty line and take away their coverage if they fail to pay their monthly premium. New Hampshire required both work and 100 hours of community service to be eligible for Medicaid. This requirement applied to people up to 64 years old.

In March 2019, HHS approved a couple of waiver for the State of Utah. The waivers came in response a 2018 election initiative in which the voters approved the ACA Medicaid expansion. The Utah state legislature rejected the initiative. One waiver gave the state the unprecedented authority to set an arbitrary cap on the number of Medicaid recipients based on the state budget. This waiver is unprecedented because Medicaid is an entitlement for families with children and with incomes below the poverty line. The other waiver allows the state to mandate work requirements.

Supporters of HHS waivers claim that they improve health outcomes and work experience. Research has demonstrated that these Medicaid waivers have succeeded in raising insurance premiums, substantially reducing access to health care and worsening health conditions in waiver states.

## Court Challenges

States have continued to challenge the ACA in court. The latest challenge arose after the Trump administration terminated the individual mandate. This mandate was eliminated in the 2018 budget bill. Opponents of the ACA insist that the court refused to allow the mandate under the commerce clause. Instead it allowed the mandate under the federal government's taxing power. Opponents now argue that since the federal tax has been eliminated, the entire constitutional foundation for the Act has collapsed and the entire bill is unconstitutional. The Texas Attorney General initiated the suit. Several other state attorney generals joined the suit. The Federal District Court accepted the argument and ruled the ACA unconstitutional. The case was appealed all the way up to the Supreme Court.

The Trump administration ordered the Justice Department to urge the Supreme Court to invalidate the entire ACA, including the provision that protected people with preexisting conditions. In an astonishing 7 to 2 decision for a conservative court, the U.S. Supreme Court reversed the lower court decision and upheld the constitutionality of the ACA.

## SUMMARY

During his 2016 presidential campaign, Trump promised to replace the ACA with something better. During his 2020 reelection campaign, President Trump claimed that he had succeeded. In two tweets on June 27, 2020, he claimed that Obamacare was too expensive and that he was asking the Supreme Court to terminate it. Shortly afterward, he tweeted a pledge that he would always protect people with preexisting conditions and that Obamacare was too expensive:

> Now that the very expensive, unpopular and unfair Individual Mandate provision has been terminated by us, many States & the U.S. are asking the Supreme Court that Obamacare itself be terminated so that it can be replaced with a FAR BETTER AND MUCH LESS EXPENSIVE ALTERNATIVE . . . Obamacare is a joke! Deductible is far too high and the overall cost is ridiculous. My Administration has gone out of its way to manage OC much better than previous, but it is still no good. I will ALWAYS PROTECT PEOPLE WITH PRE-EXISTING CONDITIONS, ALWAYS, ALWAYS, ALWAYS!!! (Trump, @realDonaldTrump, June 27, 2020)

About five weeks before the election, he issued two executive orders: One stated that "it is the policy of the United States that people who suffer from pre-existing conditions will be protected." The other order directed the secretary of health and human services to work with Congress to address the issue of surprise out of network medical bills.

Secretary of Health and Human Services, Alex Azar, claimed that President Trump, "revolutionize(d) health care in the United States to deliver better care, more choice, and lower cost." He added that Trump had "done more in three-and-a-half years to help all 331 million Americans' health care than any president in modern history" (quoted by Creitz 2020).

Trump's promises and statements regarding his healthcare policy were reminiscent of his promises regarding Trump university, much hype and little substance. Abigail Abrams of *Time Magazine* provides this summary of

Trump's plan in an article titled, "Donald Trump's Much-Hyped Health Care Plan Isn't Much of a Plan at All":

> He told the often-cheering audience on Thursday that he was glad his Administration has been able to keep the ACA's protections for pre-existing conditions even as Republicans successfully eliminated other provisions, like the so-called individual mandate. "We were able to terminate the individual mandate, but kept the provision protecting patients with pre-existing conditions," Trump said.
>
> This statement likely made the Trump Administration's own Department of Justice (DOJ) lawyers squirm. In the current ACA case before the Supreme Court, DOJ lawyers are backing an argument that is at odds with the President's words—that the Justices must find the entire ACA no longer constitutional since the individual mandate is no longer in effect.
>
> And while Trump has often talked about protecting people with pre-existing conditions, his Administration has repeatedly taken actions that would have the opposite effect. The Administration has supported Congressional Republicans' many attempts to repeal the ACA, which would eliminate protections for those with pre-existing conditions, and it championed cheaper, skimpier health insurance plans that allowed insurers to deny coverage to those with pre-existing conditions. (Abrams 2020)

Abram's statement about cheaper, skimpier health insurance is in reference to Trump allowing associated healthcare insurance plans to compete within the insurance exchange. Associated insurance plans are not just skimpier, they are example from ACA regulations, including regulations that protect people with preexisting conditions, that prohibit gender discrimination and that require the essentials: preventive care, maternal care, and hospital care.

In the final analysis, contrary to President Trump, the ACA was not a total disaster. While it did not stop increases in premiums, it succeeded in reducing the number of Americans without healthcare insurance by the millions. Indeed as table 7.1 indicates, between 2010 and 2016, the number and percentage of Americans without healthcare insurance declined from 48.6 million or 16 percent to 28.6 million or 9.0 percent. This was a decline of 20 million Americans. This policy saved the lives of thousands of Americans.

Table 7.1 also indicates that between 2017 and 2019, the number and percentage of Americans without health insurance increased from 29.3 million or 9.1 percent to 33.2 million or 10.3 percent. Close to 4 million Americans lost healthcare insurance under the Trump administration.

Trump's position on health care was duplicitous and dishonest. While he promised not to disturb protections for people with preexisting conditions, he ordered his Justice Department to get the Supreme Court to eliminate this protection. While he promised to replace the ACA with something much better, he engaged in an all-out assault to destroy this policy with no concrete replacement plan. He amplified the voices from talk radio assailing this policy as a disaster, as this same policy saved the lives of thousands of American. Whereas it may be difficult to understand Trump's intentions, it is not difficult to see the pain and suffering caused by his assault on the ACA.

## Chapter 8

# Social Welfare, Education, and Tax Cuts

The public policy agenda of the Trump administration is consistent with the expectations of a right-wing reactionary policy agenda. Trump's labor policy reduced the bargaining power of workers, weakened health and safety protections in the work place, and undermined the ability of workers to organize unions. Trump's healthcare policy amounted to nothing more than a relentless campaign to repeal the Affordable Care Act. This chapter focuses on social welfare, social support, education, and tax policy changes. Like any conservative hostile to social welfare programs, Trump proposed significant cuts for most social programs with a couple of notable exceptions. In some cases, especially in the midst of a pandemic, his proposed cuts were particularly draconian. In almost every case, his cuts and cruelty were stopped either by Congress or the courts. Overall, rather than exhibiting any real concern for workers in the inner city of Detroit or farmers in Nebraska, he demonstrated a profound insensitivity for low-income working-class families.

### SOCIAL WELFARE

This chapter focuses on select social welfare programs—Supplemental Nutrition Assistance Program (SNAP), Temporary Assistance for Needy Families (TANF), child nutrition programs, energy assistance, legal assistance, K-12 education, higher education, and the tax cuts. A cursory review of all of these programs demonstrate a president committed to redistributing income and benefits upward from the needy to the wealthy, while boasting loudly and falsely about how much he has helped the working class and the downtrodden.

145

## SNAP

Most antipoverty programs fluctuate with the economy. That is, the need for the program increases during recessions and declines during recovery. This pattern was evident in the unemployment program, but not in the SNAP. Spending for unemployment peaked in 2011 at $116.6 billion, but declined sharply to $32.5 billion by 2015. However, spending in the SNAP program peaked in 2013 at $79.9 billion, but the decline was smaller and slower. It declined to only $70.9 billion by 2016. Although more people were working and unemployment had reached an all-time low by January 2020, the number of people receiving SNAP benefits remained high.

Research on the SNAP program indicates that stagnant wages and increases in the working poor explain the persistent need for this program (Hacker 2019; Dickerson 2019). Fraud, waste, and inefficiency in this program had declined substantially since the establishment of Electronic Benefit Transfer (EBT) cards (Dickerson 2019A). Nevertheless, the Trump administration dogged this program throughout his four years as president. He proposed substantial cuts in SNAP funding and benefits through legislative and budget bill proposals. When the legislative strategy failed, he pursued these cuts through administrative rule changes.

All of the proposals were designed to cut spending and benefits.

The standard arguments were that the budget cuts were necessary because of the multitrillion dollar deficit and because of the need to reduce waste, fraud, and inefficiencies in welfare programs. Of course, the deficit was produced by the multitrillion dollar tax cuts. Although this program was assaulted many ways, four proposed changes stand out: harvest box, elevated unemployment, broad base eligibility, categorical eligibility, and standard utility allowance.

In the harvest box proposal, the U.S. Department of Agriculture would take about 40 percent of the benefits designated for households, which amounted to about $20 or $30 billion. Half of this money would be used to create harvest boxes, which would consist of about $90 or more of nonperishable foods, such as powdered milk, powdered eggs, cereal, pasta, peanut butter, dried beans, and canned foods. The idea was that the harvest boxes would provide beneficiaries with cheaper but nutritious food. The other half of the money would be cut.

Critics claim that this proposal would not reduce fraud, waste, or inefficiency. It would expand the bureaucracy, increase costs, and generate unnecessary problems for recipients. The need to assemble and store the food and to create and distribute the boxes would require increased federal, state and local resources. With over 3,000 counties throughout the nation, this expansion alone would require enormous additional resources. Moreover, new administrative agencies would have to be created, dramatically increasing administrative costs. Accessing the boxes would be a problem for the many SNAP recipients, especially those without automobiles. If boxes are delivered directly to recipients, delivery costs would skyrocket.

Critics also noted that the harvest boxes would create problems for recipients with special dietary needs. It would pose a problem for those recipients with either allergies to peanut butter and beans or intolerance to gluten.

The harvest box would hurt local communities, as well as recipients. Not only would the box demean and stigmatize recipients, it would impact the local economies of high poverty areas. As local grocery stores in these areas depend on SNAP purchases, these stores would lose a substantial proportion of their business to the harvest boxes.

The Trump administration proposed to eliminate state work requirement waivers for able-body adults without children in elevated unemployment areas. SNAP regulations require able-bodied adults between the ages of 16 and 49 to register with a SNAP employment program and work 80 hours a month. In previous administrations, SNAP offered waivers for these work requirements to states with high unemployment areas. The waiver was based on the understanding that SNAP recipients in high unemployment areas would have more difficulty getting jobs. Initially, the Trump administration proposed to eliminate this waiver in the 2018 Farm Bill. However, when Congress deleted this waiver from the bill, the U.S. Department of Agriculture proposed terminating the waiver through an administrative rule change in 2019. This change was scheduled to take effect in April 2020. It was predicted to terminate the benefits of about 700,000 adults living in high unemployment areas (Rosenbaum 2020).

In another rule change, the administration proposed to eliminate the use of "broad based categorical eligibility." About forty states allowed people who qualified for welfare assistance to automatically received food assistance. Many of these states gradually reduced benefits as individuals acquired jobs and earned more money rather than abruptly terminating benefits. Families that qualified for TANF, automatically qualified for SNAP benefits. As with the elevated unemployment area waiver, the Trump administration initially proposed eliminating this rule in the 2018 Farm Bill. When Congress rejected the proposal, the administration made the change through the rule-making process. News reports claimed that this change would kick about 3.1 million people and 500,000 children off the food program and save several billions of dollars a year (Levintova 2019; Campbell 2019). In defense of the rule change, the U.S. secretary of agriculture stated:

> States are taking advantage of loopholes that allow millions of people to receive
> Supplemental Nutrition Assistance Program (SNAP) benefits, commonly

known as food stamps, who would otherwise not qualify . . . It is my job to
ensure the people who truly need food stamps receive what they're entitled
to—but the waste must stop. (quoted by Levintova 2019)

In still another rule change, the Trump administration proposed eliminating
the standard utility allowance program. This program allowed states to con-
sider high gas and electric bills in calculating eligibility for SNAP benefits.

These rule changes were scheduled to go into effect in the spring of 2020,
in the middle of the Covid-19 pandemic and at a time when unemployment
rates were rising and millions of working-class families were suffering a food
crisis. These were not the type of rule changes characteristic of an administration that cared about working-class American families. These were the rule
changes characteristic of a plutocratic administration, incredibly detached
from working-class families and devoid of the ability to understand their pain.
Considering these circumstances, the actions and rule changes of the Trump
administration were cruel. In response to these rule changes, a number of state
attorney generals, attorneys representing New York City and Washington,
D.C., and health officials join together in federal law suits to prevent the Trump
administration from moving forward with these rule changes. The federal judge
was stunned by the icy silence of the U.S. Department of Agriculture in providing a rational basis for the rule changes scheduled to take effect in the middle
of a rapidly expanding pandemic and an "exponentially increasing food insecurity" crisis. The court ordered the cessation of the rule changes.

## Child Nutrition Programs

Trump's budget proposals for child nutrition were mixed. It called for
increases for child nutrition programs, but decreases for the Women, Infants,
and Children (WIC) program. The administration proposed an increase of
$1 billion for the National School Lunch Program, $207.7 for the School
Breakfast Program, and $25.6 million for the Summer Food Service Program.
However, it proposed a $500 million budget cut for the WIC program.
Congress accepted the former and rejected the latter.

## TANF

The Temporary Assistance for Needy Families (TANF) emerged out of the
Aid for Families with Dependent Children (AFDC), established in 1935
as part of the New Deal. Conservatives opponents engaged in a relentless
assault on the AFDC program up until 1996, the year it was replaced by
TANF. These opponents evoked racial stereotypes and racialized images
of welfare queens, women having babies to get government money, and

intergenerational welfare dependency in their attack. Conservative think tanks like the American Enterprise Institute poured out hundreds of studies to provide pseudo-intellectual support for these stereotypes, much like the old fashioned scientific racism of about a hundred years ago. See my book, *Metaracism* for examples (Wilson 2015).

The transformation of the AFDC program into the TANF program was a profound change that hurt women and working-class families in many ways. AFDC was an entitlement program. It provided benefits to families whose income fell below the poverty line. When the number of families with children falling into poverty increased, the number of families receiving AFDC benefits increased. The AFDC program acted as a social safety net for impoverished families with children had shrunk. The AFDC program empowered women. With this program women were able to escape abusive relationships. The program gave women with pre-school-aged children the option to stay home and take care of their children. Most importantly, the AFDC program enhanced women's bargaining power as workers. It allowed women to avoid low-paying and super-exploitive jobs with abusive bosses.

The transformation of the AFDC program into the TANF program changed all of this.

TANF became a block grant. Benefits were no longer an entitlement. They became a special privilege, available only to a few. The social safety net for impoverished families with children disappeared. These families could get food, but not money. In some states in the Deep South, like Alabama, Georgia, Mississippi, and North Carolina, less than 10 percent of poor women with children receive TANF benefits. In Arkansas, Louisiana, and Texas, less than 5 percent receive these benefits (Floyd 2018). The change from AFDC to TANF obliterated the bargaining power of low-skilled women with children. TANF forced millions of low-skilled women into the labor market to compete with other low-skilled women already in the market, trapped in low-paying dead end jobs. This change contributed to stagnant wages. It shifted both power and income from low-skilled workers to their employers. It allowed for greater exploitation of low-skilled women workers (Collins and Mayer 2010; Soss et al. 2011).

The TANF program devoted more resources to monitoring women, than supporting work. It did not count participating in a GED or high-school completion program as work related for women over 20 years old. It only allowed one year of participation in a vocational training program (Davetti 2012). It was more about providing disciplined labor for a low-wage labor force than it was about assisting poor women with children.

Although the real value of TANF payments to families had declined by about 40 percent since the program was established, the Trump administration proposed substantial cuts to this program. These cuts appeared in

Trump's budget proposals every year of his administration. Nevertheless, every budget year, Congress routinely rejected Trump's TANF budget cuts and restored funding. Congress even marginally increased funding for TANF.

Trump's proposed 2021 TANF budget proposal requested a cut from the main TANF program of about $1.6 billion, which amounts to a total reduction of funding of over 10 percent. The Trump administration proposed to terminate the TANF contingency fund, which amounts to a $608 million cut. This fund provided money for job-related costs such as transportation, child care, uniforms, or training. The proposal called for the creation of a new demonstration program, "Promoting Opportunity and Economic Mobility Demonstrations." It is not clear exactly what the new demonstration grants would be for. It may re-establish funding to assist businesses by subsidizing low-income jobs. This subsidy was eliminated by the Obama administration. It appears that Trump had been proposing substantial cuts in direct benefits to families, while shifting a small amount of funds to subsidize businesses (U.S. Department of Health and Human Services 2020).

## SOCIAL SUPPORT

### Energy Assistance and Legal Aid

Trump budget requests targeted more programs for elimination than Reagan's budget requests. The proposed termination of both the Low Income Home Energy Assistance Program (LIHEAP) and the Legal Service Corporation are particularly disturbing. The LIHEAP program provides low-income families, particularly the elderly, assistance for their heating bills during winter months. The administration claimed that it was proposing the elimination of this program because some states have regulations that prohibit terminating heat during the winter and other states provide assistance similar to this federal program. Despite Trump's effort to terminate this program, it survived with bi-partisan support.

The Legal Service Corporation (LSC) provides free legal services for residents of high poverty areas. Many of the cases handled by a LSC involve evictions and landlord tenant disputes. Some involve more costly class action suits against corporations and governments. The administration claimed that it was requesting the complete elimination of the LSC program because of improper spending and fraud. It cited a case in which a local LSC used money for table decorations and refreshments to attract local attorneys, an attorney who overbilled for travel expenses, and a program director who was over paid. It is not clear whether these infractions were serious enough to request repayments from the malefactors. It is clear that they are inadequate reasons for terminating the entire program. Despite all of Trump's efforts to terminate the LSC, this program enjoyed bi-partisan support in Congress.

## Housing

The U.S. Department of Housing and Urban Development posted a news release announcing the construction of its 2021 budget. The news release claimed that the budget proposal offered "a $47.9 billion plan that expands resources to prevent/end homelessness, invest record funding to reduce lead and other home health and safety hazards; and preserves rental assistance to HUD-assisted households" (U.S. Department of HUD 2020).

The 2021 HUD budget proposal requested five dramatic changes. First, the budget requests call for the complete termination of funding for the Community Development Block Grant (CDBG) and the Public Housing Capital Fund. The elimination of the CDBG would have had disastrous effects on urban areas across the country, as many had come to depend on the over $3 billion of federal assistance. The loss of about $2.9 billion for the Public Housing Capital Fund would accelerate the deterioration of existing public housing projects, as this fund contributed to the upkeep of viable projects and the demolition of uninhabitable housing. Second, to the administration's credit, this proposal called for increases in support for housing the elderly and disabled. The funding request for the elderly amounted to an increase of about 7.6 percent. For the disabled, it was about 25 percent. Third, the administration continued support for reducing lead poisoning. Although the proposals called for increased spending for some programs and decreased spending for other programs, the net change was a significant increase in spending for programs to reduce address lead poisoning. Fourth, contrary to the public statements, the budget request called for substantial cuts to housing programs designed to reduce homelessness. The Trump administration proposed cutting the Tenant-based Rental Assistance from about $24 billion to about $19 billion, a proposed cut of over 20 percent. This is HUD's largest rental assistance program. It largely constitutes the Section 8 voucher program. These cuts would not reduce homelessness. On the contrary, these cuts would increase homelessness. Finally, the budget proposal established a new program, the Move to Work program, to be funded at about $5 million. A more detailed description of this budget request states:

> The Budget incorporates the proposed reforms, which promote work, simplify program administration, reduce federal costs, and increase local choice. The reforms include increased tenant rent contributions, particularly for those able to work; reduced frequency of income recertifications; and additional flexibilities

for PHAs and property owners to develop alternative rent structures. In addition, the Budget proposes uniform work requirements for work-able households. Consistent with Administration policy, the

requirement would allow for work seeking activities and would exempt the elderly, the disabled, those caring for a disabled family member of small child, and pregnant women. (HUD 2020)

It appears that the new Moving to Work program, slated for $5 million, is not a program that provides benefits for the homeless, but a program to administer work requirements for those seeking assistance.

## K-12 EDUCATION

The Trump administration's K-12 education policy agenda focused primarily on school choice, increasing funding for charter schools and private and parochial school vouchers. In 2018, the administration proposed $500 million for a new Opportunity Grant. This grant would provide scholarships for low-income families to transfer their school-aged children from public schools to private or parochial schools. The administration also proposed to increase federal grants for charter schools from $339.8 million to $500 million (U.S. Department of Education 2020).

In 2019, the Trump administration continued to promote school choice with the Education Freedom Scholarship bill. This bill proposed a tax credit for scholarship donations to private schools. The administration continued to support this bill in 2020.

In 2020, the administration introduced a radical proposal to collapse K-12 grants, including the Elementary and Secondary Education Title I program into a single program, the Elementary and Secondary Education for the Disadvantaged Block Grant. The administration requested a 20 percent reduction in the funding for these programs. The rational given for the consolidation was to give state and local governments more flexibility over these programs. The administration claimed that state and local governments understand their needs better than the federal government. The title of this new grant, the rationale for the consolidation of the old grants, and the extent of the proposed cuts demonstrate a lack of understanding of the purpose of these federal education programs (Department of Education 2020).

The title of the new block grant, the Elementary and Secondary Education for the Disadvantaged Block Grant, is misleading. Few of the competitive grants are for disadvantaged students: Academic Enhancement, Teacher Leader Incentive, Arts in Education, School Safety, and Magnet Schools.

Not listed are the American History and Civics Education, Supporting Effective Educator Development (SEED), and Javits Gifted and Talented Education (U.S. Department of Education 2020). The American History and Civics Education program provides grants to universities to offer intensive workshops for high-school teachers. The SEED program is also designed to enhance teacher training. The Javits grant provides money for schools to develop innovative programs to enhance the education of gifted and talented students.

The rationale for the consolidation—that it would give local agencies more flexibility over the program—illustrates a profound lack of understanding of why the ESEA Title I program was initially centralized. Historically, Title I was a Great Society antipoverty, compensatory educational program. It was designed to compensate for disadvantages and to help promote the upward social mobility of disadvantaged children from impoverished families. Initially, it was a total failure. Conservative opponents claimed it wasted money and should be terminated. Research demonstrated that it failed precisely because the federal government gave local agencies more control and flexibility over the program, assuming that the local agency understood local problems better than the federal government. Instead, local agencies took advantage of the extra money. Some reduced local taxes. None put forth any effort to create programs to assist disadvantaged children. Rather than terminate the program, liberal members of Congress added an amendment to the law requiring local agencies to use the money for a specific purpose: to create programs to target disadvantaged children and provide them with additional instructions in math and reading. When these programs complied with centralized federal regulations and goals, they were effective in increasing the math and reading skills of disadvantaged participants (Mazmanian and Sabatier 1989). Consolidating these programs and giving local agencies more flexibility completely undermines federal compensatory educational goals and erases all efforts to use the program to target disadvantaged children. Whether President Trump was aware of the consequences of these proposals or not, they constituted a direct assault on compensatory educational programs.

The proposed 20 percent funding cut to ESEA Title I and the 29 grants was also an attack on federal programs designed to enhance public education and to expand opportunities for students in high poverty areas. These changes would have not only impacted urban areas. They would have impacted rural areas as well. Indeed, one of the programs proposed to be consolidated into the block grant was the Rural Education Achievement Program. This grant provided additional moneys for school in low density and high poverty rural areas. Fortunately, Congress did not approve of these extreme proposals.

However, these proposals make it clear that Trump was part of the ongoing assault on equal opportunity program.

## Higher Education

Just as the Trump administration assaulted K-12 programs, it launched multiple attacks on higher education programs. These attacks took several forms: cuts to the TRIO program, cuts to the Pell Contingency grant, weakening loan forgiveness, and deregulation of for-profit schools. Overall funding was cut about 12.8 percent. These two changes diminish these programs (Department of Education 2020). The TRIO program included Upward Bound, GEAR UP, and Talent Search and Student Support Services. These programs had a reputation for targeting low-income, first generation precollege and college students and assisting them in preparing for and succeeding in college. In Trump's first year of office, his administration targeted this program for a ten percent budget cut (Douglas-Gabriel 2017).

The Trump administration proposed a slight increase in funding for the Pell Grant, from about $29.6 billion to about $30.3, an increase of about $700 million. However, this increase is accompanied by the complete elimination of the Federal Supplemental Education Opportunity Grant, or a cut of about $1.2 billion. The explanation provided is that this grant, which is available to Pell Grant recipients, duplicates the Pell Grant. The administration also proposed to cut the Federal Work-Study program in half, decreasing it from $1.2 billion to about $500 million. The administration requested a slight increase in the Federal Direct Loans and the Teach Grants. The overall results would have been fewer resources for low-income college students (Department of Education 2020).

The Trump administration, under Secretary Betsy DeVos, has strongly opposed student loan forgiveness programs. This opposition precipitated a number of law suits, particularly those regarding the "borrower defense" rule. According to this rule, which originated in the Obama administration, students may have their student loans forgiven if they are able to demonstrate that the school or college used illegal or deceptive practices to encourage them to take out the loans. One case initiated by consumer advocate groups involved the for-profit Corinthian College, which closed down. A federal judge ordered DeVos to honor the rule and to cease all collection activities on student loans associated with the college. DeVos ignored the order. The federal government continued the collections, garnishing wages and repossessing income tax returns. The judge threatened to jail the secretary before she relented (Minsky 2019). Another case involved DeVos reluctance to honor the Public Service Loan Forgiveness program. Between May 2018 and May 2019, out of 54,000 applications for forgiveness, the department had only approved 661, which amounted to only 1.2 percent (Derysh 2019). The 2021 Department of Education budget request proposed eliminating the Public Service Loan Forgiveness program entirely.

## TAX CUTS AND JOBS ACT OF 2017

The Trump administration's response to poverty and social welfare is to grow the economy, to generate jobs, and to move people from welfare and dependency on government into the workforce. This perspective insists that more government spending on welfare is the problem, not the solution and that the most effective way to grow the economy is through tax breaks. Thus, the center piece of Trump's approach to improving the conditions of low-income Americans is the Tax Cuts and Jobs Act of 2017. This massive piece of legislation radically changed the U.S. tax code. It cut the taxes of individuals and families; it reduced the estate tax; it repealed the health insurance mandate; it established a 20 percent deduction for pass-through business income; it incentivized corporations moving jobs and capital back to the United States; and it cut corporate taxes.

Supporters of this act highlight three major features of this tax bill: an across the board income tax cut for all Americans, a reduction of corporate and business taxes, and the establishment of tax incentives to move jobs and investments back to the United States. These provisions of tax bill were calculated to produce millions of new jobs and raise the wages of American workers by $4,000. In promoting this bill, the Council of Economic Advisers issued this statement:

> Reducing the statutory federal corporate tax rate from 35 to 20 percent would, the analysis below suggests, increase average household income in the United States by, very conservatively, $4,000 annually. The increases recur each year, and the estimated total value of corporate tax reform for the average U.S. household is therefore substantially higher than $4,000. (Council of Economic Advisers 2017)

The council argued that substantial bonuses from corporate tax breaks, especially from the reduction of taxes on overseas profits, would be passed down to workers. The report estimated that workers would get about 30 percent of the profits repatriated from abroad as a result of this tax break. In another report, the CEA estimated that wages would increase by up to $9,000. Trump added to the council's promotion of the tax cut, "It is the biggest tax cut and reform in American history. And at the heart of our plan is tremendous relief for working families and for small businesses" (Trump 2017). After the passage of the bill, the president claimed, "Everywhere we look, we are seeing the effects of the American miracle" (Trump 2017).

This tax bill and the arguments supporting it suffered from several serious flaws: the individual and family tax cuts were modest and regressive; the tax bill failed to produce the surge in income and productivity; and the corporate tax cuts were excessive and regressive.

The Congressional Research Service studied the actual impacts of these tax cuts on wages. This study examined wage growth from 2013 through 2018, with a focus on 2018, the year just after the tax cuts. It found no evidence of any surge in wages. The study concluded:

> Wages, assuming full-time work, increased by $1,248 annually, but this number must account for inflation and growth that would otherwise have occurred regardless of the tax change. The nominal growth rate in wages was 3.2%, but adjusting for the GDP price deflator, real wages increased by 1.2%. This growth is smaller than overall growth in labor compensation and indicates that ordinary workers had very little growth in wage rates. (CRS 2019, 11)

The tax cuts did not produce the boost in wages that supporters claimed.

Assessments of the redistributive impact of the Tax Cut and Jobs Act of 2017 were mixed. Eric Toder of the Tax Policy Center claimed that although the initial impact might be regressive, the long-term impact would be more progressive (Toder 2018). However, Sammartino, Stallworth, and Weiner of the same center claimed that tax payers from the bottom quintile would receive the lowest percentage cut on income taxes than any other income groups:

> Taxpayers in the bottom income-quintile (those with income less than $25,000) will see an average tax cut of $40 or 0.3 percent of after-tax income. Taxpayers in the middle-quintile (those with income between about $49,000 and $86,000) will receive an average tax cut of about $800, or 1.4 percent of after-tax income. Taxpayers in the 95th to 99th income percentiles (those with income between about $308,000 to $733,000) will benefit the most as a share of after tax income, with an average tax cut of about $11,000 or 3.4 percent after tax income. (Sammartino et al. 2018)

According to their analysis, the bottom quintile received the lowest percentage tax cut and the highest quintile received the largest percentage tax cut.

Some provisions of income tax reductions are scheduled to expire in 2025 and others in 2027, while most corporate tax cuts are permanent. The Tax Policy Center examined and predicted changes in tax laws after temporary provisions expired in 2025 and concluded that there would be modest increases in taxes across the five quintiles and after 2027 changes, and the bottom two quintiles will lose money.

The Congressional Research Service also concluded that the tax cuts did not produce a surge in GDP or investment. GDP growth and capital investment in 2018 were modest.

The Institute on Taxation and Economics (ITE) produced a study on the impacts of the TCJA on corporate taxes, "Corporate Tax Avoidance in the

First Year of the Trump Tax Law" (Gardner et al. 2019). The study distinguished between the statutory corporate tax rate, the rate stated in law, and the average effective tax rate, the actual average rate paid by corporations. The study concluded that this change in corporate tax law was historic, radical, and excessive. Placing the change in historical context, the study noted that Reagan had enacted radical cuts in corporate taxes in his 1981 tax bill. However, when the effective corporate rate dropped to 14.1 percent, he raised the statutory rate in his 1986 tax bill and closed some of the corporate tax loop holes. The statutory tax rate changed from 46 percent to 34 percent. The effective rate was 26.5 percent. Changes in corporate tax law in the 1990s lowered the effective rate to 21.7 percent. Under the George W. Bush tax cuts, the average effective rate dropped down to 17.2 percent. By 2015, the effective rate had increased to 21.2 percent (Gardner et al. 2019).

The Tax Cut and Jobs Act reduced the statutory rate from 35 percent to 21 percent. The effective rate had dropped to an historic low average of 11.3 percent. However, the effective rate varied widely among industries and within industries. The ITE studied 379 corporations. Among these corporations, the effective tax rate ranged from a low of a negative 0.6 percent to a high of 22 percent. Out of the 379 companies, 91 companies paid a rate of zero or less, with an average effective rate of a negative 5.9 percent (Gardner et al. 2019). A negative tax rate means the corporation paid no taxes and received a refund or subsidy from the federal government. The study added:

- Half of the total tax-subsidy dollars in 2018–37.1 billion—went to just 25 companies, each with more than $650 million in tax subsidies in 2018.
- Bank of America topped the list of corporate tax-subsidy recipients with more than $5.5 billion in tax subsidies in 2018.
- Other top tax subsidy recipients included J.P. Morgan Chase ($3.7 billion), Wells Fargo ($3.2 billion), Amazon ($2.4 billion), and Verizon ($1.7 billion) (Gardner et al. 2019).

The effective tax rate varied widely between corporate sectors and within corporate sectors. The oil, gas and pipeline, utilities, motor vehicles, and industrial machinery sectors enjoyed the lowest effective tax rate. The rates of utility companies averaged around 0.5, and oil, gas, and pipeline corporation rates averaged around 3.6. Internet service, pharmaceutical, and medical supply companies paid an effective rate closer to the statutory rate of 21 percent. The effective rate varied within the same sectors:

For example, effective tax rates on food and beverage companies ranged from negative 1.7 percent for Molson Coors up to 28 percent for J.M. Smucker. Among aerospace and defense companies, effective tax rates ranged from a low of negative 5.5 percent for Rockwell Collins to a high of 25 percent for Spirit Aerosystems. Pharmaceutical giant Eli Lilly paid negative 9 percent, while its competitor Biogen Idec paid 30 percent, well above the statutory rate. (Gardner et al. 2019)

Corporations had been effective in using the accelerated depreciation and the investment deductions to qualify for negative tax rates or subsidies. The bottom line is that this tax bill was historic, radical, and excessive. It did more than lower taxes on corporations. It enabled corporations to extract billions of dollars of subsidies from the federal government. The tax bill also reduced the tax rate on the top quintile by a factor of seven times the tax break for the lowest quintile. That is, in addition to providing massive tax cuts for corporations, the tax cuts for families and individuals amounted to a massive shift of income from the working class to the wealth class.

## SUMMARY

Collectively, the social programs targeted for cuts by Trump's 2021 budget requests historically served four primary functions. First, many of these programs functioned to improve the quality of the lives of members of the lowest income groups. They helped those hurt most by downturns in the economy. They mitigated the harshest effects of poverty. Second, these programs provided some assistance to enable upward social mobility. Programs that ameliorated the more severe effects of poverty enabled individuals to work to improve their condition. Grants for low-income students to assist in preparation for college and to assist in the costs of college enabled upward social mobility. Third, collectively these programs contributed to a downward redistribution of resources and income. They slowed down the growth of inequality. Whereas the Tax Cut and Jobs Act has been promoted as relief for America's working-class families; the combination of cuts in social programs and the Tax Cuts and Jobs Act could only have the effect of shifting wealth and income from the lower classes to the upper classes.

Supporters of the tax breaks insisted that these cuts expanded the economy and enriched both America's workers and minorities. President Trump provided a powerful and convincing voice for this rhetoric, especially when he claimed that "at the heart of our plan is tremendous relief for working families and small businesses" (Trump 2017). Many Americans believed the president. However, they missed three important factors contradicting this rhetoric. First, the tax cuts were regressive, giving richer individuals and corporate America a larger percentage cut than poorer Americans. Second, the president's tariff war undermined many of the broad benefits of the tax cuts (The Editors of the Economist 2020). Third, the president engaged in an all-out assault on public policies designed to ameliorate the severity of poverty and to enhance the opportunities for the upward social mobility of those in the bottom-income quintiles.

# Chapter 9

# Voter Suppression

This chapter examines the twenty-first-century voter suppression movement prior to the Trump administration and the role of Trump in accelerating and intensifying this movement into a full-fledged reactionary movement and assault on democracy. Voter suppression refers to methods used by government to prevent or discourage voting-aged citizens from voting.

Despite all of his boasting about returning power back to the people and making life better for African Americans, Trump accelerated the voter suppression movement that negatively impacted black voters. From the beginning to the end of his administration, and even after he was defeated in the 2020 election, Trump persistently promoted the big lie that elections are rigged and that millions of people vote illegally. In the first year of his administration, Trump created the voter fraud commission and selected to co-chair this commission of political leaders with a reputation for minority vote suppression. During the 2020 presidential election, Trump attempted to undermined mail-in voting by calling it a magnet for fraud. He appointed a Postmaster General and CEO of the U.S. Postal Service who was committed to rolling back postal services in ways bound to slow down and obstruct the delivery of the mail during the 2020 presidential election. Trump advocated decertifying ballots delivered late to election boards.

Trump engaged in a well-organized voter suppression campaign, claiming massive voter fraud and multiple conspiracies to steal the election from him. This campaign precipitated an attack on American democracy and a direct assault on the U.S. Capitol. It also intensified the voter suppression movement after the 2020 election. This movement incited Republican leaders in more than forty states to either propose or enact new laws making it more difficult for voting-aged citizens to vote.

Trump did not start the voter suppression movement. This movement began before Trump ran for president. Just as the Southern Democratic Party as part of the Redeemer movement of the late nineteenth and early twentieth century developed techniques and mechanism to suppress the vote of African American and poor white voters, the Republican Party initiated the twenty-first century voter suppression movement. The current Republican party is following the same playbook as the white nationalist Southern Democratic Party of the early twentieth century. Both would claim they were not violating the 15th amendment, although both targeted black voters. In the first decade of the twenty-first century, the Republican Party engaged in irregular practices calculated to suppress the vote. After the 2020 election, Republicans used the claim of irregular voting practices to justify enacting stricter voter suppression laws.

## EARLY TWENTY-FIRST-CENTURY MINORITY VOTE SUPPRESSION TECHNIQUES

The twenty-first-century voter suppression movement began with the 2000 presidential election in Florida. In a report entitled "Voter Irregularities in Florida," the U.S. Civil Rights Commission documented several techniques used by Florida officials that reduced the minority vote. These techniques included spoiled ballots, false positive purges, felony disenfranchisement, police checkpoints, discrimination in the allocation of voting machines, and early closings of polling venues (U.S. Civil Rights Commission 2001). Whereas the media suggested that spoiled ballots were the fault of voters, the commission determined that in most cases of so-called dimpled chads, the voter's choice was clearly indicated by the punched indentation. Whereas the Florida Supreme Court had ruled that the state should count all votes in which the voter's choice was clear, these votes were thrown out and never counted. The commission identified a pattern of racial bias in the rejected ballots: "black voters were nearly 10 times more likely than non-black voters to have their ballots rejected" (U.S. Civil Rights Commission 2001). The State of Florida had contracted with Database Technologies to scrub the voter rolls; that is, to remove the names of people who had felony convictions, who had died, or moved out of the state. Database Technologies created a master list of the names of people with felony convictions in Florida and several nearby states. The company matched names on the master list with names on the state-voter registration list. Often one name on the master list matched several names on the state voter registration list. Even though only one person had a felony conviction, all of the names on the state's list were deleted, guaranteeing that thousands of legitimately registered voters would be purged from the state's list and denied the right to vote, without a hearing, without a right to an appeal, and without the opportunity to vote with a provisional ballot. A disproportionate number of those purged were African Americans: "For instance, in the state's largest county, Miami-Dade, more than 65 percent of the names on the purge list were African American, who represented only 20.4 percent of the population" (Commission 2001). The commission reported other problems. The state police had set up police checkpoints in major streets leading to voting polls in predominantly black areas.

In 2002, Congress responded to the Florida crisis with the Help America Vote Act (HAVA). This act required states to provide provisional ballots for voters who could not vote on election-day because of a problem with the registration roll, inadequate identification, or any other problem. This act also mandated that states require first-time voters registering by mail to show an identification card or a copy of a current utility bill, bank statement, paycheck, government check, or any document showing the name and address of the voter. It allowed for the scrubbing or purging of voter registration rolls, but provided guidelines to ensure fairness.

Over the next decade-and-a-half, a pattern emerged. The new tools of voter suppression now include felony conviction, purges, voter identification, reduced poll access, and signature matches.

## Felon Disenfranchisement

Although felony disenfranchisement laws are a relic of both the era of slavery and the Redeemer period (Manza and Uggen 2008), these laws are part of the contemporary suppression movement. Many of these laws were originally passed between 1830 and 1861. However, these laws became more restrictive during the post-Reconstruction period as about "19 states adopted or amended laws restricting the voting rights of criminal offenders" (Manza and Uggen 2008, 55). Indeed, the more expansive and onerous felon disenfranchisement laws were enacted around the same time states were enacting poll tax, literacy test, character test, and grandfather clause laws. These laws were motivated by a bias against blacks and were designed to circumvent the 15th amendment.

The number of people who lost the right to vote because of these laws declined during the civil rights era, dropping from 1.8 million in 1960 to 1.2 million by 1976 (Ugger et al. 2020). However, this number increased dramatically throughout the 1980s, 1990s, and the 2000s. This increase was not the result of new laws, but the unintended consequences of more draconian criminal justice laws that produced a dramatic increase in the incarceration rate. By the twenty-first century, seven states stood out for having both the most severe laws and the highest percentage of minority citizens disenfranchised. These states include Alabama, Florida, Kentucky, Mississippi, Tennessee, Virginia, and Wyoming. Whereas most states take away the right to vote from citizens who are in jail or prison these states either permanently disenfranchise convicted felons or require the payment of all fines and costs before restoring the right to vote, which amounts to permanent disenfranchisement for most.

Florida has fluctuated between more and less restrictive felony disenfranchising policies, as a moderate Republican governor supported democracy, while a more conservative Republican promoted strict felon disenfranchisement rules. In 2007, Florida's Clemency Board, chaired by the former governor and moderate Republican, Charlie Crist, passed a resolution to restore the right to vote to non-violent felons. In 2011, conservative Republican Floridian governor, Rick Scott, chaired the board and reversed the 2007 decision. In 2018, as a result of a bi-partisan initiative election, Florida voters approved a proposal to restore voting rights to convicted felons. However, in 2020, the Florida state legislature passed a law requiring convicted felons to pay all fines and debts before regaining the right to vote. This law was supported by the conservative Republican governor and strong Trump supporter, Ron DeSantis.

The research on felony disenfranchisement laws suggest that they have a direct impact on convicted felons, but little overall effect on voter turnout rates. Because of the strong association between poverty and felony conviction, voter turnout among the population of convicted felons tend to be low. This assumption is consistent with the literature on voting rates and convicted felons (Klumpp et al. 2017; Miles 2004).

## Purging

Purging is an old practice. States and counties purge or scrub their voter registration rolls primarily to eliminate the names of voters who have died, changed residency, or stopped voting, because they were incarcerated or mentally incapacitated. The National Voter Registration Act of 1993 provides guidelines for purges. It allows purging. However, it required voters who change their addresses within the same precinct to remain on the rolls and it recommends the use of the Postal Service's National Change of Address registry, which is less expansive than other processes. The common explanation for the purges is that they are routine ways to maintain accurate voter registration lists, to prevent voter fraud, and to secure the integrity of elections.

Since the 2000 Florida case, more states and counties have abused the purging process.

The purging process is abused when it is unnecessarily expansive, produces an excessively high error rate, and intentionally targets urban areas with substantial minority populations. The Florida purge was abusive because officials deliberately used an unnecessarily expansive process calculated to purge a substantial percentage of people who were legitimately registered to vote. Normal purges have low exclusion rates. Abusive purges have both high exclusion rates and high percentages of legitimately registered voters deleted from the registration rolls. When abusive purges disenfranchise large percentages of minority voters, they constitute minority voter suppression. In 2008, for example, the purge rate for Salt Lake County, Utah, was 0.1 percent. In contrast, the purge rate for Milwaukee County, Wisconsin, was 34 percent (Brater et al. 2020, 4). Milwaukee is the home of 240,000 African Americans, 69.7 percent of the State of Wisconsin's black population (Census 2018).

Purging has increasingly involved the Republican Party targeting minority communities. Investigative journalist Gregg Palast documented a case in Detroit, Michigan, involving the Michigan Republican Party. Just before the 2008 election, a law firm that handled mass foreclosures, Trott Brothers Law Firm, turned over its foreclosure address list to the Michigan Republican Party. The party used the list either to challenge voters or to have their names purged from the rolls for not filing the change of address (Palast 2012, 270).

After the 2012 election, purging intensified. Kris Kobach, Kansas's secretary of state, played a major role in promoting these purges. He helped develop the Interstate Voter Registration Crosscheck System, a system far more expansive and error-prone than the Postal Service's National Change of Address registry. This system matched the names of registered voters with the same name within a state and among the states in order to detect voters registered more than once. Kobach claimed that this system has identified millions of voters registered in more than one state and engaged in double or triple voting. Kobach has supported President Trump's claim that millions of people have voted illegally.

Greg Palast argued that Kris Kobach's claims of voter fraud are used to justify a scheme to target and disenfranchise minority voters. Palast maintained that Crosscheck targets names that have a high probability of flagging and purging people of color. For example, the system targets names like Garcia, 95 percent of whom are Hispanic American; Nguyen, 99 percent of whom are Asian American; and Williams, over half of which are African American. Palast demonstrated several false positives by interviewing several people whose names had been purged by Crosscheck. He found that there are about 30,000 people in the United States named James Brown. Thousands of these names are on the Crosscheck list of double voters who are slated to be purged. He located and interviewed several of them and found that they all are false positives and the system did not check birthdates, social security numbers, middle names, juniors, seniors, or any other indicator that would have caught the mistakes as false positives. Palast concluded that Kobach's system was designed to suppress minority votes.

In 2019, several states like Georgia, Ohio, and Wisconsin deleted over 200,000 names each from their voter registration rolls. Georgia deleted 313,243. According to a Palast Investigative Fund report, 198,000 of the names were deleted in error. In other words, they were legitimately registered to vote. There was no legitimate reason for them to have been removed. Although the secretary of state for Georgia claimed that the state had used the Postal Service's National Change of Address registry, 75 percent of the names were not on the Postal list (Palast 2020).

Purges are becoming a standard method used to suppress voters. The Republican Party has become more aggressive in promoting purges. In December 2019, the Republican Party of Wisconsin sued the Democratic governor for not purging names before the 2020 election. The suit forced the purging of 234,000 names. The state sent out letters to verify addresses and registrations. Some of the letters were returned undeliverable, for others there were no responses. The state had decided to wait until after the 2020 election before enforcing the purge. In December 2019, a local judge ordered the purge. A *U.S. Today* article pointed out that a disproportionate number of the purges were concentrated in Milwaukee and Madison, the state's stronghold for the Democratic Party. These two cities constituted 14 percent of the state's populations, but about 23 percent of the purges (Marley and Vielmetti 2019). Democratic governor Tony Evers stated, "I won the race for governor by less than 30,000 votes. This move pushed by Republicans to remove 200,000 Wisconsinites from the voter rolls is just another attempt at overriding the will of the people and stifling the democratic process" (quoted by Marley and Vielmetti 2019).

## Voter ID

Laws requiring identification before voting increased dramatically after the 2008 presidential election. These laws vary in strictness in terms of the difficulty of getting an identification card and the range and variety of cards allowed. Initially, many states did not require identification to vote and those that did allowed most forms of identification such as a utility bill, a check book, or a pay stub. The requirement of strict state photo identification cards was part of the voter suppression movement because most states required a birth certificate. Older African Americans born in the south during the Jim Crow era had more difficulties obtaining a birth certificate. For many, the costs were prohibited. Moreover, the distribution of state photo IDs is racially biased. For example, 19 percent of Native Americans in North Dakota do not have state IDs. Nation-wide, about 25 percent of voting-aged African Americans U.S. citizens do not have the qualifying state photo IDs (Johnson and Feldman 2020).

Some states were discriminatory in the types of ID they would or would not accept. For example, Texas' ID law allowed the use of a permit to carry a concealed weapon ID card, but not a college ID card. As most concealed carry IDs were held by white males who were more likely to vote Republican and college IDs were more likely held by young people and minorities who were more likely to vote Democrat, the partisan and racial biases of the IDs seemed obvious. More than 80 percent of handgun licenses issued in Texas in 2018 went to whites (Johnson and Feldman 2020).

A number of journalists tied the rise of this movement to a number of different organizations with the American Legislative Exchange Council playing a central role in generating, disseminating, and promoting model legislation. Most of the new tools for voter suppression came from the ALEC committee, the Public Safety and Elections Task Force. In an article for the *Nation*, John Nichols provided some insight into the public relations strategy and the motives for the movement. In terms of public relations, the rational for voter suppression laws would be voter fraud, although voter fraud is largely a myth:

> Republicans have argued for years that "voter fraud" (rather than unpopular policies) costs the party election victories. A key member of the Corporate Executive Committee for ALEC's Public Safety and Elections Task Force is Sean Parnell, president of the Center for Competitive Politics, which began highlighting voter ID efforts in 2006, shortly after Karl Rove encouraged conservatives to take up voter fraud as an issue. Kansas Republican Kris Kobach, who along with ALEC itself helped draft Arizona's anti-immigration law, has warned of "illegally registered aliens." ALEC's magazine, Inside ALEC, featured a cover story titled "Preventing Election Fraud" following Obama's election. Shortly afterwards in the summer of 2009, the Public Safety and Elections Task Force adopted voter ID model legislation. And when midterm elections put Republicans in charge of both chambers of the legislature in twenty-six states (up from fifteen, GOP legislators began moving bills resembling ALEC's model. (Nichols 2011)

In regards to motive, the corporate-dominated organizations had been committed to making voting more difficult for working-class voters because these voters tend to support raising the minimum wage and workers' rights. Nichols added, "Horrified by the success of living-wage referendums and other projects that allowed voters to enact protections for workers and regulations for businesses, ALEC's corporate sponsors have pushed to toughen the rules for voter initiatives."

The literature on the effects of voter ID laws is mixed. A number of studies indicate that these laws do not suppress the minority vote (Hood and Bullock 2012; Muhlhausen and Sikich 2007; Vercellotti 2006; Vercellotti and Anderson 2006; Lott 2006; Jones et al. 2017). Vercellotti and Anderson use Census Bureau Current Population Survey data on the 2004 presidential election to develop a complex, multi-variate regression model to assess the impacts of voter identification laws on voter turnout rates. They apply statistical analyses to aggregate data at several levels: state, county, and individual. Their analysis of the data indicates that these laws had no effect on minority voter turnout. However, they did have some impact on low-income voters (Vercellotti 2006; Vercellotti and Anderson 2006).

Muhlhausen and Sikich re-evaluate Vercellotti and Anderson's data. They identify several problems. They claim that Vercellotti and Anderson apply a one-tail test for statistical significance when they should have used a two-tail test and that they had placed two states, Illinois and Arizona, in the wrong category. They conclude, "Controlling for factors that influence voter turnout, voter ID laws largely do not have the negative impacts on voter turnout that the Eagleton Institute suggest" (Muhlausen and Skich 2007).

Hood and Bullock examine the effect of Georgia's 2005 photo ID law on the 2008 election. They note that civil rights groups challenged the law, demonstrating the 289,622 registered voters in Georgia did not have a valid driver's license. After the state complied with the Crawford decision and allowed qualifying voters to attain free state photo ID cards, a federal court approved the law.

As Georgia was one of the few states with data on the race of registered voters, Hood and Bullock used actual voting data rather than Census Bureau Current Population Survey data. They used data from both the 2004 and the 2008 elections. They developed a complex multi-variate model to test whether the ID law suppressed the minority vote in the 2008 election. They demonstrate that the law had a direct effect on registered voters who did not have a state photo identification card. The law had a marginal effect on overall turnout. They conclude, "Although the law does slightly depress the overall turnout, this effect does not disproportionately affect racial or ethnic minority groups" (Hood and Bullock 2012).

Researchers at University of Houston studied the effects of the Texas voter ID law on voters in Harris County and Congressional District 23. They discovered that only 1.5 percent of the non-voters in Harrison County did not vote because of a lack of a state-approved photo ID. Only 0.5 percent of non-voters in Congressional District 23 did not vote because of a lack of this

ID. In Texas, during the 2016 presidential election, the photo ID law was an insignificant factor in explaining non-voting.

In 2014, the United States Government Accountability Office (GAO) published a major study of the effects of voter ID laws. The study was based on a quasi-experimental design method, using a treatment and comparison group. The GAO selected Kansas and Tennessee for the treatment group and Alabama, Arkansas, Delaware, and Maine for the comparison group. As with this method, the GAO was careful to select treatment and comparison groups that were as much alike as possible in terms of election conditions. The main difference was that the treatment group had enacted strict voter ID laws prior to the 2012 election. The GAO relied on multiple datasets, especially the Census Bureau Current Population Survey and the United States Elections Project's (USEP) databases. The databases included outcomes for both the 2008 and the 2012 elections. The GAO examined changes in voter turnout data for several demographic groups in both the treatment and comparison groups from the 2008 presidential election and the 2012 presidential election. Relevant to our student, the GAO concluded:

> In both Kansas and Tennessee we found that turnout was reduced by larger amounts among African-American registrants, as compared with Asian American, Hispanic, and White registrants. We estimate that turnout was reduced among African-American registrants by 3.7 percentage points more than among Whites in Kansas and 1.5 percentage points more than among Whites in Tennessee. However, we did not find reductions in turnout among Asian-American or Hispanic registrants, as compared to White registrants, thus suggesting the laws did not have larger effects on these registrants. (GAO 2014, 52)

Recent studies challenge advocates of stricter voter regulations and contradict earlier statistical analyses that claim no effect of voter ID laws (Atkeson et al. 2014; Rogowski and Cohen 2014; Zoltan et al. 2017; Palast 2016).

Using data from the Brennan Center, Palast estimates that the requirement of presenting a government-issued photo ID card would have a severe impact on low-income, aged, and minority voters. He notes that about 15 percent of voters whose household incomes are below $35,000 lack this form of ID. About 6 million seniors, 8.1 million Hispanic, and about 5.5 black voters lack this form of ID (Palast 2016, 223–224). Palast expects the implementation of these laws to have substantial impacts on low-income, minority, and aged voters.

Most of the research suggests that voter ID laws may not have the substantial effect that their critics claim. However, these do seem to have a marginal effect on select groups. Moreover, more research needs to be done on the effects of multiple methods of voter suppression. Several other methods have emerged during the 2016–2020 period. These methods include signature match, actual residency, and poll access.

Signature match involves comparing the voter's signature at the time of registration with the voter's signature during voting. The actual address requirement, which denies the right to vote of citizens who use the Post Office address rather than the residency address, is likely to have a significant suppressing effect on Native American voters. As significant numbers of Native Americans live on reservations and use a Post Office box, this new policy is likely to have a suppressing effect (Ashoka Mukpo 2018). The signature match can be subject to abuse.

## Reduced Poll Access

Poll access is a significant problem. Deliberately reducing the number of polling places in large metropolitan areas has the effect of substantially increasing the waiting time to vote. One study conducted by the Leadership Conference Education Fund, "Democracy Diverted: Polling Place Closure and the Right to Vote," documents massive closings of polling places. The study identifies 1,688 polling place closings between 2012 and 2018. Many of these closings occurred in Southern states. Arizona lost 320, Georgia lost 214, and Louisiana lost 126. Texas closed down 750 polling places. Harris County anchored by Houston, Texas, is 42 percent Latino and 19 percent African American. It lost 52 polling places. In the 2020 primary election, voters waited several hours to vote. A local newspaper pointed out that after the closings, two-thirds of all the polling places were located in GOP areas. Consequently, Democratic voters were forced to wait several hours to vote (Despart and Morris 2020). Milwaukee, Wisconsin, lost 177 polling places. By 2016, this city had only five polling places. When voter turnout increases and the number of polling places decline, the length of time for voting increases substantially. Targeting minority communities for poll closing has emerged as a common voter suppression technique.

## The Courts and Voter Suppression

The courts have played a major role in setting the parameters of voting rights rules. *Richardson v Ramirez* (1974) allowed felony disenfranchisement laws, even if they have a disparate impact on minorities.

The *Crawford v Marion County* (2008) case upheld Indiana's voter ID law. The court found the law to be a reasonable exercise of the state's power to regulate the time, place, and manner of elections (553 U.S. at 201). The Indiana Voter ID law required the presentation of a photograph ID before casting an in-person vote. There was no phase in period, but there were exceptions for residents of state-licensed nursing homes. Individuals who wanted to vote, but did not have a photo ID, could cast a provisional ballot, which would be processed, if within ten days, they swore out an affidavit of indigence or religious objection before a court clerk. In the alternative, they could provide a photo ID to the court clerk within ten days. The law also eliminated fees for a state-issued photo ID—though fees could be assessed for obtaining the documents required for the issuance of that ID.

*NAACP v McCrory* is important because the U.S. Fourth Circuit Court blocked North Carolina from implementing an omnibus voting bill that required voters to present a state photo ID before voting, reduced early voting from 17 days to 10 days and eliminated same day registration. In this case, plaintiffs not only demonstrated that this law would have a disproportionate negative impact on minority voters, they presented evidence that white Republican legislators deliberately targeted black voters.

The court noted that the day after the Supreme Court Shelby decision (discussed below) struck down the preclearance provision of the Voting Rights Act, the Republican Chairman of the North Carolina Senate Rules Committee announced that it was preparing the omnibus bill. Shortly afterward, Republican leaders requested and received racial data on the usage of state issued IDs, participation in early voting, same-day registration, teen pre-registration, and cross precinct voting. Republicans deliberately eliminated government-issued IDs and other forms of IDs that black voters were likely to possess and required voters to present a Department of Motor Vehicles photo ID because whites were more likely to have this form of ID and blacks were less likely to have it. Republicans reduced early voting because blacks disproportionately used early voting, while whites were less likely to use it. These changes to the voter regulation laws were found to have been racially motivated, with the legislature having "targeted African-Americans with almost surgical precision." The court went on to say that the asserted justifications of the law could not conceal the state's "true motivation"—"minority disenfranchisement" (*NAACP v McCrory* 2016).

When given a chance to review the Fourth Circuit decision, the Supreme Court passed, with the following statement from the chief justice, denial of cert "imports no expression of opinion on the merits of the case." It appears that the court denied standing due to issues of *locus standi* after the newly elected Democratic North Carolina attorney general and governor filed a motion to dismiss the petition for a *writ of certiorari*.

The *Shelby v Holden* decision set voting rights back significantly. This decision invalidated Section 4 of the Voting Rights Act, which pertained to preclearance. Because of the brazen and shameless behavior of former Confederate States to deliberately disenfranchise African Americans and to continue to fight efforts to extend voting rights to them, Congress added a provision in the Act to require these states to get special permission before changing voting policies. The court believed that times had changed, that minority voter disenfranchisement was buried in the past, that there was more bad behavior in Northern States, and that the law unnecessarily impinged on the sovereignty of the Southern states. However, since this provision was invalidated, Southern states intensified their campaign to make voting more difficult for African Americans. Select Northern states joined the campaign.

## TRUMP'S ACCELERATED ASSAULT ON DEMOCRACY

From the beginning of his 2016 campaign for president and continuing after his defeat in the 2020 presidential election, Trump engaged in an attack on the right to vote. This attack involved two parts: a campaign of disinformation and conspiracy theories and the promotion of actions and public policy change to undermine the vote and democracy. Most of the disinformation centered on several issues related to voter fraud. These issues found some support among well-intentioned public officials and scholars. Collectively, they form a series of myths about voter fraud that have been debunked. Most were related to Trump's persistent claim that millions of people vote illegally—non-citizens, impostors, illegally registered. This claim has several parts.

### Voter Fraud Myths

Donald Trump promoted several voter fraud myths and conspiracy theories. Four myths stand out and help precipitate voter suppression laws:

*Myth 1: Massive Numbers of Undocumented Immigrants Voting*

Trump popularized the myth that millions of undocumented immigrants vote and steal elections from Republicans. This myth is not without support from well-intentioned scholars and public officials. In 2014, three scholars published an article in a highly regarded peer-reviewed journal, *Electoral Studies*. This article, "Do Non-Citizens Vote in U.S. Elections?" used the Cooperate Congressional Election Study survey to demonstrate that up to14 percent of non-citizens voted in the 2008 election (Richman et al. 2014). In 2017, Trump's press secretary, Sean Spicer, and his senior adviser, Stephen Miller, referenced this article to claim that Trump was right in claiming that millions of immigrants vote illegally and steal elections. Two serious problems make this claim a myth or lie. First, because of the extremely small sample size of non-citizens, the 14 percent did not translate into a figure anywhere close to a million or even a thousand, making the statement false. Second, the authors later caught an error in the survey which invalidated their results (Weiser and Keith 2017; Koerth 2019).

As mentioned above, Kris Kobach, former secretary of state for Kansas and former co-chair of Trump's voter fraud commission, supported Trump's claim that millions of people voted illegally. He also promoted the claim that 18,000 non-citizens immigrants were registered to vote in Kansas. This claim was used to past and implement a new Kansas law that required voters to demonstrate proof of citizenship. In 2013, the American Civil Liberties Union challenged this claim and the law. It sued Kobach. The court mandated a study of non-citizens in Kansas registered to vote. The study found that between 1999 and 2013, thirty-nine non-citizens had registered to vote. There was no evidence that they had voted. The study also found that as a result of this law, 32,000 U.S. citizens in Kansas were prevented from voting.

The Brennan Center posted a report debunking several other cases related to the myth of rampant cases of millions of immigrants voting illegally. The report documented a case in Virginia in which a public interest group, Public Interest Legal Foundation (PILF), published two documents claiming that thousands of immigrants had voted illegally. A voter rights advocacy sued PILF and demonstrated the inaccuracy of the claim of illegal voters. Another case involved the State of Texas claiming that 95,000 immigrants had registered to vote illegally and 58,000 had voted illegally. The report demonstrated that the immigrants in question had become naturalized citizens. In another case, they demonstrated that the Heritage Foundation had grossly overestimated the number of actual cases of voter fraud (Feldman 2020).

The claim of massive numbers of immigrants voting is patently false. There have been documented cases of immigrants registering to vote. The National Voter Registration Act required states to allow residents to register to vote at the time they apply for a driver's license. Indeed, some immigrants were registered to vote. The federal government and most states prohibit non-citizens from voting.

When real cases of voter fraud are discovered, people are prosecuted. For example, in 2016 Rosa Maria Ortega, a documented non-citizen brought to the United States when she was a baby, a 39-year-old mother of four and a registered Republican voted in the 2014 election in the State of Texas. She was arrested, prosecuted, and sentenced to eight years in prison for voting illegally (Wines 2017; Levine 2018).

## Myth 2: Massive Number of People Voting on Behalf of Dead People

This myth may have been true in the early twentieth century in the city of Chicago; however, in the twenty-first century with the event of modern technology, it is largely a myth that has hurt some Trump supporters. In one case in the State of Pennsylvania in October 2020, Robert Lynn requested an absentee ballot for his deceased mother (Marans 2020). His mother had died in 2015. The commuted caught the attempt. Lynn was arrested and prosecuted. In another case, in May 2021, Bruce Bartman casted a vote for his dead mother and dead mother-in-law. He was caught, arrested, and prosecuted for voter fraud and perjury. The county prosecutor stated that these cases of voter fraud are extremely rare. It appeared that both men were influence by Trump's claims of widespread and rampant voter fraud, as they wanted to make sure that Trump won (Marans 2020; Gstalter 2021).

### Myth 3: People Vote in Multiple States

The Brennan Center debunked the claim of cases of massive numbers of college students bussed into neighboring states to vote illegally. This case was investigated by the New Hampshire Attorney General and officials from Trump's initial voter fraud commission. There was absolutely no evidence supporting this claim.

### Myth 4: Mail-in Voting Is a Fraud Magnet

This is another one of Trump's baseless fraud claim. Although as noted above, there are indeed cases of this form of fraud, they are rare.

## POLITICAL ACTION AND PUBLIC POLICY

During his first year in office, Trump established a special commission to investigate and remedy voter fraud. He made Kris Kobach the co-chair of this organization, along with Mike Pence. Kobach had a reputation for promoting voter suppression laws and his ties to Koch-related organizations. The commission was eventually dissolved during Trump's second year in office.

As part of the attack on mail-in ballots, Trump hired a Postmaster General who engaged in a series of actions that undermined the capacity of the Post Office to deliver the mail. Trump's Postmaster, Louis DeJoy, instituted a hiring freeze, eliminated overtime, reduced staff, and removed mail-sorting machines. He targeted thousands of mailboxes throughout the country for removal. While DeJoy promised to desist in these actions, the damage was already done. Mail delivery had slowed. The ability of the Post Office to successfully deliver the mail on Election Day had already been undermined.

Several Republican governors and Republican state legislators engaged in an aggressive effort to pass new voter suppression laws. For example, Tennessee governor William Lee signed a bill into law that restricts organizations engaged in voter registration drives. The law prohibits groups from paying workers for meeting quotas for a set number of registration forms and criminalizes turning in incomplete or inaccurate forms. A number of civic organizations sued the governor and the state over this new law. A court issued an injunction which temporarily prevented the enforcement of the law (Gardner 2019). In the summer of 2020, after a series of riots precipitated by anti-police brutality demonstrations sponsored by the Black Lives Matter movement in the summer of 2020, Tennessee pasted a law making it a felony punishable for up to six years in prison for demonstrating outside the state Capitol. Such a conviction would not only lead to a long prison term, but also to the permanent disenfranchisement of the convicted protestor.

After losing the presidential election to Joe Biden by close to 7 million votes and despite the fact that Republican officials supported the legitimacy of the election, Trump and his allies engaged in a shameless and baseless campaign of lies, disinformation, and conspiracy theories alleging that the election was stolen from Trump. Trump's attorney general, William Barr, ordered the investigation of the election. After the investigation, Barr concluded that he had "not seen fraud on a scale that could have effected a different outcome in the election" (quoted by Zapotosky 2020). Chris Krebs, Trump's head of the Cybersecurity and Infrastructure Security Agency in the U.S. Department of Homeland Security, issued a joint statement with other federal, state, and local public officials responsible for the security of elections, including Republican governors and Republican secretary of states. The statement verified that the election was neither stolen nor hacked. Krebs said that it was the most secure election in history (Peiser 2020). Shortly after Krebs issued the statement, Trump fired him. Gabriel Sterling, Georgia's Voting System Manager urged Trump to reign in his supporters and stop promoting the big lie that the election was stolen. Sterling's concern was that the lies would provoke violence and someone would get hurt.

Despite public statements from key Republican public officials and loyal supporters that the election was legitimate and that Trump lost, Trump intensified his campaign of lies. The Trump propaganda machine accelerated the pace of spewing out conspiracy theories, ranging from the complex and nefarious to the simple. Typical of right-wing conspiracy theories, the more complex ones either alleged an international conspiracy or blamed a racial minority. Dominion Voting Machines were alleged to have connections with Venezuelan socialists.

Just after the November election, Trump's adviser and attorney, Rudy Giuliani, gave a news conference and presented several conspiracy theories claiming that the 2020 presidential election was stolen from Donald Trump. One conspiracy theory had racist overtones. This theory alleged that fraud was concentrated in Atlanta, Georgia; Detroit, Michigan; Milwaukee,

Wisconsin; and Philadelphia, Pennsylvania. All four of these cities have substantial or predominantly black populations. Giuliani claimed that the fraud from these cities caused Trump to lose Georgia, Michigan, Wisconsin, and Pennsylvania, and consequently stole the election from Trump. While Giuliani did not mention that these were predominantly black cities, he did claim that they were controlled by Democrats (Timm 2020).

The simple lies alleged that the Dominion Voting Machines switched votes for Trump to votes for Biden; Sharpies Markers were used to change votes in Arizona; many dead people voted everywhere; many people voted multiple times; poll watchers were prevented from watching the vote count allowing people to discard ballots or to bring in bags and suitcases of fake ballots; and U.S. Postal Service workers were told to backdate late arrival ballots. All of these allegations were lies. Just after the election, Trump claimed that more people voted in Detroit than lived in Detroit (Seth 2020). Trump and his supporters either confused Detroit, Michigan, with Detroit, Minnesota, or deliberately manipulated the figures to promote another lie. The point is that Trump and his supporters promoted multiple lies about election fraud.

Trump attorneys filed sixty law suits alleging voter fraud. Judges dismissed fifty-nine of the cases because of the lack of evidence. Trump's propaganda machine alleged that the judges failed to examine any of the evidence and dismissed the cases on procedural grounds. This allegation was false. The cases were dismissed precisely because there was no evidence. In the one case, Trump attorneys won, there was no fraud, just a violation of election procedures. The results of winning the case did not change the results of the election.

Trump lost the 2020 presidential election. Trump's own attorney general claimed that there was no fraud that rose to a level that would have changed the outcome of the election. Trump lost plain and simple.

Trump's big lies and the conspiracy theories served three functions. They delegitimized the 2020 election. They provoked outrage among Trump supporters and incited the January 6, 2021 insurrection and the assault on the Capitol. They intensified the Republican Party's efforts to continue to pass voter suppression laws.

# Chapter 10

# Trumpism

## Race, Class, and Police Policy

With few exceptions, most of Trump's public policies followed the neoliberal playbook. This playbook was designed to weaken the bargaining power of American workers. It hacked away at the Affordable Care Act. It eroded the social safety net. It diminished compensatory educational programs. It enacted a more regressive federal tax. It put a great deal of energy and effort into making it more difficult for the more vulnerable citizens to vote.

One of Trump's policies followed the right-wing nationalist playbook: criminal justice and police policy. Although Trump promised criminal justice reform, like most of his promises, this one was largely symbolic. As mentioned in chapter 1, Trump secured the passage of the First Step Act. This act provided small changes and incremental progress. It prohibited the shackling of pregnant women, shortened the sentences for a few thousand non-violent prisoners convicted of drug offenses, and allowed convicts to be imprisoned no more than 500 miles from their families. It secured the early release of over 3,000 federal prisoners and impacted a couple of thousand more. However, in just over a year after the passage of this act, Trump's Justice Department prosecutors began objecting to the early releases (Satija 2020). Moreover, other criminal justice changes, like the use of DHS police officials to target journalists and Black Lives Matter protesters, moved the Trump administration in the direction of establishing a repressive police state.

This chapter sums up both Trump's criminal justice police policy and the theme of this text. The theme is simple: Trump was a right-wing reactionary populist who engaged in a public policy agenda that exacerbated inequality and hurt low-income white workers and minorities. In regards to his criminal justice and policing policy, he racialized violent crime and supported police violence. This chapter begins with a discussion of the racialization of violent crime in the United States, which obstructs efforts to reduce violent crime and enables police violence. It summarizes the problem of police violence. It illustrates the ways in which Trump racialized violent crime, encouraged police violence, and operated to undermine efforts toward police reform. It exposes Trump's efforts to move the United States in the direction of establishing a racially and class-repressive police state.

## RACIALIZING VIOLENT CRIME

Violent crime in the United States is no different from violent crime anywhere in the world. It is not a racial problem. It is a social problem. Homicide is strongly associated with excessive inequality and pockets of concentrated poverty, aggravated by an inadequate social safety net, a harsh and ineffective criminal justice system, and easy access to fire arms.

Table 10.1 illustrates the association between inequality and homicide. What stands out in this table is that countries with extraordinarily high rates of inequality have extraordinarily high rates of homicide. Countries with Gini coefficients above 48 percent tend to have homicide rates above 25 per 100,000. South Africa, Brazil, and Honduras have substantially higher levels of inequality than the United States and substantially higher levels of homicide. The United States has the highest level of inequality among

**Table 10.1   Gini Index and Homicide Rates by Select Countries**

| Country | Gini (%) Index* | Date | Homicide Rate (per 100,000)** |
|---|---|---|---|
| South Africa | 63.0 | 2014 | 33.97 |
| Brazil | 53.9 | 2018 | 29.53 |
| Honduras | 52.1 | 2018 | 56.52 |
| Guatemala | 48.3 | 2014 | 27.60 |
| United States | 41.1 | 2016 | 5.35 |
| United Kingdom | 34.8 | 2016 | 1.20 |
| Canada | 33.3 | 2017 | 1.68 |
| Japan | 32.9 | 2013 | .28 |
| Germany | 31.9 | 2016 | 1.18 |
| France | 31.6 | 2017 | 1.35 |
| Sweden | 28.8 | 2017 | 1.08 |
| Denmark | 28.7 | 2017 | .98 |
| Netherlands | 27.0 | 2017 | .55 |
| Norway | 27.0 | 2017 | .51 |
| Slovakia | 25.2 | 2016 | .48 |

*Central Intelligence Agency. 2021. The World Fact Book, Gini Index Co-efficient Distribution
Htttps://www.cia.gov/the-world-factbook/field/gini-index-coefficient-distribution-of-family-income/country
   -comp.
**World Population Review. 2021. "Murder Rate By Country."
https://worldpopulationreview.com/country-rankins/murder-rate-b-country.

developed nations and the highest homicide rate among developed nations. With a Gini coefficient of 41.1, the United States has a homicide rate of 5.34 per 100,000. The UK has a Gini coefficient of 34.8, with a homicide rate of 1.20 per 100,000. In contrast, Scandinavian and Nordic countries with Gini coefficients below 29 percent have homicide rates below 1.1 per 100,000.

Homicide rates per 100,000 vary widely among the cities and regions of the world. Homicide rates are higher in cities and regions of the world with extreme inequality, extremes in wealth and poverty, and pockets of concentrated poverty. Cities like Caracas, Venezuela, Guatemala City, Guatemala, and Tegucigalpa, Honduras have homicide rates above 100 per 100,000. The prominent criminal justice scholar, Elliot Currie, said, "In Russia, homicide rates range from 6 per 100,000 in one region to 130 per 100,000 in another" (Currie 2016; Lysova et al. 2012).

Currie demonstrated that in most countries with high homicide rates, these rates are associated with excessive inequality, weak social safety nets, easy access to firearms, concentrated poverty, and marginal work. He pointed out that in Estonia where homicide rates were high, over 80 percent of the homicides were committed by offenders who had no jobs. Generally, offenders lived in isolated and concentrated poverty areas, experienced unstable and marginal work, and suffered stressed family relations (Currie 2016). High homicide rates are associated with excessive inequality, concentrated poverty, marginal employment, weak social safety nets, harsh and ineffective criminal justice systems, and easy access to firearms (Currie 2016).

Despite the overwhelming evidence that violent crimes are associated with non-racial social factors, right-wing political leaders and a significant proportion of Americans associate violent crime with two unrelated factors: immigrants and blacks. They explain the higher rates of violent crime in American compared to rich developed European countries in terms of racial diversity. They are oblivious of the fact that some areas of Europe have no racial diversity, but substantially higher rates of violent crime than the United States. They deliberately ignore the fact that European countries with lower rates of violent crime have more robust social safety nets and more lenient and effective criminal justice systems. This tendency to associate violent crime with racial groups defines the process of racializing violent crime. This process is a function of America's racist political culture (Unnever and Cullen 2012; Cazenave 2018). This culture is promoted by right-wing media personalities and political leaders. It enables state violence against minorities.

Over the past four years, Trump did more to racialize violent crime and to promote this racist culture than any other right-wing political leader or media personality. He promoted this culture through many of his statements about immigrants and violence, and blacks and violence.

Trump began his race for the presidency with his infamous statement about a flood of Mexican murders and rapists coming across the border into the United States. He supported this statement with an actual case in which an undocumented Mexican shot and killed a young, bright, and attractive American woman, Kathryn Steinle (Arkin and Siemasko 2017). About 42 percent of Americans believed Trump when he claimed that immigrants are making America worse by bringing violent crime to America (Gallup 2019).

The research on immigrants and crime contradicts Trump's claim. Immigrants tend to have lower crime rates than American citizens. Cities that have experienced the most increases in immigrants over the past thirty years have also enjoyed the greatest decline in crime rates (Flagg 2018).

In addition to associating immigrants with violent crimes, Trump associates blacks with violent crimes. He promoted two racialized narratives about blacks and violent crimes, a mainstream narrative and a white supremacist narrative.

The mainstream narrative is that violent crime rates are high in predominantly black neighborhoods. During the 2016 election campaign, while attempting to court black voters, Trump said that you cannot walk down the street in a black neighborhood in Chicago without getting shot (Bump 2016). He told blacks that they had nothing to lose by voting for him.

Trump promoted this narrative throughout his term in office. He claimed that other predominantly black cities experienced nothing but increases in violent crime under Democratic administrations (Jake 2020). He dehumanized the city of Baltimore, Maryland, and criminalized its black U.S. Representative, Elijah Cummings. Trump stated, "Why is so much money sent to Elijah Cummings' district when it is considered the worst run and most dangerous anywhere in the United States. No human being would want to live there. Where is all this money going? How much is stolen? Investigate this corrupt mess immediately" (Quoted by Kimball 2019).

The residents of Baltimore are decent, law abiding, and middle-class citizens. About 64 percent are black. When Trump falsely claims that Baltimore is the worst run and most dangerous city anywhere in the United States, he is promoting a racial stereotype and a racist narrative that predominantly black cities are led by incompetent and corrupt black leaders, with dangerous black inhabitants who must be less than human, because, "no human being would want to live there." His characterization of the people provokes fear and revulsion.

During the 2016 campaign, Trump promoted a white supremacist narrative. He claimed that blacks were a direct threat to whites. He re-tweeted a message that came straight from a white supremacist website: "97 percent of blacks killed are killed by other black people and that 80 percent of white people killed are killed by black people" (quoted in Bump 2015). This was the same false and racist narrative that provoked white supremacist, neo-Nazi, Dylann Roof, to go inside a black church in Charleston, South Carolina, and gun down nine people who had welcomed him to their prayer meeting (Zapotoshy 2017).

The claim that violence is high in predominantly black neighborhoods is a mainstream perspective. The claim that blacks are a direct threat to whites and are killing whites is a white supremacist perspective. The difference between the mainstream perspective and the white supremacist perspective is that the former takes data out of context and the latter promotes a blatant lie. In regards to the mainstream perspective, it is true that rates of violence are high in predominantly black, concentrated poverty inner city areas. However, the context is that rates of violence are high in concentrated poverty areas. In regards to race, poverty, and violence, a Justice Department report stated, "Poor urban blacks (51.3 per 1,000) had rates of violence similar to poor urban whites (56.4 per 1,000)" (Harrell et al. 2014). Just as there is a high rate of violent crime among blacks living in concentrated urban poverty areas, there is a high rate of violent crime among whites living in concentrated urban poverty areas (Currie 2016; Harrell et al. 2014). Race is a spurious variable. Concentrated poverty is the explanatory variable. Racializing violence involves making race the causal variable. Making race the causal variable while ignoring concentrated poverty contributes to a racist narrative.

In regards to the lie that blacks are killing whites, the data demonstrate that 82.4 percent of whites are killed by whites and 90 percent of blacks are killed by blacks and 78.1 percent of murder victims, black and white, are killed by someone they know (Bump 2015). By re-tweeting this racist lie, Trump brought a dangerous racist lie into mainstream political discourse. Even though he deleted this re-tweet, there was no correction, no apology, and no remorse. The damage was never undone.

From the beginning of his 2016 campaign and throughout his administration, Trump promoted narratives of violent urban blacks. When the president of the United States characterizes predominantly black urban areas as inhabited by violent thugs, this characterization provokes fear and revulsion. It makes police shootings appear as normal reactions to extremely violent areas.

## ENABLING POLICE VIOLENCE

In addition to having a problem with violence, the United States has a problem with police violence. Compared to other developed countries, the United States has an extremely high rate of police officers killing civilians. The Prison Policy Initiative gathered data on the number of civilians killed by police officers from government reports, advocacy groups, and news sources to prepare a report on police killings from the United States and select developed countries. The report was based on the total number of people and the number of people per 10 million killed by the police, by gun, asphyxiation, blunt instrument, or other means. In the United States in 2019, police officers killed over a thousand civilians. In the same year, police officers in England and Wales killed three civilians. This figure translated into U.S. police killing 33.5 people per 10 million, compared to a figure for England and Wales of 0.5 per 10 million (Jones and Sawyer 2020).

Not only does the United States have a substantially higher rate of police killings per population than any other developed country, there are racial and class biases in police killings. This point was demonstrated by Feldman (2020). He gathered data on police killings that occurred from January 1, 2015 to June 9, 2020. The data included people who died from gunshot, taser shock, blunt force, asphyxiation, or any other means as a result of their encounters with police. He used only data in which he could verify the race of the deceased and the census track of the fatal encounter. He identified fifteen types of census tracks ranked from the lowest income census tracks to the highest income census tracks. About 6,451 police killings met the criteria. Of the 6,451 people killed by U.S. police officers, 3,353 were white, 1,746 were black, and 1,152 were Latino. Feldman discovered that the level of the income of the census tract was associated with the incidents of fatal police encounters. Whites from the lowest income census tracks were disproportionally more likely to die from fatal police encounters than whites from the other census tracks. Similarly, blacks from the lowest income census tracks were disproportionately more likely to die from fatal police encounters than blacks from other census tracks. Low-income class was a factor in explaining incidents of police killings. Moreover, race had an independent effect. Blacks from low-income areas were slightly more likely to die from fatal police encounters than whites from similar low-income areas. Race and class interacted to enhance the probability of blacks dying from fatal police encounters. A Rutgers University study added, "Among all groups, black men and boys face the highest lifetime risk of being killed by police. Our models predict that about 1 in 1,000 black men and boys will be killed by police over the life course" (Edwards et al. 2019).

Egregious cases of racial prejudice in police killings have become more visible to the public in the age of cell phones. Videos allow the public to see how frequent and egregious police killings of young black males have become. Videos allow for the debunking of myths surrounding these shootings. The 2016 case of Philando Castile defied the common myths that these shootings would not occur if black males simply cooperated with police officers and complied with their commands. Contrary to this myth, the video shows that Castile responded to the police officer in a cooperative and polite manner. When he complied with state law and informed the officer that he had a concealed carry permit, the police officer shot and killed him. The Walmart store videos captured the police shooting of John Crawford III. The video showed Crawford talking on his cell phone with his right hand and grasping the barrel of a BB gun with his left hand. As his finger was nowhere near the trigger, he posed no threat. In a matter of seconds, the police officers came around a corner and shot and killed Crawford. In another video, a police officer shot Walter Scott in the back as he fled the scene of a traffic stop for a broken taillight. Scott had a misdemeanor warrant for black child support. In another video, a 12 year old Tamir Rice was playing with a toy gun in a park. A police car pulled up. A police officer jumped out of the car and shot and kills Tamir. Although defenders of this police shooting claim that the police officer could not have known that this 12 year old child's gun was a harmless toy, in this same year (2014) there was a major confrontation between federal police representing the Bureau of Land Management and heavily armed and hostile white male protesters defending Cliven Bundy's right to graze his cattle on federal land without paying a grazing fee. In the case of the white male protesters, the police demonstrated enough regard for human life to exercise restraint and caution. In the case of Tamir Rice, the police officer displayed no regard for the human life of this back child. In the case of John Crawford III, the police officer displayed no regard to the life of this Walmart shopper.

The Justice Department's 2017 report on the Chicago Police Department provides further insights into the problems of urban violence and police violence. Chicago is the third largest metropolitan area in the United States, with 9.5 million residents and 2.7 million living inside the city. Because the city is so large, its homicide rate of about 15 per 100,000, is much lower than the rates for Caracas, Venezuela (122 per 100,000), Baltimore (37 per 100,000), or Detroit (45 per 100,000). In 2015, Chicago had 478 homicides. In 2016, this figure jumped to 762. Chicago has a homicide problem concentrated in a select few high-poverty areas (Sampson and Wilson 1995/2012).

Chicago's homicide problem is exacerbated by another problem: an ineffective and excessively violent police department. After the release of a video of a Chicago police officer shooting a 17 year old, black male suspect, the Illinois Attorney General requested a U.S. Justice Department investigation. The Chicago Police Department had ruled the shooting justifiable. The video contradicted the police report. The video featured the suspect walking backward, away from the police officer. The police officer rapidly approached and fired upon the suspect, shooting him sixteen times.

The U.S. Department of Justice (DOJ) engaged in an extensive investigation of the Chicago Police Department (CPD). Justice Department officials reviewed thousands of pages of police training manuals, police policies, reports, orders, memos, civilian complaints, and other documents. DOJ investigators interviewed hundreds of people including police officers, police supervisors, the police chief, police union officials, political and community leaders, and others. The DOJ report on the CPD documented a pattern and practice of unreasonable, excessive, and unconstitutional use of force targeted primarily on minority neighborhoods, a lack of a working system of accountability, and a deep sense of distrust of CPD officers within minority neighborhoods. The report defined unreasonable and unconstitutional use of excessive force:

> In determining whether force used by a law enforcement officer is reasonable, courts look to "the severity of the crime at issue, whether the suspect poses an immediate threat to the safety of the officers or others, and whether he is actively resisting arrest or attempting to evade arrest by flight." Whether a particular use of force is reasonable is judged from the perspective of a reasonable officer on the scene rather than with 20/20 vision of hindsight. (U.S. Department of Justice 2017, 23)

The report made it clear that police officers do not have the unfettered authority to shoot a member of the public or a suspect simply because that person has a weapon or is fleeing a scene.

> Instead, deadly force may only be used by a police officer when, based on a reasonable assessment, the officer or another person is threaten with the weapon . . . Where the suspect poses no immediate threat to the officer and no threat to others, the harm resulting from failing to apprehend him does not justify the use of deadly force to do so. (U.S. Department of Justice 2017, 26)

The report identified numerous incidents in which CDP officers shot and killed people who posed no threat to anyone. Several incidents involved officers chasing a fleeing person who posed no immediate threat to the officer or the public and sometimes when no crime was committed:

> In one case, a man had been walking down a residential street with a friend when offices drove up, shined a light on him, and ordered him to freeze, because he had been fidgeting with his waistband. The man ran. Three officers gave chase and began shooting as they ran. In total, the officers fired 45 rounds, including 28 rifle rounds, toward the man. Several rounds struck the man, killing him. The officers claimed the man fired at them during the pursuit. Officers found no gun on the man. However, officers reported recovering a handgun nearly one block away. The gun recovered in the vicinity, however, was later determined to be fully-loaded and inoperable, and forensic testing determined that there was no

gunshot residue on the man's hands. IPRA found the officers' actions were justified without addressing the efficacy of the pursuit or the number of shots fired. (U.S. Department of Justice 2017, 26)

This was not an isolated case. It was part of a pattern that the Justice Department found occurring over the five years it investigated, 2011–2016. The report also documented numerous cases of the use of non-lethal excessive force. Some of these cases involved the unnecessary use of tasers and physical assaults.

The problem of excessive and unconstitutional use of force by the CPD is aggravated by an inadequate or dysfunctional system of accountability. Police officers are required to file a formal report after the use of lethal force. The DOJ report documented 203 incidents and 223 civilians shot. Police reporting on the shootings tended to be inaccurate. There were cases in which the report claimed that the suspect was facing the police officer when shot, while the autopsy report indicated that the suspect was shot multiple times in the back.

The CPD rarely investigates citizen complaints. The DOJ report noted over 30,000 complaints filed each year to a complaint board that routinely filed the complaints without any investigation. Three factors undermine any system of accountability. There is a code of silence among police officers. Union rules prohibit any investigation of a complaint, unless there is sworn testimony. Supervision is inadequate.

Because of the pattern and practice of excessive use of force targeting minority communities, these communities do not trust the police, and police and community relations are strained. This distrust and strained relationship contributes to an ineffective criminal justice system. This ineffectiveness is evident by the fact that the CPD has a 29 percent rate for identifying homicide suspects (DOJ 2017). Ineffective policing, defined by low rates of identifying suspects, is associated with higher rates of crime (Wilson 2013). In addition to an ineffective system, police violence and misconduct costed the City of Chicago about a half a billion dollars in law suits over a period of about five years (DOJ 2017).

The DOJ report resulted in an agreement between the DOJ and the CPD, mediated by the federal court. The court-mediated agreement became a consent decree. The CPD agreed to undertake a series of reforms designed to establish clear directives prohibiting the excessive and unconstitutional use of force, to create a system of accountability, and to engage in community policing to improve police–community relations.

The Chicago investigation and consent decree was not an isolated event. Obama's DOJ had engaged in about twenty-five other investigations, resulting in about fourteen other consent decrees with local police departments (Berman and Werner 2020).

## TRUMP ENCOURAGES POLICE VIOLENCE

Trump and his administration enabled and encouraged police violence several ways. First, as noted above, Trump promoted racialized images of violent predominantly black urban areas. The claim that you can't walk down the street in a black neighborhood makes police shootings of young black males seem like a normal response to arbitrary and irrational urban violence.

Second, Trump tolerated racist violence. When a white supremacist neo-Nazi murdered Heather Heyer in Charlottesville, Virginia, in 2017, Trump said there were good people on both sides. When Kyle Rittenhouse went from Antioch, Illinois, to Kenosha, Wisconsin, and shot three Black Lives Matter protesters, killing two, Trump claimed Kyle was acting is self-defense (Philip 2020). During the presidential debate, Chris Wallace asked Trump to condemn white supremacists and Biden mentioned the Proud Boys, a white nationalist group noted for engaging in armed violence at protest demonstration, Trump said, "Proud Boys, stand back and stand by" (quoted by Green 2020). During the weekend before the November 2020 election, a caravan of Trump supporters accosted a Biden–Harris campaign bus. One Trump supporter in the caravan hit a SUV driven by a Biden campaign staffer. Trump responded by tweeting, "I love Texas" (Boblotz 2020).

Third, Trump directly encouraged police violence. This encouragement began in Trump's first year in office and continued throughout his administration. In a speech before police officers on Long Island in 2017, Trump said, "When you see these thugs being thrown into the back of a paddy wagon . . . Please don't be too nice" (quoted by Serwer 2020). He added that it was ok for them to hit their heads. He also claimed that the police could end the violence in Chicago if they were given the authority. He claimed that the problem was that laws restricted what the police could do. He added, "For years and years, [laws have] been made to protect criminals. Totally protect the criminal, not the officers. You do something wrong, you're in more jeopardy than they are. These laws are stacked against you. We're changing those laws" (quoted by Reilly 2017).

Trump's message is clear: Police need more power and suspects deserve fewer rights. In the summer of 2020, when peaceful protests in Minneapolis turned into a riot, Trump called the protesters thugs and he called for violent intervention. He stated, "Any difficulty and we will assume control, but when the looting starts, the shooting starts" (quoted by Visser 2020).

Fourth, Trump's administration engaged in a campaign to undermine all of the programs established by the Obama administration designed to address problems of police violence. Trump's Attorney General, Jeff Sessions attempted to rescind agreements. He succeeded in rescinding the Chicago agreement, with Mayor Rahm Emmanuel's approval. However, the Illinois

Attorney General stepped in and secured an agreement that was more restrictive than Obama's. It included provisions for restricting the use of firearms on unarmed suspects. Sessions issued an administrative order severely restricting the pursuit of consent agreements. Sessions claimed that these agreements undermined the safety, morale, and respect of police officers (Reilly 2018). The Trump administration marginalized the DOJ Office of Community-Oriented Policing Services. This department switched from mediating conflicts and investigating civil rights violations to defending police departments (Berman and Werner 2020; Pilkington 2020).

Trump defined himself as the law and order president. He is not the first president to embrace law and order. Nixon defined himself as the law and order president. However, Nixon added, "To me law and order must be combined with justice. Now that's what I want for America. I want the kind of law and order that deserves respect" (quoted by Serwer 2020). Serwer adds,

> Reporters today do not bother asking Trump what law and order means, because everyone already understands that it simply means violence. Trump has dispensed with any pretense of seeking justice, and the Trump-era Republican Party has closed every possible path for reforming the police. Federal oversight of police is oppression. Elected officials who seek police reform have "blood on their hands." (Serwer 2020)

William Barr, the Attorney General who replaced Jeff Sessions, had considered punishing communities that did not have enough respect for police. He stated that communities "have to start showing more than they do, the respect and support that law enforcement deserves, and if communities don't give that support and respect, they might find themselves without the police protection they need" (quoted in Strauss 2009).

In a democratic society, the police get their power from the people and are there to serve and protect the people. It is generally in an autocratic or fascist society that the police have power independent of the people and that people are required to obey and respect the police regardless of how unlawful, repressive, and violent police behavior becomes. Indeed, in a repressive police state, peaceful protesters and journalists become targets of the national police power.

## THE SPECTER OF A POLICE STATE

Whether done intentionally or not, Donald Trump laid the foundation for a police state, lethal to any democratic system. In their book, *How Democracies Die*, Levitsky and Ziblatt identified four key indicators of forms of authoritarian political behavior that precede or presage the emergence of an anti-democratic police state: rejection of democratic rules, denial of the legitimacy of political opponents, toleration or encouragement of police violence, and readiness to curtail civil liberties. They pointed out that contemporary autocratic leaders rarely seize control of the state by military force. These leaders exploit democracies. They engage in mass propaganda campaigns. They promote conspiracy theories and lies to demonize opposing political parties and opponents. They precipitate extreme polarization. They characterize the media as the enemy of the people. They exploit crises. They exaggerate threats and generate enough fear to make the excessive expansion of police power and police repression seem like a normal and rational response to a real threat.

The Trump administration engaged in all of these practices. Not only did Trump deny the legitimacy of his opponents, he attempted to criminalize them. His 2016 campaign centered on criminalizing Clinton. He led large crowds of his supporters in chants of lock her up. He got caught attempting to criminalize Joe Biden. Throughout his presidency, Trump defined the press as the enemy of the people. He characterized Democrats as extreme leftist and socialists. He did more to intensify partisan conflict than any president since Andrew Johnson. Even after he lost the 2020 election, he continued to promote the big lie there was massive voter fraud and Biden stole the election. He used this lie to encourage his supporters to storm the U.S. Capitol and stop a process essential to American democracy, the peaceful transfer of power from one duly and legitimately elected president to another duly and legitimately elected president. This assault on the Capitol was a direct assault on America's democratic system.

Trump exploited crises to expand federal police powers. In response to a series of protests and demonstrations against confederate monuments and in favor of the Black Lives Matter (BLM) movement, Trump issued a series of executive orders underscoring the legal power of the Department of Homeland Security (DHS) to protect federal property. In response to multiple BLM protest and demonstration, some of which deteriorated into riots, Trump deployed DHS police officers to multiple cities. The deployment of officers to Portland, Oregon, is a prime example.

In the summer of 2020, a peaceful BLM demonstration in Portland turned violent. Although the violence was contained in a small area and although both the governor of Oregon and the mayor of Portland objected to Trump sending federal police, Trump deployed a large federal police force to Portland. This force consisted of officers from Custom and Border Protection (CBP), Immigration and Custom Enforcement (ICE), and a few other federal agencies. Many of these agents were dressed in combat uniforms without clearly identifying insignias. There were many reported cases of groups of these federal police agents in Portland and several other cities driving up to groups of protesters, grabbing them, and forcing them into a van. There were many incidents of federal agents targeting passive by-standers and journalists (Kanno-Youngs 2020; Olmos et al. 2020). The American Civil Liberties Union filed a federal law suit against the Trump administration and the acting DHS secretary.

The suit challenged the constitutionality of deploying the agents and targeting the journalists and peaceful protesters. A *Newsweek* article provided this summary of the ACLU law suit against the deployments:

> The ACLU is involved in several other lawsuits in Oregon and across the country over allegedly violent behavior from police and federal agents some of which specifically targets journalists, a group Trump had dubbed "the enemy of the people." There have been over 500 documented aggressions against journalist attempting to cover the demonstrations as of Thursday according to the U.S. Press Freedom Tracker. (Slisco 2020)

The federal court issued an injunction to prohibit DHS police officers from harassing and seizing journalists. The court did not prohibit the targeting of protesters.

Movements toward repressive police states are never abrupt in the contemporary period. They occur in increments, in bits and pieces. The Trump administration has come closer to establishing a repressive police state than any other modern U.S. president.

## TRUMPISM IN HISTORICAL PERSPECTIVE

Trump's public policy agenda was similar to Reagan's. Both agendas were heavily set by the Heritage Institute. Both agendas included redistributive tax cuts, regulatory rollbacks, cuts in social welfare programs, spending caps on Medicaid, and a conversion of AFDC into a block grant run by the states (Palmer and Sawhill 1984; Peterson 1986). The Democrats and moderate Republicans blocked most of Reagan's and Trump's policy proposals.

There were several important differences between Reagan and Trump. Reagan, unlike Trump, established bi-partisan task forces. Reagan's Social Security Task Force is a prime example. This task force produced the bi-partisan Social Security Act of 1983. In contrast, Trump not only avoided bi-partisan task forces, he exacerbated partisan conflicts. He has called Democrats socialists and extremists. Reagan, unlike Trump, listened to scientists and experts and responded to facts and data. For example, when his tax cuts produced substantial deficits, Reagan restored some of the cuts.

In response to concerns from environmentalists, Reagan backed off on his more aggressive efforts to target environmental scientists and dismantle environmental regulations (Tolchin and Tolchin 1983) In contrast, Trump has doubled down on his tax cuts, even though they produced a much larger deficit than Reagan's cuts. Trump attacked his own scientists in the middle of the covid-19 pandemic. He called the world renowned virologist, Anthony Fauci, an idiot. He denied global warming, promoted the lie that climate change was a hoax, censored federal environmental scientists and suppressed scientific research that contradicted his anti-environment agenda (Carter et al. 2019). Reagan, unlike Trump, supported voting rights. Reagan supported and signed the Voting Rights Act of 1982. In contrast, Trump's lies about voter fraud accelerated the minority voter suppression movement. This movement intensified after the 2020 presidential election.

Trumpism as a political movement is similar to the Redeemer movement that emerged in reaction to the Reconstruction era. Both movements entailed alliances among the Christian right, white nationalist, and economic elite. Both were committed to rolling back progressive public policies that improved the quality of the lives of minorities and low-income working-class whites. Both promised to restore a mythologized past. Both engaged in campaigns to delegitimize the opposition party and to suppress the minority vote. Both promoted false narratives characterizing minority groups as rapists and murderers. Both encouraged racially motived violence. Both produced a form of upper class ruled, masked by popular support from white nationalists and conservative Christians. Both increased inequality, eviscerated labor power, and underinvested in public schools. In both eras, white workers accepted low wages, poor health, inferior schools, and extreme inequality. They were more likely to identify with white patricians than low-income blacks, because white identity gave them a greater sense of worth. It empowered them especially when economic elites like Donald Trump identified with them (DuBois 1998; Roediger 2007). Both exploited white identity and denied class divisions in order to attain the support of white workers. Both characterized government programs that assisted low-income families as government taxing whites and giving to underserving minorities. Through this characterization, economic elites enlisted the support of the white working class in political backlashes calculated to restore both racial and class hierarchy. Nancy Isenberg offers this summary:

> Even when it's denied, politicians engage in class issues. The Civil War was a struggle to shore up both a racial and a class hierarchy. The Confederacy was afraid that poor whites would be drawn in by Union appeals and would vote to end slavery—because slavery was principally a reflection of the wealthy planters' self-interests.

Today as well we have a large unbalanced electorate that is regularly convinced to vote against its collective self-interest. These people are told that East Coast college professors brainwash the young and that Hollywood liberals make fun of them and have nothing in common with them and hate America and wish to impose an abhorrent, godless life-style. The deceivers offer essentially the same fear-laden message that the majority of southern whites heard when secession was being weighed. Moved by the need for control, for an unchallenged top tier, the power elite in American history has thrived by placating the vulnerable and creating for them a false sense of identification—denying real class differences wherever possible. (Isenberg 2016)

Historian Heather Richardson also describes the Trump administration as reminiscent of southern patricians, committed to restoring racial and class hierarchy. She offers this summary of the public policy changes of the Trump administration:

The Trump administration slashed regulations and gutted the Affordable Care Act passed by the Democrats under the Obama administration, a popular health-care reform that nonetheless had stood as Movement Conservatives' prime example of the misuse of government to create a form of socialism in America . . . He put in charge of government departments officials whose only qualification was great wealth, and they proceeded to use those departments for their own profit or for those of their friends . . .

In that, most of all, the Trump administration reflected the ideology of oligarchy. Government was not designed to promote equality of opportunity by guaranteeing equality before the laws. Rather, such meddling interfered with the ability of a few to arrange society as they saw fit: they, and they alone, truly understood what was best for everyone (Richardson 2020, 200).

# Bibliography

Abramowitz, Alan. 2018. *The Great Alignment: Race, Party Transformation, and the Rise of Donald Trump*. New Haven: Yale University Press.

Abramowitz, Alan and Jennifer McCoy. 2018. "United States Racial Resentment, Negative Partisanship and Polarization in Trump's America." *The Annuls of the American Academy of Political and Social Sciences*. December 20.

Abrams, Abigail. 2020. "Donald Trump's Much-Hyped Health Care Plan Isn't Much of a Plan at All." *Time*. September 24. https://time.com/5893032/donald-trump-health-care-plan/ accessed September 27, 2020.

Acemoglu, Daron and James Robinson. 2000. "Why Did the West Extend the Franchise? Democracy, Inequality, and Growth in Historical Perspective." *The Quarterly Journal of Economics*, 115(4, November), 1167–1199.

———. 2001. "A Theory of Political Transitions." *The American Economic Review*, 91(4), 938–963.

Adorno, Theodore. 1950. *The Authoritarian Personality*. New York: Harper.

Ahler, Douglas and Guarav Sood. 2018. "The Parties in Our Heads: Misperceptions About Party Composition and Their Consequences." *Journal of Politics*, 80(3), 964–981.

Akdenizli, Banu. 2007. "News Coverage and Immigration 2007: A Political Story Not an Issue, Covered Episodically." https://www.pewresearch.org/wp-content/uploads/sites/8/legacy/PEJ-Immigration-2007-Report.pdf

Al-Gharbi, Musa. 2018. "Race and the Race for the White House: On Social Research in the Age of Trump." *The American Sociologist*, 49(4), 496–519.

Alexander, Daniell. 2004. "Forty Acres and a Mule: The Ruined Hope of Reconstruction." *Humanities*. January/February.

Alexander, Michelle. 2012. *The New Jim Crow: Mass Incarceration in the Age of Color Blindness*. New York: The New Press.

Allegretto, Sylvia and David Cooper. 2014. "Twenty-Three Years and Still Waiting for Change: Why It's Time to Give Tipped Workers the Regular Minimum Wage." *Economic Policy Institute*. July 10. https://www.epi.org/publication/waiting-for-change-tipped-minimum-wage/

Altemeyer, Bob. 1988. *Enemies of Freedom: Understanding Right-wing Authoritarianism.* Hoboken, NJ: John Wiley Publisher.

American Enterprise Institute for Public Policy and Research. 2020. "History of AEI." July 26. https://web.archive.org/web/20090708195505/http://www.aei.org/history

American Immigration Council. 2020. "The Costs of Immigration Enforcement and Border Security." July. https://www.americanimmigrationcouncil.org/sites/default/files/research/the_cost_of_immigration_enforcement_and_border_security.pdf

Appelbaum, Eileen and Rosemary Batt. 2014. *Private Equity at Work: When Wall Street Manages Main Street.* New York: Russell Sage Foundation.

Arendt, Hannah. 1951. *The Origins of Totalitarianism.* New York: Harcourt, Brace and Company.

Arkin, David and Corky Siemasko. 2017. "Shooting of Kathry Steinle: San Francisco Pier Killing Suspect Found Not Guilty of Murder: Donald Trump Seized on the Case During the Campaign as Proof that U.S. Needs His Proposed Border Wall." *U.S. News.* https://www.nbcnews.com/news/us-news/jose-ines-garcia-zarate-san-francisco-pier-killing-suspect-found-n823351

Arria, Michael. 2017. "Meet Trump's Anti-Worker Labor Department Nominees." *Truthout.* November 1. https://truthout.org/articles/meet-trump-s-anti-worker-labor-department-nominees/

Atkeson, Lonna Rae, Yann P. Kerevel, R. Michael Alvarez and Thad E. Hall. 2014. "Who Asks For Voter Identification? Explaining Poll-Worker Discretion." *Journal of Politics,* 76(4), 944–957.

Austin v Michigan Chamber of Commerce. 494 U.S. 652 (1990).

Autor, David. 2019. "Work of the Past, Work of the Future." *American Economic Association, Papers and Proceeding,* 109, 1–32. https://1257/panelp.20191110

Avery, Michael. 2008. "The Rise of the Conservative Legal Movement." *Suffolk University Law Review,* 42(Winter), 1.

Baretto, Matt, Stehpen Nuno and Gabriel Sanchez. 2007. "Voter ID Requirements and the Disenfranchisement of Latino, Black and Asian Voters." *Paper Prepared for the Annual Meeting of the American Political Science Association.* September.

———. 2009. "The Disproportionate Impact of Voter ID Requirements on the Electorate: New Evidence from Indiana." *PS Political Science and Politics,* 42(1), 111–116.

Bartels, Larry. 2008. *Unequal Democracy: The Political Economy of the New Gilded Age.* Princeton, NJ: Princeton University Press.

Baum, Eric. 2015. "5 Noteworthy Quotes About First U.S. Minimum Wage." *Newsmax.* June 2. https://www.newsmax.com/FastFeatures/minimum-wage-quotes/2015/06/02/id/648236/

Baumgartner, Frank and Bryan Jones. 2009. *Agendas and Instability in American Politics,* 2nd ed. Chicago: University of Chicago Press.

———. 2015. *The Politics of Information Problem Definition and the Course of Public Policy in America.* Chicago: University of Chicago Press.

Baynes, Norman, ed. 1942. *The Speeches of Adolf Hitler, 1922–1939.* New York: Oxford University Press.

Beard, Charles. 2014/1913. *An Economic Interpretation of the Constitution.* New York: Macmillian Company.

Bedard, Paul. 2012. "Coke Caves in Face of Democratic Boycott Threat." *Washington Examiner*. April 4.

Berlin, Isaiah. 1969. *Four Essays on Liberty*. Oxford, England: Oxford University Press.

Berman, Ari. 2015. *Give Us the Ballot: The Modern Struggle for Voting Rights in America*. New York: Picador Paperback.

Berman, Mark and Erica Werner. 2020. "The Trump Administration Abandoned Obama-era Police Reform Efforts. Now Critics Want Them Restored." *Washington Post*, June 2.

Bernstein, Harry. 1987. "Airlines Devise a New Way to Bust Unions." *Los Angeles Times*. May 20. https://www.latimes.com/archives/la-xpm-1987-05-20-fi-759-st ory.html#:~:text=Continental%20Airlines%20pioneered%20a%20way%20to%20 break%20union,benefits%20they%20were%20entitled%20to%20under%20their %20agreements.

Blanchflower, David. 2021. *Not Working: Where have all the Good Jobs Gone?* Princeton, NJ: Princeton University Press.

Bloom, Jack. 1987. *Class, Race and the Civil Rights Movement: The Changing Political Economy of Southern Racism*. South Bend, IN: Indiana University Press.

Bluestone, Harry and Bennett Harrison 1990. *The Great U-Turn: Corporate Restructuring and the Polarizing of America*. New York: Basic Books.

Blumenthal, Max. 2007. "Agent of Intolerance." *The Nation*. May 28. https://www .thenation.com/AgentofIntolerance|TheNation

Bobltz, Sara. 2020. "Trump Supporters Swarm Biden Campaign Bus on Texas Highway." *HuffPost*. October 31. https://www.huffpost.com/entry/trump-supporte rs-biden-bus-texas_n_5f9dcae5c5b658b27c3b04a3

Bochetti, Mark. 2019. "Scalia, Skilled at Upending Rules, May Soon Write Them at Labor." *Roll Call*. August 5. https://www.rollcall.com/news/policy/scalia-skilled -at-upending-rules-may-soon-write-them-at-labor

Bokhari, Allum and Milo Yiannopoulos. 2016. "An Establishment Conservative's Guide to the Alt-Right." *Breitbart*. March 29. https://www.breitbart.com/tech/2016 /03/29/an-establishment-conservatives-guide-to-the-alt-right/

Bolton, John. 2020. *The Room Where It Happened: A White House Memoir*. New York: Simon and Schuster.

Book, Robert. 2017. "Yes, It Was The 'Affordable' Care Act that Increased Premiums." *Forbes*. March 22. https://forbes.com/sites/theapothecary/2017/03/22/ yes-it-was-the-affordable-care-act-that-increased-premiums/#46940b11d2

Bottari, Mary. 2018. "Behind Janus: Documents Reveal Decade-long Plot to Kill Public Sector Unions." *In These Times*. February/March. http://inthesetimes.com/f eatures/janus_supreme_court_unions_investigation.html

Brater, Jonathan, Kevin Morris, Myrna Perez and Christopher Deluzio. 2020. "Purges: A Growing Threat to the Right to Vote." *Brennan Center for Justice*. https://www.bre nnancenter.org/our-work/research-reports/purges-growing-threat-right-vote

Brecher, Jeremy. 1997. *Strike*. New York: South End Press.

Brecher, Jeremy and Stephanie Adler-Paindiris. 2018. "Restaurant Industry Association Files Suit Challenging 80/20 Rule." *Wage & Hour Law Update*, July 13.

Brewer, Mark. 2016. "Populism in American Politics." *Forum*, 14(3), 249–264.

Broaddus, Matt and Aviva Aron-Dine. 2019. "Medicaid Expansion Has Saved at Least 19,000 Lives, New Research Finds." *Center on Budget and Policy Priorities.* November 6. https://www.cbpp.org/research/health/medicaid-expa nsion-has-saved-at-least-19000-lives-new-research-finds Accessed September 19, 2020.

Brock, David. 2005. *The Republican Noise Machine: Right-wing Media and How It Corrupts Democracy.* New York: Crown Publishers.

Brock, David and Ari Rabin-Havt. 2012. *The Fox Effect: How Roger Ailes Turned a Network Into a Propaganda Machine.* New York: Random House, Inc.

Bump, Philip. 2015. "Donald Trump Retweeted a Very Wrong Set of Numbers on Race and Murder." *Washington Post.* November 22. https://www.wp.com/news/t he-fix/wp/2015/11/22/trump-retweeted-a-very-wrong-set-of-numbers-on-race-and -murder/

———. 2016. "The Numbers behind Trump's 'You Walk Down the Street, You Get Shot' Pitch to Black Voters." *Washington Post.* August 24. https://www.washingt onpost.com/news/the-fix/wp/2016/08/24/the-numbers-behind-trumps-you-walk-do wn-the-street-you-get-shot-pitch-to-black-voters/

Burdick v Takushi, 504 U.S. 428 (1992).

Bureau of Labor Statistics. 2019.

BLS. 2018. https://www.bls.gov/news.release/archives/union2_01192018.pdf

Burnham, Walter Dean. 1970. *Critical Elections and the Mainspring of American Politics.* New York: W.W. Norton Company.

Burke, Alison. 2017. "Working Class White Americans Are Now Dying in Middle Age at Faster Rates than Minority Groups." *Brookings.* March 23. https://www.bro okings.edu/blog/brookings-now/2017/03/23/working-class-white-americans-are-now-dying-in-middle-age-at-faster-rates-than-minority-groups/.

Burke, Daniel. 2016. "The Guilt-Free Gospel of Donald Trump." C*NN Politics.* October.

Butler, Stuart. 1989. "Assuring Affordable Health Care for All Americans." *The Heritage Foundation.* https://www.heritage.org/social-security/report/assuring-aff ordable-health-care-all-americans

Campbell, Sierra. 2019. "Trump Administration Proposes Cuts to SNAP Benefits and School Lunches." *Children Defense Fund.* August 2. https://www.childrensdefe nse.Org/blog/trump-admin-proposes-cuts-to-snap-benefits-and-schoollunches/? gclid=EAIaIQobChMI2MeVkP3W5wIVy8DAch2c4wOuEAAYASAAEgJSU _D_BwE.

Card, David and Alan Kruger. 1994. "Minimum Wages and Employment: A Case Study of the Fast-Food Industry in New Jersey and Pennsylvania." *The American Economic Review*, 84(4), 772–793.

———. 1995. *Myth and Measurement: The New Economics of the Minimum Wage.* Princeton, NJ: Princeton University Press.

Carmine, Edward and James Stimson 1990. *Issue Evolution: Race and the Transformation of American Politics.* Princeton, NJ: Princeton University Press.

Carter, Jacob, Emily Berman, Anita Desikan, Charise Johnson and Gretchen Goldman. 2019. "The State of Science in the Trump Era: Damage Done, Lessons

Learned and a Path to Progress." *Union of Concerned Scientists*. January 23. https://www.ucsusa.org/sites/default/files/attach/2019/01/ucs-trump-2yrs-report. pdf.

Carter, Jimmy and James Baker, ed. 2005. "Building Confidence in U.S. Elections: Report of the Commission on Federal Election Reform." http://www.american.edu /cfer/report/full_report.pdf.

Case, Anne and Angus Deaton. 2017. "Mortality and Morbidity in the 21st Century." *Brookings Institute*. https://www.brookings.edu/wp-content/uploads/2017/08/ca setextsp17bpea.pdf.

———. 2020. *Deaths of Despair and the Future of Capitalism*. Princeton, NJ: Princeton University Press.

Cavenave, Noel. 2018. *Killing African Americans: Police and Vigilante Violence as a Racial Control Mechanism*. New York: Routledge.

Center for Responsible Politics/OpenSecrets.Org. 2021. "Top Spenders." https://ww w.opensecrets.org/federal-lobbying/top-spenders

Centers for Medicare and Medicaid Services. 2021. "National Health Expenditure Accounts, National Health Expenditure Data: Historical." June 24. https://cms.gov/ Research-Statistics-Data-and-Systems/statistics-Trends-and-Reports/NationalHeal thExpenData/NationalHealthAccountsHistorical.

Citizens United v Federal Election Commission, 558 U.S. 310 (2010).

Cobbs, Roger and Charles Elder. 1983. *Participation in American Politics: The Dynamics of Agenda Building*. Baltimore: Johns Hopkins University Press.

Cohen, Adam. 2020. *Supreme Inequality: The Supreme Court's Fifty Year Battle for a more Unjust America*. New York: Penguin Press.

Cohen, Michael. 2020. *Disloyal: A Memoir: The True Story of the Former Personal Attorney to President Donald J. Trump*. New York: Skyhorse Publishing

Colby, Gerard. 1984. *Du Pont Dynasty: Behind the Nylon Curtain*. New York: Open Road.

Collins, Jane and Victoria Mayer. 2010. *Both Hands Tied: Welfare Reform and the Race to the Bottom of the Low Wage Labor Market*. Chicago: University of Chicago Press.

Congressional Budget Office. 2014. *The Effects of a Minimum Wage Increase on Employment and Family Income*. Washington, DC: Government Printing, February. file:///C:/Users/carwilso/Documents/MinimumWageCBO.pdf

———. 2021. "The Budgetary Effects of Raising the Wage Act of 2021." *The Budgetary Effects of the Raise the Wage Act of 2021 (cbo.gov)*. February. https:// www.cbo.gov/system/files/2021-02/56975-Minimum-Wage.pdf

Corsi, Jerome. 2008. *The Obama Nation: Leftist Politics and the Cult of Personality*. New York: Simon & Schuster.

———. 2011. *Where's the Birth Certificate? The Case that Barack Obama is not Eligible to be President*. Washington, DC: Wind Books.

Council of Economic Advisers. 2017. "Corporate Tax Reform and Wages: Theory and Evidence." https://www.whitehouse.gov/sites/whitehouse.gov/files/documents /Tax%20Reform%20and%20Wages.pdf

Crary, David. 2020. "Trump's Prayer Breakfast Jibes Jolt Many Faith Leaders." *ABC News*. February 6, 2020.

Crawford v Marion County Election Board, 553 U.S. 181 (2008).

Creitz, Charles. 2020. "Azar Blatsts ObamaCare as 'Not Affordable Health Care' as Supreme Court Battle over 2010 Law Looms." *Fox News*. https://www.foxnews.com/politics/azar-obamacare-not-affordable-health-care

Crenson, Matthew. 1971. *The Un-politics of Air Pollution: A Study of Non-Decisionmaking in the Cities.* Baltimore: Johns Hopkins University Press.

Currie, Elliot. 2016. *The Roots of Danger: Violent Crime in Global Perspective.* New York: Oxford University Press.

Dahl, Robert. 1989. *Democracy and Its Critics*. New Haven: Yale University Press.

———. 2005. *Who Governs? Democracy and Power in an American City.* New Haven: Yale University Press.

Dahl, Ryan. 2007. "Collective Bargaining Agreements and Chapter 9 Bankruptcy." https://www.kirkland.com/-/media/publications/article/2007/11/collective-bargaining-agreements-and-chapter-9-ban/ecd988879cd62726751863c380ee6977.pdf

Danziger, Sheldon and Robert Haveman. "The Reagan Budget: A Sharp Break with the Past." *Challenge*, 24, May–June 1981, 5–13.

Davetti, LaDonna. 2012. "Five Thins to Know About the TANF Work Rules." *Center for Budget Policy and Priorities.* https://www.cbpp.org/blog/five-things-to-know-about-the-tanf-work-rules#:~:text=Five%20Things%20To%20Know%20About%20the%20TANF%20Work,to%20find%20work%20with%20one.%20More%20items...%20

Davis, Ben. 2020. "Worker Endangerment in the Meat Industry during COVID-19." April 30. http://www.jurist.org/comentary/2020/04/ben-davis-worker-endangerment-during-covid-19/

Davis, Julie, Sheryl Stolberg and Thomas Kaplan. 2018. "Trump Alarms Lawmakers with Disparaging Words for Haiti and Africa." *New York Times*. January 11. https://www.nytimes.com/2018/01/11/us/politics/trump-shithole-countries.html

Davidson, Joe. 2017. "Obama's Orders Protecting Federal Contract Workers Face Reversal by Trump." *Washington Post*. January 18. https://www.washingtonpost.com/news/powerpost/wp/2017/01/18/obamas-orders-protecting-federal-contract-workers-face-reversal-by-trump/

Delsol, Jean-Phalippe, Nicolas Lecaussin and Emmanuel Martin. 2017. *Anti-Piketty: Capital for the 21$^{st}$ Century.* Washington, DC: The Cato Institute.

Derysh, Igor. 2019. "Student Loan Forgiveness Program for Public Servants Has So Much Complex Red Tape Almost No One Qualifies." *Salon*. September 5. https://www.salon.com/2019/09/05/betsy-devos-education-department-rejects-99-of-applications-for-loan-forgiveness-program/

Diamond, Sara. 1989. *Roads to Dominion: Right-wing Movements and Political Power in the United States.* New York: Gilford Press.

Dickinson, Maggie. 2019. "The Ripple Effects of Taking SNAP Benefits from One Person." *The Atlantic*, December.

Dixon, Thomas. *The Clansman: A Historical Romance of the Ku Klux Klan.* New York: Doubleday.

Downs, Anthony. "Up and Down with Ecology—The "Issue-Attention Cycle." *The Public Interest*, 28 (Summer), 37–80.

Dred Scott v Sanford, 60 U.S. 393 (1857).

DuBois, W. E. B. 1998. *Black Reconstruction, 1860–1880*. New York: Frist Free Press.

Dunn, Megan and James Walker. 2016. "Union Membership in the United States." *Bureau of Labor Statistics*. https://www.bls.gov/spotlight/2016/union-membership -in-the-united-states/pdf/union-membership-in-the-united-states.pdf

Dyer, Joel. 1997. *Harvest of Rage: Why Oklahoma City is Only the Beginning*. Boulder, CO: Westview Press.

Economists Editors. 2020. "Grading Trumponomics: How to Judge President Trump's Economic Record." *The Economists*. October 17. https://www.economist .com/leaders/2020/10/17/how-to-judge-president-trumps-economic-record

Edsell, Mary and Thomas Edsell. *Chain Reaction: The Impact of Race, Rights and Taxes on American Politics*. New York: Norton Press.

Edwards, Frank, Hedwig Lee and Michael Esposito. 2019. "Risk of Being Killed by Police Use of Force in the United States by age, Race-Ethnicity, and Sex." *Proceedings of the National Academy of Science*, 116, August 20. https://www.pna s.org/content/pnas/116/34/16793.full.pdf

Ehle, John. 1989. *Trail of Tears': The Rise and Fall of the Cherokee Nation*. New York: Anchor Books.

Elk, Mike and Bo Sloan. 2011. "The Hidden History of ALEC and Prison Labor." *The Nation*. August 1. https://www.thenation.com/article/archive/hidden-history -alec-and-prison-labor/?print=1

Emanuel, Ezekiel. 2015. Reinventing American Health Care: How the Affordable Care Act Will Improve Our Terribly Complex, Blatantly Unjust, Outrageously Expensive, Grossly Inefficient, Error Prone System. New York: Perseus Books.

Encyclopedia Britannica. "Racism." https://www.britannica.com/topic/racism.

Epstein, Reid and Linda Qui. 2019. "Fact-checking Trump's Claims that Democrats Are Radical Socialists." *New York Times*. July 20. https://www.nytimes.com/2019 /07/20/us/politics/trump-democrats-socialists.html?searchResultPosition=1

Fang, Lee. 2013. *The Machine: A Field Guide to the Resurgent Right*. New York: The New Press.

Feagin, Joe. 2012. *White Party, White Government: Race, Class and U.S. Politics*. New York: Routledge Taylor & Francis Group.

Feldman, Glenn. 2004. *The Disfranchisement Myth: Poor Whites and Suffrage Restrictions in Alabama*. Athens: University of Georgia Press.

Feldman, Justin. 2020. "Police Killings in the United States: Inequalities by Race/ Ethnicity and Socioeconomic Position." *People's Policy Project*. https://www.peo plespolicyproject.org/wp-content/uploads/2020/06/PoliceKillings.pdf

Feldman, Max. 2020. "Ten Voter Fraud Lies Debunked." *Brennan Center for Justice*. May 27 https://www.brennancenter.org/our-work/research-reports/10-voter-fraud -lies-debunked

Flagg, Anna. 2018. "The Myth of the Criminal Immigrant." *New York Times*. March 30. https://www.nytimes.com/interactive/2018/03/30/upshot/crime-immig rant-myth.html.

Floyd, Ife. 2018. "TANF Reaches Few Poor Families." *Center for Budget Policy and Priorities*. https://www.cbpp.org/research/family-income-support/tanf-reaching-few-poor-families

Foner, Eric. 1982. *Organized Labor and the Black Worker 1619–1981*. New York: International Publishers.

———. 2014. *Reconstruction: America's Unfinished Revolution, 1863–1877*. New York: Harper.

Foroohar, Rana. 2016. *Makers and Takers: How Wall Street Destroyed Main Street*. New York: Penguin Random House.

Fouhy, Beth. 2011. *Trump: Obama a "Terrible Student" Not Good Enough for Harvard*. New York: NBC Trump: Obama a "Terrible Student" Not Good Enough for Harvard – NBC New York.

Frances, Allen. 2018. *Twilight of American Sanity: A Psychiatrist Analyzes the Age of Trump*. New York: Harper Collins Publishers.

Frank, P., Clancy, C. M., Gold, M. R. 1993. "Health Insurance and Mortality: Evidence from a National Cohort." *Journal of American Medical Association*, 270, 223–233.

Frank, Thomas. 2020. *The People, No: A Brief History of Anti-Populism*. New York: Henry Holt and Company.

Freedland, Jonathan. 2017. "The New Age of Ayn Rand: How She Won Over Trump and Silicon Valley." *The Guardian*. April 10. https://www.theguardian.com/books/2017/apr/10/new-age-ayn-rand-conquered-trump-white-house-silicon-valley

Friedman, Milton. 1955. "The Role of Government in Education." In Robert Solo (Ed.), *Economics and the Public Interests*, 123–144. Rutgers University Press.

———. 1962. *Capitalism and Freedom*. Chicago: University of Chicago Press.

Friedman, Milton and Rose Friedman. 1990. *Free to Choose: A Personal Statement*. New York: Harvest Books, Harcourt, Inc.

Frizell, Sam. 2019. "Here's How Bernie Sanders Explained Democratic Socialism." *Time*. February 20. Here's How Bernie Sanders Explained Democratic Socialism | Time

Fromm, Erich. 1994. *Escape from Freedom*. New York: Henry Holt and Company.

Furman, Jason and Betsey Stevensen. 2014. "Congressional Budget Office Report Finds minimum Wage Lifts Wages for 16.5 Million Workers." White House Office Newsrelease. February. Congressional Budget Office Report Finds Minimum Wage Lifts Wages for 16.5 Million Workers | whitehouse.gov (archives.gov).

Gajanan, Mahita. 2017. "Donald Trump's Legal Team won a 'Russia Law Firm of the Year' Award." *Fortune*. January 11. https://fortune.com/2017/01/11/donald-trumps-morgan-lewis-russia-award/

Gallup. 2019. "Immigration." *Gallup Polls*. https://news.gallup.com/poll/1660/immigration.aspx

Galston, William. 2018. *Anti-Pluralism: The Populist Threat to Liberal Democracy*. New Haven: Yale University Press.

Gayner, Jeffrey. 1995. "The Contract with America: Implementing New Ideas in the U.S." *The Heritage Foundation*. October 12.

Gerber, Alan and Gregory Huber. 2010. "Partisanship, Political Control, and Economic Assessments." *American Journal of Political Science*, 54(1, January), 153–173.

Gest, Justin. 2016. *The New Minority: White Working Class Politics in an Age of Immigration and Inequality*. New York: Oxford University Press.

Gilder, George. 2012. *Wealth and Poverty*. Washington, DC: Regnery Publishing Company.

Gilens, Martin. 1999. *Why Americans Hate Welfare: Race, Media, and the Politics of Antipoverty Programs*. Chicago: University of Chicago Press.

Gingrich, Newt. 2018. *Trump's America: The Truth About Our Nation's Great Comeback*. New York: Center Street.

Goldberg, David. 1993. *Racist Culture: Philosophy and the Politics of Meaning*. Oxford, UK: Blackwell.

Golshan, Tara. 2019. "Bernie Sanders's Definition of Democratic Socialism, Explained." *Vox*, June 12. Bernie Sanders's speech defining democratic socialism, explained - Vox

Goodwyn, Lawrence. 1978. *A Populist Movement: A Short History of the Agrarian Revolt in America*. New York: Oxford University Press.

Gordon, Linda. 1994. *Pitied but not Entitled: Single Mothers and the History of Welfare 1890–1935*. Cambridge: Harvard University Press.

Government Accountability Office. 2019. "Health Insurance Exchanges: Claims Costs and Federal and State Policies Drove Insurer Participation, Premiums and Plan Design." January. https://www.gao.gov/assets/gao-19-215.pdf

Graham, David, Adrienne Green, Cullen Murphy and Parker Richards. 2019. "An Oral History of Trump's Bigotry." *Atlantic*. June.

Gramlich, John. 2020. "How Border Apprehension, ICE Arrest and Deportations Have Changed under Trump." *Pew Research Center*. March 2. https://www.pewresearch.org/fact-tank/2020/03/02/how-border-apprehensions-ice-arrests-and-deportations-have-changed-under-trump/

Gramsci, Antonio. 1987. *Select ion from the Prison Notebooks of Antonio Gramsci*. New York: International Publishers.

Grant, Madison. 1916. *The Passing of the Great Race of the Racial Bases of European History*. New York: Charles Scribner's Sons.

Gray, Wayne and John Scholz. 1993. "Does Regulatory Enforcement Work? A Panel Analysis." *Law and Society Review*, 27(1), 177–214.

Green, Emma. 2020. "Why Can't He Just Say it." *Atlantic*. September 30. https://www.theatlantic.com/politics/archive/2020/09/trump-white-nationalism-proud-boys-debate/616546/

Green, Joshua. 2018. *Devil's Bargain: Steve Bannon, Donald Trump, and the Nationalist Uprising*. New York: Penguin Books.

Gross, Wendy, Tobias Stark, John Krosnick, Josh Pasek, Gaurav Sood, Trevor Tompson, Jennifer Agiesta and Dennis Junius. 2012. "Americans' Attitudes Toward the Affordable Care Act: Would Better Public Understand Increase or Decrease Favorability." *Unpublished Paper*. http://web.stanford.edu/dept/commun

icationfaculty/krosnick/docs/2012/health%20care%202012-%20knowledge%20
and20favorability.pdf

Grossmann, Matt and David Hopkins. 2016. *Asymmetric Politics: Ideological Republicans and Group Interest Democrats*. New York: Oxford University Press.

Gstalter, Morgan. 2021. "Trump Supporter Admits to Voter Fraud After Casting Dead Mother's Ballot in 2020." *The Hill*. May 4. Trump supporter admits to voter fraud after casting dead mother's ballot in 2020 | TheHill

Gumbel, Andrew. 2016. *Down for the Count: Dirty Elections and the Rotten History of Democracy in America*. New York: The New Press.

Hacker, Jacob and Paul Pierson. 2011. *Winner-Take-All Politics: How Washington Made the Rich Richer—and Turned Its Back on the Middle Class*. New York: Simon & Schuster Paperbacks.

———. 2016. *American Amnesia: How the War on Government Led Us to Forget What Made America Prosper*. New York: Simon & Schuster.

———. 2020. *Let Them Eat Tweets: How the Rich Rules in an Age of Extreme Inequality*. New York: Liveright Publishing Corporation, W.W. Norton & Co.

Hajnal, Zoltan, Nazita Lajevardi, and Lindsay Nielson. 2017. "Voter Identification Laws and the Suppression of Minority Votes." *The Journal of Politics*, 79(2), 363–379.

Hammer v Daghenhart, 247 U.S. 251 (1918).

Hannah-Jones, Nikole. 2015. "Living Apart: How the Government Betrayed a Landmark Civil Rights Law." *ProPublica*, June 25. https://www.propublica.org/art icle/living-apart-how-the-government-betrayed-a-landmark-civil-rights-law

Harrell, Erika, Lynn Langton, Marcus Berzofsky, Lance Couzens and Hope Smiley-McDonald. 2014. "Household Poverty and Nonfatal Violent Victimization, 2008–2012." *Special Report, U.S.D.J. Office of Justice Programs, Bureau of Justice Statistics*. https://www.bjs.gov/content/pub/pdf/hpnvv0812.pdf

Harris, Harriet. 1998. *Fundamentalism and Evangelicals*. Oxford: Clarendon Press.

Harris, Richard and Sidney Milkis. 1996. *The Politics of Regulatory Change: A Tale of Two Agencies*. New York: Oxford University Press.

Harvey, David. 2005. *A Brief History of Neoliberalism*. New York: Oxford University Press.

Hauter, Wenonah. 2012. *Foodopoly: The Battle Over the Future of Food and Farming*. New York: The New Press.

Hawley, George. 2017. *Making Sense of the Alt-Right*. New York: Columbia University Press.

Hayek, Friedrich. 1944. *The Road to Serfdom*. Chicago: University of Chicago Press.

Heritage Action Website. 2021. https://heritageaction.com/about.

The Heritage Foundation. 2021. "A Sampling of Recent Election Fraud Cases from Across the United States." May 15, 2021. https://www.heritage.org/voterfraud

Hertel-Fernandez, Alexander. 2019. *State Capture: How Conservative Activists, Big Businesses, and Wealthy Donors Reshaped the American States—and the Nation*. New York: Oxford University Press.

Hetherington, Marc and Jonathan Weiler. 2009. *Authoritarianism and Polarization in American Politics*. New York: Cambridge University Press.

Hicks, William, Seth McKee and Mitchell Sellers. 2015. "A Principle or a Strategy? Voter Identification Laws and Partisan Competition in the American States." *Political Research Quarterly*, 68(1, March), 18–33.

Hill v Gautreaux, 425 U.S. 284 (1976).

Hitchens, Christopher. 2008. *Thomas Paine's Rights of Man: A Biography*. New York: Grove Press.

Hochschild, Arie. 2016. *Strangers in Their Own Land: Anger and Mourning on the American Right*. New York: The New Press.

Hofstadter, Richard. 1963. *Anti-intellectualism in American Life*. New York: Vintage Books.

———. 1967. *The Paranoid Style in American Politics and Other Essays*. New York: Vintage Books.

———. 1995. *The Age of Reform from Bryan to FDR*. New York: Vintage Books.

Hogue, James. 2006. *Uncivil War: Five New Orleans Street Battles and the Fall of the Radical Reconstruction*. Baton Rouge: Louisiana State University

Hood III, M. V. and Charles Bullock III. 2012. "Much Ado About Nothing? An Empirical Assessment of the Georgia Voter Identification Statute." *State Politics and Policy Quarterly*, 12(4, December), 394–414.

Horton, Jake. 2020. "Are U.S. Cities Seeing a Surge in Violent Crime as Trump Claims?" *BBC News*. September 1. https://www.bbc.com/news/world-us-canada-53525440

Horwitz, Steven. 2015. "Inequality, Mobility and Being Poor in America." *Social Philosophy and Policy*. Spring.

Hudson, Michael. 2011. *The Monster: How a Gang of Predatory Lenders and Wall Street Bankers Fleeced America and Spawned a Global Crisis*. New York: Times Books.

Irons, John and Isaac Shapiro. 2011. "Regulation, Employment and the Economy: Fears of Job Loss are Overblown." *Economic Policy Institute*. April 12.

Isenberg, Nancy. 2016. *White Trash: The 400-Year Untold History of Class in America*. New York: Penguin Books.

Jacobs, Lawrence and Theda Skocpol. 2005. *Inequality and American Democracy: What We Know and What We Need to Learn*. New York: Russell Sage Foundation.

Jamieson, Kathleen and Joseph Cappella. 2008. *Echo Chamber: Rush Limbaugh and the Conservative Media Establishment*. New York: Oxford University Press.

Janik, Rachel. 2018. "Michael Savage Promotes White Nationalist Conspiracy on his Radio Show, Wins Praise from Racist Author." *Southern Poverty Law Center, Hate Watch* https://www.splcenter.org/hatewatch/2018/02/01/michael-savage-promotes-white-nationalist-conspiracy-his-radio-show-wins-praise-racist

Janus v ASCME, 585 U.S. __ (2018).

Jardina, Ashley. 2019. *White Identity Politics*. Cambridge, UK: Cambridge University Press.

Jason, Lemon. 2019. "MLK's Niece Defends Donald Trump against Racism Accusations: 'All That News Is Absolutely Fake'" *Newsweek*. July 30.

Johnson v California, 543 U.S. 499 (2005).

Johnson, Haynes. 1991. *Sleepwalking through History: America in the Reagan Years.* New York: Anchor Books.

Johnson, Marty. 2020. "Federal Judge Temporarily Bars Federal Officers in Portland from Taking Action against Journalists, Observers." *The Hill.* July 23. https://thehill.com/homenews/administration/508834-federal-judge-temporarily-bars-fed eral-officers-in-portland-from

Johnson, Theodore and Max Feldman. 2020. "The New Voter Suppression." *The Brennan Center for Justice.* https://www.brennancenter.org/our-work/research-re ports/new-voter-suppression

Jones, Alexi and Wendy Sawyer. 2020. "Not Just 'a Few Bad Apples': U.S. Police Kill Civilians a Much Higher Rates than Other Countries." *Prison Policy Initiative.* Not Just "a Few Bad Apples": U.S. Police Kill Civilians at Much Higher Rates Than Other Countries | Prison Policy Initiative.

Jones, Bryan and Lynn Bachelor. 1993. *The Sustaining Hand: Community Leadership and Corporate Power.* Lawrence, KS: University of Kansas Press.

Jones, Mark, Renee Cross and Jim Granato. 2017. "The Texas Voter ID Law and the 2016 Election: A Study of Harris County and Congressional District 23." Hobby School of Public Affairs, University of Houston.

Jost, John and Jamie Napier. 2009. "Political Ideologies: Its Structures, Functions, and Elective Affinities." *Annual Review of Psychology*, 60, 307–337.

Judis, John. 2016. *The Populist Explosion: How the Great Recession Transformed American and European Politics.* New York: Columbia Global Reports.

Kakutani, Michiko. 2018. *The Death of Truth: Notes on Falsehood in the Age of Trump.* New York: The Duggan Books.

Kanno-Youngs, Zolan. 2020. "Were the Actions of Federal Agents in Portland Legal?" *New York Times*, July 24. https://www.nytimes.com/2020/07/17/us/politic s/federal-agents-portland-arrests.html

Kennedy, Merrit. 2020. "U.S. Charges Suspect in El Paso Walmart Shooter with Hate Crimes." *NPR.* February 6. https://www.npr.org/2020/02/06/803503292 /u-s-charges-walmart-gunman-in-el-paso-with-hate-crimes#:~:text=Federal%20pr osecutors%20have%20charged%20Patrick%20Wood%20Crusius%20with,driven %20to%20the%20store%20intending%20to%20kill%20%22Mexicans.%22

Kennedy Jr., Robert F. 2006. "Was the 2004 Election Stolen?" *Rolling Stone*, June 1.

Kertscher, Tom. 2020. "Facebook Post Misrepresents Obama's Use of Pardon Power." *Politifact, The Poynter Institute*, February 24. https://www.politifact.co m/factchecks/2020/feb/24/facebook-posts/misleading-based-numbers-say-obama- and-not-trump-a/

Kessler, Glenn. 2016. "Donald Trump and David Duke: For the Record." *The Washington Post.* March 1. https://www.washingtonpost.com/news/fact-checker/ wp/2016/03/01/donald-trump-and-david-duke-for-the-record/

Key, V.O. 1955. "A Theory of Critical Elections." *Journal of Politics*, 17, 3–18.

Keyssar, Alexander. 2000. *The Right to Vote: The Contested History of Democracy in the United States.* New York: Basic Books.

Kharakh, Ben and Dan Primack. 2016. "Donald Trump's Social Media Ties to White Supremacists: Its More than Just a Couple of Retweets." *Fortune*. March 22.

Kimball, Spencer. 2019. "Trump Calls Baltimore a 'Disgusting, Rat and Rodent Infested Mess in Attack on Rep. Elijah Cummings." *CNMB*. July 17. https://www.cnbc.com/2019/07/27/trump-calls-baltimore-a-disgusting-rat-and-rodent-infested-mess-in-attack-on-rep-elijah-cummings.html

King, Alveda. 2020. "Why Trump." *Atlantic Tribune*. October 6. Alveda King, niece of Dr. Martin Luther King, Jr. supports Trump - Atlanta Tribune.

Klumpp, Tilman, Hugo Mialon, Michael Williams. 2019. "The Voting Rights of Ex-Felons and Election Outcomes in the United States." *International Review of Law and Economics*, 59, 40–56, September.

Kobach, Kris. 2011. "The Case for Voter ID." *The Wall Street Journal*. May 23. https://www.wsj.com/articles/sb10001424052748704816604576333650886790480

Koerner, Claudier. 2018. "These Tipping Activists Deny Being Funded by the Restaurant Lobby." *BuzzFeed News*. https://www.buzzfeednews.com/article/claudiakoerner/rwa-restaurant-workers-america-grassroots-astroturf-berman

Koerth, Maggie. 2019. "The Tangled Story behind Trump's False Claims of Voter Fraud." *FiveThirtyEight*. May 11. https://fivethirtyeight.com/features/trump-noncitizen-voters/

Kovel, Joel. 1984. *White Racism: A Psychohistory*. New York: Columbia University Press.

Krieg, Gregory. 2016. "14 of Trump's Most Outrageous 'Birther Claims—Half From 2011." *CNN Politics*. September 16. https://www.cnn.com/2016/09/09/politics/donald-trump-birther/index.html

Krugman, Paul. 1994. *Peddling Prosperity: Economic Sense and Nonsense in the Age of Diminished Expectations*. New York: W.W. Norton.

Krugman, Paul. 2009. *The Conscience of a Liberal*. New York: W.W. Norton.

Krugman, Paul. 2021. *Arguing with Zombies: Economics, Politics and the Fight for a Better Future*. New York: W.W. Norton.

Kuhner, Thomas. 2014. *Capitalism and Democracy: Money in Politics and the Free Market Constitution*. Stanford, CA: Stanford Law Books.

Lafer, Gordon. 2017. *The One Percent Solution: How Corporations Are Remaking America One State at a Time*. Ithaca: Cornell University Press.

Lanard, Noah. 2017. "Trump's Labor Board Appointments are Another Blow for Unions." *Mother Jones*. July 19. https://www.motherjones.com/politics/2017/07/trumps-labor-board-appointments-are-another-blow-for-unions/

Leadership Conference Education. 2019. "Democracy Diverted: Polling Place Closure and the Right to Vote." http://civilrightsdocs.info/pdf/reports/Democracy-Diverted.pdf

Lee, Ye Hee. 2016. "A Guide to All of Donald Trump's Flip-Flops on Minimum Wage." *Washington Post*. August 3. http://www.washingtonpost.com/news/fact-checker/wp/2016/08/03/a-guide-to-all-of-donald-trump's-flip-flops-on-minimum-wage.

Levine, Sam. 2016. "This Woman Got 8 Years in Prison for illegally Voting. Texas is Showing No Mercy." *Huffington Post*. November 30. https://www.huffpost.com/entry/kris-kobach-trial-voting-rights_n_5a9a072fe4b0a0ba4ad37328

———. 2018. "Trump's Voter Fraud Czar and His Claims About Illegal Voting Are About to Go on Trial." *Huffington Post*. March 5. https://www.huffpost.com/entry/kris-kobach-trial-voting-rights_n_5a9a072fe4b0a0ba4ad37328

Levintova, Hannah. 2019. "The Trump Administration Just Proposed kicking 3.1 Million People Off Food Stamps." *Mother Jones*. July 23. https://www.motherjones.com/food/2019/07/trump-food-stamp-cuts/

Levitt, Justin. 2008. "In-person Voter Fraud Myth: Myth and Trigger for Disenfranchisement." Testimony before the U.S. Senate Committee on Rules and Administration. Brennan Center for Justice. https://www.brenancenter.org/analysis/in-person-voter-fraud-myth-justin-levitt-senate-committee

———. 2014. "A Comprehensive Investigation of Voter Impersonation Finds 31 Credible Incidents Out of One Billion Ballots Cast." *Washington Post*. August 6. https://www.washingtonpost.com/news/wonk/wp/2014/08/06/a-comprehensive-investigation-of-voter-impersonation-finds-31-credible-incidents-out-of-one-billion-ballots-cast/?utm_term=.10146ccc8203

Lindblom, Charles. 1980. *Politics and Markets: The World's Political Economic Systems*. New York: Basic Books.

Lochner v New York, 198 U.S. 45 (1905).

Logan, Rayford. 1965. *The Betrayal of the Negro*. New York: Collier-Macmillan.

Lopez, German. 2020. "Donald Trump's Long History of Racism from the 1970s to 2020." *Vox*. August 13. https://www.vox.com/2016/7/25/12270880/donald-trump-racist-racism-history

Lopez, Ian. 2014. *Dog Whistle Politics: How Coded Racial Appeals Have Reinvented Racism and Wrecked the Middle Class*. New York: Oxford University Press.

Lott, John. 2006. "Evidence of Voter Fraud and the Impact that Regulations to Reduce Fraud have on Voter Participation Rates." Department of Economics SUNY Binghamton, August.

Lowi, Theodore. 1969. *End of Liberalism: Ideology, Policy and the Crisis of Public Authority*. New York: Norton.

Lysova, Alexandra, Nikolay Shchitov, and William Pridemore. 2012. "Homicide in Russia, Ukraine, and Belarus." In Marike Liem and William Pridemore (Eds.), *Handbook of European Homicide Research: Patterns, Explanations, and Country Studies*, Vol. 29, 451–469. New York: Springer.

MacLean, Nancy. 2017. *Democracy in Chains: The Deep History of the Radical Right's Stealth Plan for America*. London: Scribe Publications.

Macpherson, C. B. 1975. *Democratic Theory: Essays in Retrieval*. New York: Oxford University Press.

MacWilliams, Matthew. 2016. *The Rise of Trump: America's Authoritarian Spring*. Amherst, MA: The Amherst College Press.

Madland, David, Karla Walter, Alex Rowell, Zoe Willingham, and Malkie Wall. 2019. "President Trump's Policies are Hurting American Workers." *American*

*Progressive Action.* Blog Downloaded. December 24, 2019. https://www.american progressaction.org/issues/economy/reports/2018/01/26/168366/president-trumps -policies-hurting-american-workers/

Mahler, Jonathan. 2018. "How One Conservative Think Tank Is Stocking Trump's Government." *The New York Times.* June 20.

Mann, Thomas and Norman Ornstein. 2012. *It's Even Worse That It Looks: How the American Constitutional System Collided with the New Politics of Extremism.* New York: Basic Books.

Manza, Jeff and Ned Crowley. 2017. Working Class Hero? Interrogating the Social Baes of the Rise of Donald Trump." *Forum,* 15(1), 3–28. https://as.nyu.edu/conten t/dam/nyu-as/sociology/documents/manza-publications/Forum.pdf

Manza, Jeff, and Christopher Uggen. 2008. *Locked Out: Felon Disenfranchisement and American Democracy.* New York: Oxford University Press, Inc.

Marans, Daniel. 2020. "Trump Supporter Arrested for Requesting Absentee Ballot for Dead Mother." *Huffington Post.* October 22.

Marley, Patrick and Bruce Vielmetti. 2019. "Judge Orders 234,000 purged from Wisconsin Voter Rolls." *U.S. Today.* https://www.usatoday.com/story/news/nation/2019/12/13/w isconsin-voter-registration-judge-orders-234-000-purged-rolls/2643852001/

Martin, Jeffrey. 2020. "President Trump Says Democratic Platform's 'Probably Communist.'" *Newsweek,* September 22. https://www.msn.com/en-us/news/politics/ president-trump-says-democratic-platform-is-probably-communist/ar-BB19hxzi

Mascaro, Lisa. 2016. "Trump Made Promises to Blue-collar Voters. Democrats Plan to Make Sure He Follows Through." *Los Angeles Times.* November 29.

Mayer, Jane. 2016. *Dark Money: The Hidden History of the Billionaires Behind the Rise of the Radical Right.* New York: Random House.

Mayhew, David. 2002. *Electoral Realignment: A Critique of an American Genre.* New Haven: Yale University Press.

Mazmanian, David and Paul Sabatier. 1989. *Implementation and Public Policy.* Lanham, MD: University Press of America.

McConnell, Grant. 1966. *Private Power and American Democracy.* New York: Knopf.

McEnany, Kayleigh. 2018. *The New American Revolution: the Making of a Populist Movement* New York: Simon & Schuster.

McNicholar, Celine, Heidi Shierholz and Marni von Wilpert. "Workers' Health, Safety, and Pay Are Among the Casualties of Trump's War on Regulations: A Deregulation Year in Review." *Economic Policy Institute.* January 29. https://ww w.epi.org/publication/deregulation-year-in-review/

McNicholas, Celine, Lynn Rhinehart, and Margaret Poydock. 2020. "50 Reasons the Trump Administration is Bad for Workers. Economic Policy Institute." Epi.org /207624.

McNicholas, Celine, Margaret Poydock and Lynn Rhinehart. 2019. "Unprecedented: The Trump NLRB's Attack on Workers' Rights." *Economic Policy Institute.* U.S. Chamber of Commerce. 2017. "Restoring Common Sense to Labor Law: Ten Policies to Fix at the National Labor Relations Board." February 28.

Meacham, Jon. *The Soul of America: The Battle for Our Better Angels.* New York: Random House.

Merritt, Keri. 2017. *Masterless Men: Poor Whites and Slavery in the Antebellum South*. Cambridge, UK: Cambridge University Press.

Metzl, Jonathan. 2019. *Dying of Whiteness: How the Politics of Racial Resentment is Killing America's Heartland*. New York: Basic Books.

Michaels, David. 2020. "What Trump Could Do Right Now to Keep Workers Safe From Coronavirus." *The Atlantic*. March 2. https://www.theatlantic.com/ideas/a rchive/2020/03/use-osha-help-slow-covid-19-pandemic/607312

Michener, Jamila. 2020. "Race, Politics, and the Affordable Care Act." *Journal of Health Politics, Policy ad Law*, 45(4, August), 547–566.

Miles, Thomas. 2004. "Felon Disenfranchisement and Voter Turnout." *The Journal of Legal Studies*, 33, 85–129.

Miller, Sarah, Sean Altekruse, Norman Johnson, and Laura Wherry. 2019. "Medicaid and Mortality: New Evidence from Linked Survey and Administrative Data." *National Bureau of Economics Research Working Paper*, August. https://www .nber.org/papers/w26081

Minsky, Adam. 2019. "Judge Threatens Betsy DeVos with Jail in Student Loan Case." *Forbes*, October 8.

Mishel, Lawrence and Julia Wolfe. 2019. "CEO Compensation Has Grown 94% Since 1978 Typical Worker Compensation Has Risen Only 12 % During that Time." *Economic Policy Institute Report*, August 14.

———. 2021. "Preliminary Data Show CEO Pay Jumped Nearly 16 % in 2020, While Average Worker Compensation Rose 1.8%." *Economic Policy Institute Report*, May 27.

Mitchell, Chris. 2017. "Evans Has 30M Evangelicals Praying for Jerusalem." *Christian Broadcasting Nation News*. December 10. https://www1.cbn.com/cbnn ews/israel/2017/december/mike-evans-we-rsquo-re-in-the-middle-of-prophecy

Morgan, Stephen, and Jiwon Lee. 2018. "Trump Voters and the White Working Class." *Sociological Sciences*, 5, 234–245

Mounk, Yascha. 2018. *The People vs Democracy: Why Our Freedom Is in Danger and How to Save It*. Cambridge, MA: Harvard University Press.

Mower, Lawrence and Langston Taylor. 2020. "Florida Ruled Felons Must Pay to Vote. Now, It Doesn't Know How Many Can." *Tampa Bay Times*. October 12. https://www.tampabay.com/news/florida-politics/elections/2020/10/07/florida-rule d-felons-must-pay-to-vote-now-it-doesnt-know-how-many-can/

Mudde, Cas. 2007. *Populist Radical Right Parties in Europe*. Cambridge, UK: Cambridge University Press.

Muddle, Cas and Cristobal Kaltwasser. 2017. *Populism: A Short Introduction*. New York: Oxford University Press.

Muhlhausen, David and Kari Sikich. "New Analysis Shows Voter Identification Laws Do Not Reduce Turnout." *A Report of the Heritage Center for Data Analysis*. www .heritage.org/research/legalissues/cda07-04.cfm

Mukpo, Ashoka. 2018. "Supreme Court Enables Mass Disenfranchisement of North Dakota's native Americans." *ACLU*. October 12. https://www.aclu.org/blog/voting-ri ghts/supreme-court-enables-mass-disenfranchisement-north-dakotas-native-americans

Muller, Jan-Werner. 2016. *What is Populism?* Philadelphia: University of Pennsylvania Press.

Mutz, Diana. 2018. "Status Threat, Not Economic Hardship, Explain the 2016 Presidential Vote." *Proceedings of the National Academies of Science* 115: E4330–E4339.

Murray, Charles. 1984. *Losing Ground: American Social Policy, 1950–1980*. New York: Basic Books.

Murray, Charles and Richard Herrnstein. 1994. *The Bell Curve: Intelligence and Class Structure in American Life*. New York: Free Press.

NAACP v McCory. 2016. WL4053033.

Nakamura, David. 2017. "Trump Denounces KKK, Neo-Nazis as 'Repugnant' As He Seeks to Quell Criticism of His Response to Charlottesville." *The Washington Post*. August 14. https://www.washingtonpost.com/news/post-politics/wp/2017/08/14/trump-denounces-kkk-neo-nazis-as-justice-department-launches-civil-rights-probe-into-charlottesville-death/

National Conference of State Legislatures. 2020. "Health Insurance Premiums and Increases." October 26. https://www.ncsl.org/research/health/health-insurance-premiums.aspx.

Neiwert, David. 2018. *Alt-America: The Rise of the Radical Right in the Age of Trump*. New York: Verso.

Nelson, Anne. 2019. *Shadow Network: Media, Money and the Secret Hub of the Radical Right*. New York: Bloomsbury Publishing.

Nichols, John. 2011. "ALEC Exposed: Rigging Elections." *The Nation*. July 12.

Nichols, John and Robert McChesney. 2013. *Dollarocracy: How the Money-and-Media Election Complex is Destroying America*. New York: Nation Books.

NLRB, Velox Express, Inc and Jeannie Edge, August 29, 2019, Case 15-CA-184006.

Norris, Pippa and Ronald Inglehart. 2019. *Cultural Backlash: Trump, Brexit and Authoritarian Populism*. Cambridge, UK: Cambridge University Press.

NW Austin Municipal Utility District No. One v Holder. 557 U.S. 193 (2009).

O'Connor, Rory. 2008. *Shock Jocks: Hate Speech and Talk Radio*. San Francisco: AlterNet Books.

O'Connor, Lydia and Daniel Marans. 2019. "Here are 13 Examples of Donald Trump Being Racist." *HuffPost*. August 5. https://www.huffpost.com/entry/donald-trump-racist-examples_n_56d47177e4b03260bf777e83?

O'Donnell, John. 1991. *Trumped: The Inside Story of the Real Donald Trump—His Cunning Rise and Spectacular Fall*. New York: Simon & Schuster.

Office of Management and Budget. 2016. *Draft 2016 Report to Congress on the Benefits and Costs of Federal Regulations*. Washington, DC: Government Printing Office.

———. 2020. "Budget for America's Future: Major Savings and Reforms." Budget of the U.S. Government, FY, 2021. OMB. https://www.whitehouse.gov/wp-content/uploads/2020/02/msar_fy21.pdf

Oliver, J. Eric and Wendy Rahn. 2016. "Rise of the Trumpenvolk: Populism in the 2016 Election." *Annals of the American Academy of Political and Social Sciences*, 667(1), 189–706.

Olmos, Sergio, Mike Baker and Zolan-Kanno-Youngs. 2020. "Federal Agents Crackdown on Portland." *New York Times*. July 17. https://www.nytimes.com/2 020/07/17/us/portland-protests.html.

Page, Benjamin and Martin Gilens. 2017. *Democracy in America: What Has Gone Wrong and What we Can Do About It*. Chicago: University of Chicago Press.

Palast, Greg. 2012. *Billionaires and Ballot Bandits: How to Steal an Election in 9 Easy Steps*. New York: Seven Stories Press.

———. 2016. *The Best Democracy Money Can Buy: A Tale of Billionaires and Ballot Bandits*. New York: Seven Stories Press.

———. 2020. "Georgia Voter Purge Errors' Report Likely Removed Nearly 200,000 Citizens from Voter Rolls." *Palast Investigative Fund*. https://www.gregpalast.com /aclu-releases-palast-fund-georgia-voter-purge-errors-report/.

Palmer, John and Isabel Sawhill, ed., 1984. *The Reagan Record: An Assessment of America's Changing Domestic Priorities*. Washington, DC: Urban Institute.

Papenfuss, Mary. 2020. "Trump Administration Failed Dry Run 'Crimson Contagion' Pandemic Exercise." *HuffPost*. March 20. https://www.huffpost.com/entry/crim son-contagion-exercise-trump-administration-failures_n_5e744105c5b6eab77945 60e6

Parker, Christopher and Matt Barreto. 2013. *Change They Can't Believe In: The Tea Party and Reactionary Politics in America*. Princeton: Princeton University Press.

Peiser, Jaclyn. 2020. "Trump Lashes Out as Top Former DHS Official Reasserts That Election was 'Secure.'" *The Washington Post*. December1.

Peterson, George, Randall Bonbjerb, Barbara Davis, Walter Davis and Eugene Durman. 1986. *The Reagan Block Grants: What Have We Learned?* Washington, DC: Urban Institute.

Pew Charitable Trusts. 2016. "Colorado Voting Reforms: Early Results." *Pew Charitable Trusts*, March 22. https://www.pewtrusts.org/en/research-and-analysis/ issue-briefs/2016/03/colorado-voting-reforms-early-results

Philip, Bump. 2020. "Over and Over, Trump Focused on Black Lives Matter as a Target of Derision or Violence." *Washington Post*, September 1. https://www.was hingtonpost.com/politics/2020/09/01/over-over-trump-has-focused-black-lives -matter-target-derision-or-violence/

Phillips-Fein, Kim. 2009. *Invisible Hands: The Businessmen's Crusade Against the New Deal*. New York: W. W. Norton.

Piketty, Thomas. 2014. *Capital in the Twenty-First Century*. Cambridge: The Belknap Press of Harvard University Press.

———. 2020. *Capital and Ideology*. Cambridge, MA: Harvard University Press.

Piketty, Thomas and Emmanuel Saez. 2013. "Income Inequality in the United States, 1913–1998." *Quarterly Journal of Economics*, 118, 1–39.

———. 2014. "Inequality in the Long Run." *The Science of Inequality,* 344(6186, May).

Pilkington, ed. 2020. "Trump's Scrapping of Obama-era Reforms Hinders Police Reform." *Guardian*. June 7. https://www.theguardian.com/us-news/2020/jun/07/ police-consent-decrees-trump-administration-oversight

Punish, Johnny. 2020. "Top 4 Evidence-Based Reasons Donald Trump is Racist." *Veterans Today*. October 31. TOP 4 Evidence-Based Reasons Donald Trump is Racist – Veterans Today | Military Foreign Affairs Policy Journal for Clandestine Services.

Qiu, Linda. 2020. "Giuliani Peddles Election Conspiracy Theories and Falsehoods." *New York Times*. November 18.

Quinnipiac University Poll. 2018. "Economy Lifts Trump to Best Score in Seven Months." https://poll.qu.edu/images/polling/us/us02072018_uefy24.pdf

———. 2019. "Trump Is Racist, Half of U.S. Voters Say, Quinnipiac University National Polls Finds; But Voters Say Almost 2 to 1 don't Impeach President." *Quinnipiac University National Polls*. July 30. https://poll.qu.edu/images/polling/us/us07302019_uxug2111.pdf

Ramsey, Priscilla, Peggy McConnell, Betsy Palmen, and Glenn Lee. 1996. "Nurses' Compliance with Universal Precautions before and After Implementation of OSHA Regulations." *Clinical Nurse Specialist*, 10(5, September), 234–239.

Rana, Aziz. 2010. *Two Faces of American Freedom*. Ithaca: Hull Memorial Publication Fund of Cornell University.

Reagan, Ronald. 1980. "Ronald Reagan's Neshoba County Fair Campaign Speech." *The Closed Captioning Project*. https://www.youtube.com/watch?v=5I-JZwEPRzs&t=5s

Reese, Richard and Eleanor Krause. 2018. "Social Mobility Memos: Raj Chett in 14 Charts: Big Finding on Opportunity and Mobility We Should Know." *Brookings Institute*. https://www.brookings.edu/blog/social-mobility-memos/2018/01/11/raj-chetty-in-14-charts-big-findings-on-opportunity-and-mobility-we-should-know/

Reich, Michael, Sylvia Allegretto, Ken Jacobs and Clair Montialoux. 2016. "The Effects of a $15 Minimum Wage in New York States." *Center on Wage and Employment Dynamics, Policy Brief*, March.

Reich, Robert. 2007. *Supercapitalism: The Transformation of Business, Democracy, and Everyday Life*. New York: Alfred A. Knopf.

———. 2012. *Beyond Outrage: What Has Gone Wrong With Our Economy and Our Democracy and How to Fix It*. New York: Vintage Books.

———. 2016. *Saving Capitalism for the Many, Not the Few*. New York: Vintage Books.

———. 2020. *The System: Who Rigged It. How We Fix It*. New York: Alfred A. Knopf.

Reilly, Ryan. 2017. "Donald Trump Endorses Police Brutality in Speech to Cops." *HuffPost*. July 28. https://www.huffpost.com/entry/trump-police-brutality_n_597b840fe4b02a8434b6575a

———. 2018. "Jeff Sessions Dealt Police Reform One Final Blow On His Way Out the Door." *Huffington Post*. November 9. https://www.huffpost.com/entry/jeff-sessions-doj-police-reform-consent-decrees_n_5be5ae51e4b0e84388973547

Relman, Eliza. 2020. "The 26 Women Who Have Accused Trump of Sexual Misconduct." *Business Insider*. September 17. https://www.businessinsider.com/women-accused-trump-sexual-misconduct-list-2017-12

Reny, Tyler, Loren Collingwood and Alia Valenzuela. 2019. "Vote Switching n the 2016 Election: How Racial and immigration Attitudes, Not Economics, Explain Shifts in White Voting." *Public Opinion Quarterly*, 83(1, Spring), 91–113.

Richard v Ramirez, 418 U.S. 24 (1974).

Richardson, Heather. 2020. *How the South Won the Civil War: Oligarchy, Democracy, and the Continuing Fight for the Soul of America.* New York: Oxford University Press.

Richman, Jesse, Gulshan Chattha and David Earnest. 2014. "Do Non-Citizens Vote in U.S. Elections?" *Electoral Studies*, 36(December), 149–157.

Robin, Cory. 2018. *The Reactionary Mind: Conservatism from Edmund Burke to Donald Trump.* New York: Oxford University Press.

Rochefort, David and Roger Cobb. 1994. *The Politics of Problem Definition.* Lawrence: University of Kansas Press.

Roediger, David. 2007. *The Wages of Whiteness: Race and the Making of the American Working Class.* New York: Verso.

Rogowski, Jon C. and Cathy J. Cohen. 2014. "Black and Latino Youth Disproportionately Affected by Voter Identification Laws in the 2012 Election." In Black Youth Project. voter_id_effect_2012.pdf (blackyouthproject.com).

Rolston, Bill. 1993. "Training Ground: Ireland, Conquest and Colonization." *Race and Class*, 34(4), 13–24.

Romeo, Peter. 2021. "DOL Delays Discontinuation of 80/20 Rule on Servers Day." *Restaurant Business Online.* https://www.restaurantbusinessonline.com/workforce /dol-delays-discontinuation-8020-rule-servers-pay

Rosen, Philip and Howard Bloom. 2018. "Labor Board: Secondary Picketing Not Protected, Subcontracted Janitors Lawfully Fired." *The National Law Review.* October 23.

Rosenstone, Steven and John Hansen. 1993. *Mobilization, Participation and Democracy in America.* New York: MacMillan Publishing Company.

Rosenwald, Brian. 2019. *Talk Radio's America: How an Industry Took Over a Political Party that Took Over the U.S.* Cambridge, MA: Harvard University Press.

Roth, Zachary. 2016. *The Great Suppression: Voting Rights, Corporate Cash and the Conservative Assault on Democracy.* New York: Penguin Random House.

Rucker, Philip. 2019. "How Do You Stop These People?: Trump's Anti-immigrant Rhetoric Looms Over El Paso Massacre." *The Washington Post.* August 4. https ://www.washingtonpost.com/politics/how-do-you-stop-these-people-trumps-anti -immigrant-rhetoric-looms-over-el-paso-massacre/2019/08/04/62d0435a-b6ce-11 e9-a091-6a96e67d9cce_story.html

Rutenberg, Jim, Nick Corasaniti and Alan Feuer. 2020/2021. "Trump's Fraud Claims Died in Court, But the Myth of Stolen Elections Lives On." *The New York Times.* December 26/January 7.Trump's Fraud Claims Died in Court, but the Myth of Stolen Elections Lives On - The New York Times (nytimes.com).

Saad-Filho, Alfredo and Deborah Johnston, ed. 2005. *Neoliberalism: A Critical Reader.* London: Pluto Press.

Sakahara, Tim. 2011. "President Obama's Birth Certificate Delivers News to Doctor's Family." *Hawaii News Now.* April 27. President Obama's Birth Certificate Delivers

News to Doctor's Family (hawaiinewsnow.com) https://www.hawaiinewsnow.com/ story/14529568/president-obamas-birth-certificate-delivers-news-to-doctors-family.

Sammartino, Frank, Philip Stallworth and David Weiner. 2018. "The Effect of the TCJA Individual Income Tax Provisions Across Income Groups and Across the States." *Tax Policy Center*, March 28. www.txpolicycenter.org.sales/default/files /publication/154006/the_effectof_the_individual_income_tax_provisions_across_i ncome_groups and across the states.pdf

Sampson, Robert and William J. Wilson. 1995/2012. "Toward a Theory of Race, Crime and Urban Inequality." In John Hogan and Ruth Peterson (Eds.), *Crime and Inequality*, 37–54. Stanford, CA: Stanford University Press.

Satija, Neena. 2020. "Trump Boasts That His Landmark Law Is Freeing These Inmates: His Justice Department Wants Them to Stay in Prison." *Washington Post*. May 23.

Schattschneider, Elmer. 1975. *The Semi-sovereign People: A Realist's View of Democracy in America*. Boston, MA: Wadsworth.

Schlesinger, Arthur. 2003. *The Coming of the New Deal: 1933–1935: The Age of Roosevelt*. New York: Houghton Mifflin Co. Skocpol and Hertel-Fernandez. 2016. *The Koch Effect*.

Schwartz, Michael. 1988. *Radical Protest and Social Structure: The Southern Farmers' Alliance and Cotton Tenancy, 1880–1890*. Chicago: The University of Chicago Press.

Serwer, Adam. 2020. "Trump Gave Police Permission to Be Brutal." *Atlantic*. June 3. https://www.theatlantic.com/ideas/archive/2020/06/chauvin-did-what-trump-as ked-him-do/612574/.

Seth, Herald. 2020. "Fact Check: Trump's Bogus Claim of More Voters in Detroit Than People." *nbcnews.com*. https://www.nbcnews.com.fact-check-trumps-bogus -claim-of-more-voters-in-detroit-than-people

Setzler, Mark and Alixandra Yanus. 2018 "Why Did Women Vote for Donald Trump?" *PS: Political Science and Politics*, 51(3, July), 523–527.

Shaw, Greg. 2017. *The Dysfunctional Politics of the Affordable Care Act*. Santa Barbara, CA: Praeger.

Shear, Michael, Katie Brenner and Michael Schmidt. 2020. "'We Need to Take Away Children,' No Matter How Young, Justice Dept. Officials Said." *New York Times*. October 6. https://www.nytimes.com/2020/10/06/us/politics/family-separation- border-immigration-jeff-sessions-rod-rosenstein.html.

Shear, Michael and Maggie Haberman. 2017. "Trump Defends Initial Remarks on Charlottesville; Again Blames 'Both Sides.' *The New York Times*. August 15. https://www.nytimes.com/2017/08/15/us/politics/trump-press-conference-charl ottesville.html.

Shear, Michael and Sarah Mervosh. 2020. "Trump Encourages Protest Against Governors Who Have Imposed Virus Restrictions." *New York Times*, April 17.

Shelby County v Holder, 570 U.S. 2 (2013).

Shen, Megan and Jordan La Borff. 2016. "More than Political Ideology: Subtle Racial Prejudice as a Predictor of Opposition to Universal Health Care among U.S. Citizens." *Journal of Social and Political Psychology*, 4(2), 493–520.

Shepherd, Michael. 2020. "The Politics of Pain: Medicaid Expansion and the Opioid Epidemic." Paper Delivered at the Southern Political Science Association. January 2.

Shierholz, Heidi and David Cooper. 2019. "Trump's Labor Department Has Declared War on Tipped Workers." *In These Times*. December 3. https://inthesetimes.com/working/entry/22190/trump-labor-dept-tipped-workers-wage-theft.

Shropshire, Terry. 2018. "This Many White People Think Trump is Racist." *Rollingout*. July 8. https://rollingout.com/2018/07/08/this-many-white-people-think-donald-trump-is-racist/.

Sides, John, Michael Tesler and Lynn Vavreck. 2018. *Identity Crisis: The 2016 Presidential Campaign and the Battle for the Meaning of America*. Princeton, NJ: Princeton University Press.

Skocpol, Theda. 2016. "The Elite and Popular Roots of Contemporary Republican Extremism." In Theda Skocpol and Caroline Tervo (Eds.), *Upending American Politics: Polarizing Parties, Ideological Elites, and Citizen Activists from the Tea Party to the Anti-Trump Resistance*, 3–28. New York: Oxford University Press.

Skocpol, Theda and Alexander Hertel-Fernandez. 2016. "The Koch Effect: The Impact of a Cadre-Led Network on American Politics." Paper Presented at the Southern Political Science Association. January 8.

Skocpol, Theda and Venessa Williamson. 2012. *The Tea Party and the Remaking of Republican Conservatism*. New York: Oxford University Press.

Slisco, Aila. 2020. "ACLU Sues DHS Over Federal Agents' Response to Portland Protests." *Newsweek*. July 17. https://www.newsweek.com/aclu-sues-dhs-over-federal-agents-response-portland-protests-1518803.

Smedley, Audrey and Brian Smedley. 2018. *Race in North America: Origin and Evolution of a Worldview*. New York: Routledge.

Smith, David. 2018. "Can Kushner's Work on Criminal Justice Reform Overhaul Save His Reputation?" *The Guardian*. December 21. https://www.theguardian.com/us-news/2018/dec/21/jared-kushner-criminal-justice-reform.

Smith, David and Joanna Walter. 2020. "Donald Trump Declares National Emergency Over Coronavirus Pandemic." *The Guardian*. March 13. https://www.theguardian.com/world/2020/mar/13/donald-trump-coronavirus-national-emergency.

Smith, Hedrick. 2012. *Who Stole the American Dream?* New York: Random House.

Snyder, Timothy. 2018. *The Road to Unfreedom: Russia, Europe, America*. New York: Tim Duggan Books.

Sobel, Richard and Robert Smith. 2009. "Voter-ID Laws Discourage Participation, Particularly Among Minorities, and Trigger a Constitutional Remedy in Lost Representation." *PS: Political Science & Politics*, 42(January), 107–110.

Sommers, Benjamin, Anna Goldman, Robert Blendon, John Orav, Arnold Epstein. 2019. "Medicaid Work Requirements—Results from the First Year in Arkansas." *The New England Journal of Medicine*, 1073–1082. September 12. https://www.nejm.org/doi/pdf/10.1056/NEJMsr1901772. Accessed September 19, 2020.

Soss, Joe, Richard Fording, and Sanford Schram. 2011. *Disciplining the Poor: Neoliberal Paternalism and the Persistent Power of Race*. Chicago: University of Chicago Press.

Spivak, John. 2021. "The Crusaders." *Coat Magazine*. June 28. http://coat.ncf.ca/o ur_magazine/links/53/crusaders.html.

Stanley, Jason. 2018. *How Fascism Works: The Politics of Us and Them*. New York: Random House.

Steinberg, Jeffrey and John Hoefle. 2009. "Fascists, Then and Now, Stalk the FDR Legacy." *Executive Intelligence Review*, 36(8, February 27). https://larouchepub. com/eiw/public/2009/eirv36n08-20090227/eirv36n08-20090227_052-fascists _then_and_now_stalk_the.pdf.

Stiglitz, Joseph. 2012. *The Price of Inequality*. New York: W.W. Norton & Company.

———. 2020. *People, Power, and Profits: Progressive Capitalism for an Age of Discontent*. New York: Penguin Random House.

Strang, Stephen. 2020. *God, Trump, and the 2020 Election: Why He Must Win and What's at Stake for Christians if He Loses*. Lake Mary, FL: Frontline, House Book Group.

Strauss, Larry. 2019. "AG Barr's Nods to Hypocrisy and Fascism: Respect Police or they Might Not Protect You." *USA News*. December 9. https://www.usatoday.com/ story/opinion/2019/12/09/ag-william-barr-respect-police-if-you-want-their-protec tion-column/4374696002/.

Sundquist, James. 1983. *Dynamics of the Party System: Alignment and Realignment of Political Parties in the United States*. Washington, DC: Brookings Institution Press.

Tanner, Michael. 2016. "Five Myths about Economic Inequality in America. Policy Analysis." Cato Institute, September 7, no. 797. Five Myths about Economic Inequality in America (cato.org) https://www.cato.org/sites/cato.org/files/pubs/p df/pa797_.pdf.

Taylor, Stuart. 1983. "Bankruptcy and the Unions." *New York Times*. September 29. https://www.nytimes.com/1983/09/29/business/bankruptcy-and-the-unions.html.

Temin, Peter. 2017/2018. *The Vanishing Middle Class: Prejudice and Power in a Dual Economy*. Cambridge: MIT Press.

Tenenhaus, Sam. 2017. "The Architect of the Radical Right: How the Nobel Prize-winning Economist James m. Buchanan Shaped Today's Antigovernment Politics." *The Atlantic*. July/August. https://www.theatlantic.com/magazine/arc hive/2017/07/the-architect-of-the-radical-right/528672/.

Tesler, Michael. 2012. "The Spillover of Racialization into Health care: How President Obama Polarized Public Opinion by Race and Racial Attitudes." *American Journal of Political Science*, 56(3), 690–704.

Thornbury v Gingles, 478 U.S. 30 (1986).

Timm, June. 2020. "Rudy Giuliani Baselessly Alleges 'Centralized' Voter Fraud at Free-Wheeling News Conference." *NBC News*. November 19. Rudy Giuliani base-lessly alleges 'centralized' voter fraud at free-wheeling news conference (nbcnews .com)

Timpone, Richard. 1998. "Structure, Behavior and Voter Turnout in the United States." *American Political Science Review*, 92(1), 145–158.

Todd, Chuck and Donald Trump. 2016. "Meet the Press." *Transcript*. May 2008. https://www.nbcnews.com/meet-the-press/meet-press-may-8-2016-n570111.

Toder, Eric. 2018. "Despite the Tax Cuts and Jobs Act, the Federal Tax System is Becoming More Progressive over Time." *Tax Policy Center*, September 18.

Tolchin, Susan and Martin Tolchin. 1983. *Dismantling America: The Rush to Deregulate*. Boston: Houghton Mifflin.

Tolliday, Steven and Jonathan Zeitlin. 1987. *The Automobile Industry and Its Workers: Between Fordism and Flexibility*. New York: St. Martin's Press. Red Lion Broadcasting Company v Federal Communications Commission, 395 U.S. 367, 1969.

Truman, David. 1950/1993. *The Governmental Process: Political Interests and Public Opinion*. Berkeley, CA: Institute of Governmental Studies.

Trump, Donald. 2005. *The Art of the Deal*. New York: Ballantine Books.

———. 2008. *Think Big: Make It Happen in Business and Life*. New York: HarperCollins.

———. 2015. *Crippled America: How to Make America Great Again*. New York: Threshold Editions.

———. 2019. "White House Briefing Statements." April 4. https://www.whitehouse.gov/briefings-statements/tax-cuts-jobs-act-generating-economic-resurgence-communities-across-country/.

———. 2019. "Whitehouse Briefings Statements." April 15. https://www.whitehouse.gov/briefings-statements/president-donald-j-trumps-tax-cuts-helping-american-families-get-ahead/.

———. 2020. *Tweeter@#realTrump*. July 29, 12:19 PM.

Tupy, Marian. 2016. "Bernie Is Not a Socialist." *The Atlantic*. March 1.

Uggen, Chris, Ryan Larson, Sarah Shannon and Arleth Pulido-Nava. 2020. "Locked Out 2020: Estimates of People Denied Voting Rights Due to Felony Convictions." *Sentencing Project*. https://www.sentencingproject.org/publications/locked-out-2020-estimates-of-people-denied-voting-rights-due-to-a-felony-conviction/.

Uhrmacher, Kevin, Devin Schaul and Dan Keating. 2016. "These Former Obama Strongholds Sealed the Election for Trump." *The Washington Post*. November 9. https://www.washingtonpost.com/graphics/politics/2016-election/obama-trump-counties/.

United States Civil Rights Commission. 2001. *Voting Irregularities in Florida During the 2000 Presidential Election*. Washington, DC: Government Printing Office. www.usccr.gov/pubs/vote2000/report/main.htm.

United States Government Accountability Office. 2014. "Elections: Issues Related to State Voter Identification Laws." https://wwwgao.gov/assets/670/665966.pdf

United States House Judiciary Committee. 2005. "What Went Wrong in Ohio: The Conyers Report on the 2004 Presidential Election." https://www.loc.gov.item/2009284117.

Unnever, James and Francis Cullen. 2012. "White Perceptions of Whether African Americans and Hispanics are Prone to Violence and Support for the Death Penalty." *Journal of Research in Crime and Delinquency*, 49(4), 519–544.

U.S. Department of Education. 2018. ""Fiscal 2019 Budget Summary and Background Information." https://www2.ed.gov/about/overview/budget/budget19/summary/19summary.pdf.

U.S. Department Of Education. 2020. "U.S. Department of Education Fiscal Year 2021 Budget Summary." https://www2.ed.gov/about/overview/budget/budget21 /summary/21summary.pdf#:~:text=Overall%2C%20the%20President%E2%80 %99s%20fiscal%20year%202021%20Budget%20includes,year%202021%20R equest%20includes%20the%20following%20key%20initiatives%3A.

U.S. Department of Health and Human Services. 2020. "Budget in Brief." February. https://www.hhs.gov/sites/default/files/fy-2021-budget-in-brief.pdf.

U.S. Department of Housing and Urban Development. 2020. "HUD's Proposed 2021 Budget." *New Release*. February. https://www.hud.gov/budget#:~:text=On %20February%2010%2C%202020%2C%20the%20Trump%20Administration %20announced,hazards%3B%20and%20preserves%20rental%20assistance%20to %20HUD-assisted%20households.

U.S. Department of Labor, Wage and Hour Division. 2019. "Today the U.S. Department of Labor Announced a Final Rule to Make 1.3 million American Workers Eligible for Overtime Pay Under the Fair Labor Standard Act (FLSA)." September 24. https://www.dol.gov/newsroom/releases/whd/whd20190924.

U.S. Department of Labor, Wage and Hour Division. 2019. "Tip Regulations Under the Fair labor Standards Act (FLSA)." 84 FR 53956-53980. October 8.

Urevich, Robin. 2017. "Judging Janus: The Money Machine Behind the Attacks on Labor." *Capital and Main*. November 15. https://capitalandmain.com/judging-janus-the-money-machine-behind-the-attacks-on-labor-1115.

Valencia-Garcia, Louie. 2019. "This is What 'Peaceful Ethnic Cleansing Looks Like." *Center for Analysis of the Radical Right*. October 4. https://www.radicalr ightanalysis.com/2019/10/04/this-is-what-peaceful-ethnic-cleansing-looks-like/.

Valeo v Buckley, 424 U.S. 1 (1976)

VanBooven, Valerie. 2019. "CMS Deals Blow to Unions that Had Been Automatically Deducting Dues from Medicaid-Paid Home Health Care Workers." *Home Care Daily.com*. May 14. https://www.homecaredaily.com/2019/05/14/cms-deals-blow -to-unions-that-had-been-automatically-deducting-dues-from-medicaid-paid-home -healthcare-workers/.

Vercellotti, Timothy. 2006. "Appendix C: Analysis of Effects of Voter ID Requirements on Turnout." In Report to the U.S. Election Assistance Commission on Best Practices to Improve Voter Identification Requirements pursuant to the Help America Vote Act of 2002.

Vercellotti, Timothy and David Anderson. 2006 "Protecting the Franchise or Restricting It? The Effect of Voter Identification Requirements on Turnout." American Political Science Association Conference Paper, Philadelphia, Pennsylvania.

———. 2009. "Voter-Identification Requirements and the Learning Curve." *PS: Political Science & Politics*, 42(January), 117–120.

Visser, Nick. 2020. "Trump Calls George Floyd Protesters 'Thugs,' Threatens Violent Intervention in Minneapolis." *HuffPost*. May 29. https://www.huffpost.com/entry/ trump-minneapolis-thugs-george-floyd_n_5ed0a6cac5b6ebd583bed6be.

Vogtman, Julie. 2019. "Five Reasons Eugene Scalia Is a Terrible Choice to Lead the Department of Labor." *National Women's Law Center*. September 18. https://nw

lc.org/blog/five-reasons-eugene-scalia-is-a-terrible-choice-to-lead-the-department
-of-labor/.

Volker, Ullrich. 2017. *Hitler: Ascent: 1889–1939*. New York: Vintage Books.

Wallnau, Lance. 2016. *God's Chaos Candidate: Donald Trump and the American Unraveling*. Keller, TX: Killer Sheep Media, Inc.

Watson, Tom. 1892. "The Negro Question in the South." In George Tindall (Ed.), *A Populist Reader: Selections form the Works of American Populist Leaders*. New York: Harper & Row, 1966. https://msuweb.montclair.edu/~furrg/spl/tomwatson.html.

Weiser, Wedny and Douglas Keith 2017. "Non-Citizens Re Not Voting. Here are the Facts." *Brennan Center for Justice*.

Weissburg, Daniel. 1992. "Do the Benefits of the New OSHA HIV/HBV Standard Justify the Costs?" *Physician Executive*, 18(2), 48–49.

Wheeler, Lydia. 2017. "Trump's Labor Nominee to Withdraw, Reports." *The Hill*. February 15. https://thehill.com/homenews/administration/319717-trumps-labor-n ominee-to-withdraw-reports.

Wilkinson, Richard and Kate Pickett. 2010. *The Spirit Level: Why Greater Equality Makes Societies Stronger*. New York: Bloomsbury Press.

Wilkerson, Isabel. 2020. *Caste: The Origins of Our Discontents*. New York: Random House.

Wilkinson, Richard and Kate Pickett. 2010. *The Spirit Level: Why Greater Equality Makes Societies Stronger*. New York: Bloomsbury Press.

Wilper, Andrew, Steffie Woolhandler, Karen Lasser, Danny McCormick, David Bor and David Himmeistein. 2009. "Health Insurance and Mortality in U.S. Adults." *American Journal of Public Health*, 99(12, December), 2289–2295.

Wilson, Carter. 2000. "Policy Regimes and Policy Change." *Journal of Public Policy*, 20(3), 247–274.

———. 2015. *Metaracism: Explaining the Persistence of Racial Inequality*. Boulder, CO: Lynne Rienner.

———. 2019. *Public Policy: Continuity and Change*. Long Grove, IL: Waveland Press.

Wilson, James Q. 2013. *Thinking About Crime*. New York: Basic Books.

Wines, Michael. 2017. "Illegal Voting Gets Texas Woman 8 Years in Prison, and Certain Deportation." *The New York Times*. February 10. https://www.nytimes. com/2017/02/10/us/illegal-voting-gets-texas-woman-8-years-in-prison-and-cer tain-deportation.html.

Wiseman, Paul. 2020. "What Trump's New Northern American Trade Deal Actually Does." *AP*. January 29.

Wittner, Lawrence. 2018. "Trump Administration's War on Workers." *Counter Punch*. February 20. https://www.counterpunch.org/2018/02/20/the-trump-admin istrations-war-on-workers/.

Wolfinger, Raymond and Steven Rosenston. 1980. *Who Votes?* New Haven, CT: Yale University Press.

Wood, Thomas. 2017. "Racism Motivated Trump Voters more than Authoritarianism." *The Washington Post*, April 17.

Woodward, Bob. 2020. *Rage*. New York: Simon and Schuster.

Woodward, C. Vann. 1938. *Tom Watson: Agrarian Rebel*. New York: The Macmillan Company.

Wuthnow, Robert. 2018. *The Left Behind: Decline and Rage in Small-Town America*. Princeton, NJ: Princeton University Press.

Ye, Hee Lee, Michelle, Haisten Willis and Amy Gardner. 2020. "Long Lines Mark First Day of Early Voting in Georgia as Voters Flock to the Polls." *Washington Post*. October 12.

Yglesias, Matthew. 2020. "Trump's Disappearing Populism Was on Full Display at Thursday's Debate." *Vox*. October 22. https://www.vox.com/2020/10/22/2152 9733/donald-trump-minimum-wage-debate.

Zach, Despart and Mike Morris. 2020. "Harris County Democrats Waited for Hours to Vote: Two-thirds of the Polling Sites Were in GOP Areas." *Houston Chronicle*. March 4. https://www.houstonchronicle.com/news/houston-texas/houston/article/ Harris-County-Democrats-waited-in-line-for-hours-15105465.php.

Zapotoshy, Matt. 2017. "Charleston Church Shooter: 'I Would Like to Make It Crystal Clear, I Do Not Regret What I Did.'" *Washington Post*. January 4.

———. 2020. "Barr Says He Hasn't Seen Fraud that Could Affect the Election Outcome." *The Washington Post*. December 1. https://www.washingtonpost.com/ national-security/barr-no-evidence-election-fraud/2020/12/01/5f4dcaa8-340a-11eb -8d38-6aea1adb3839_story.html.

Zhirkov, Kirill and Nicholas Valentino. 2017. "Blue Is Black and Red Is White? Affective Polarization and the Racialized Schemas of U.S Party Coalitions." Paper presented at the Midwest Political Science Association, Chicago, IL.

Zito, Salena and Brad Todd. 2018. *The Great Revolt: Inside the Populist Coalition Reshaping American Politics*. New York: Crown Forum.

# Index

# About the Author

**Carter A. Wilson** is professor and head of the Department of Political Science and Public Administration at Northern Michigan University. He is the author of *Public Policy: Continuity and Change; Metaracism: Explaining the Persistence of Racial Inequality;* and *Racism from Slavery to Advanced Capitalism.*

www.ingramcontent.com/pod-product-compliance
Lightning Source LLC
Chambersburg PA
CBHW022309280326
41932CB00010B/1038